Spiritual Gifts

Spiritual Gifts

by

John MacArthur, Jr.

WORD OF GRACE COMMUNICATIONS

P.O. Box 4000

Panorama City, CA 91412

All Scripture quotations, unless noted otherwise, are from the *New Scofield Reference Bible,* King James Version, © 1967 by Oxford University Press, Inc. Reprinted by permission.

Library of Congress Cataloging-in-Publication Data

MacArthur, John F.
  Spiritual gifts.

  (John MacArthur's Bible studies)
  Includes index.
  1. Gifts, Spiritual.   I. Title.   II. Series:
MacArthur, John F.   Bible studies.
BT767.3.M29   1983   234'.13   85-28404
ISBN 0-8024-5121-7 (pbk.)

1 2 3 4 5 6 7 Printing/GB/Year 90 89 88 87 86 85

Printed in the United States of America

Contents

These Bible studies are taken from messages delivered by Pastor-Teacher John MacArthur, Jr., at Grace Community Church in Panorama City, California. These messages have been combined into a 12-tape album entitled *Spiritual Gifts*. You may purchase this series either in an attractive vinyl cassette album or as individual cassettes. To purchase these tapes, request the album *Spiritual Gifts* or ask for the tapes by their individual GC numbers. Please consult the current price list; then, send your order, making your check payable to:

WORD OF GRACE COMMUNICATIONS
P.O. Box 4000
Panorama City, CA 91412

Or, call the following toll-free number:
1-800-55-GRACE

1

Concerning Spiritual Gifts—Part 1

Outline

Introduction
A. The Basis of the Church
  1. The misconceptions of the church
  2. The makeup of the church
    a) Its supernatural manifestations
    b) Its spiritual gifts
      (1) Their critical function
B. The Background of the Corinthian Church
  1. The problems in Corinth
    a) The source of Paul's information
      (1) 1 Corinthians 1:11
      (2) 1 Corinthians 16:17
      (3) 1 Corinthians 7:1*a*
    b) The severity of their problems
      (1) Their crimes against the Spirit
      (2) Their corruption from society
      (3) Their confusion of the Spirit
        (*a*) Their exploitation
        (*b*) Their extremism
  2. The prominence of the mystery religion
    a) Its infiltration of Corinth
      (1) Divisions
        (*a*) Philosophers
        (*b*) Philosophies
      (2) Sex
      (3) Lawsuits
      (4) Marital conflict
      (5) Abuse of liberty
      (6) Feminism
    b) Its impact on the world
      (1) The single origin
        (*a*) The final form
        (*b*) The first form

7

(2) The spawned network
    (*a*) Semiramis
    (*b*) Tammuz
(3) The sophisticated rites
    (*a*) Baptismal regeneration
    (*b*) Sacrificial systems
    (*c*) Feasts and fasts
    (*d*) Mutilations and flagellations
(4) The specifics of ecstasy
    (*a*) An explanation of its effect
    (*b*) An example of its effect
3. The perception of the source
  a) The dilemma
  b) The declaration
  c) The delusion
  d) The disclosure

Lesson
I. The Importance of Spiritual Gifts
  A. The Concern of Paul
    1. An infallible source
      a) "Now concerning"
      b) "Spiritual gifts"
        (1) The definition
        (2) The determination
        (3) The differences
    2. An intelligent understanding

Introduction

Beginning at 1 Corinthians 12:1 is one of the most interesting, important, and controversial sections of Scripture—the section relative to spiritual gifts. In order to interpret the meaning and the use of spiritual gifts, I want to pursue this subject from the teaching aspect, being concerned about supporting each position and each view carefully.

A. The Basis of the Church

Nothing has been more abused and misunderstood in evangelical Christianity than this whole area of spiritual gifts. It is critical that we understand it because it is absolutely vital to the life of the church. There is nothing more vital apart from the divine energy of God Himself than the ministry that the believers have by way of their spiritual gifts from God for ministry.

8

1. The misconceptions of the church

   Some people think that the church is a visible religious organization governed by a hierarchy of semiofficial-type people. Other people think that the church is an efficient social or quasi-social agency designed to disperse to the community those things that will meet their needs. Other people think that the church is the building going up across the street that they would like to stop from being built. Other people think that the church is a useful place to go if you die, get married, have a baby, or want to get baptized. Some people think that the church is nothing more than a social club—a group of people who all agree about the same things religiously and then get together and have parties. In some sense, there is an element of truth in all of those views.

2. The makeup of the church

   May it be established at the very beginning of our study that biblically the church is seen as a living organism. It is the Body of Christ, and Christ is the head of that living Body. It is the fullness of Him that fills all in all (Eph. 1:23). The church is not a human institution or an earthly organization—it is an organism, and as such it is eternal. The church cannot die—it is eternal and supernatural. Its head is Christ, who lives forevermore. Its members are believers who have been given eternal life. In Matthew 16:18 Jesus says that the gates of hell could not destroy the church. It is indestructible, eternal, and supernatural. This supernatural character becomes manifest in many ways.

   a) Its supernatural manifestations

   We worship a supernatural God. We believe in a supernatural intervention in human history in terms of the revelation of God's Word and of the living Christ. We believe in a supernatural Holy Spirit, who indwells us. We are the result of a supernatural transformation that has made us new creatures. And we have been given by the Holy Spirit a supernatural endowment of gifts, by which we can minister within the organism to the building and edifying of the church, until it comes to the fullness of the stature of Christ and has a powerful witness in the world.

   b) Its spiritual gifts

   (1) Their critical function

   Since the church has been endowed by the Spirit of God with supernatural gifts for its ministry of edification and evangelism, they then become critical to its operation. That is why we must understand spiritual gifts and understand that Satan counterfeits them. He counterfeits them because they are absolutely necessary to the life and function of the church.

The church is not a spectator sport, and it is not professional pulpitism financed by lay spectators who sit and watch it happen. The church is a living, breathing organism that functions as life and breath on the basis of the ministry of each member to minister to the others. This is why the church is seen as a body and every one of us as a member of that body. We have a function in harmony and symphony with every other member. So, it is critical that we understand how it works, how we operate within it, and how the spiritual gifts function in order that the church might be built up. We must also understand how Satan counterfeits and how to recognize the counterfeit as opposed to the genuine gift. The end result of the counterfeit is the tearing down of the church and not its building up.

(2) The clarifying questions

There are many questions that surround spiritual gifts: What are spiritual gifts? How many are there? Are they important? How many do I have? How do I get them? How do I know what they are? Can I seek certain gifts? How do I understand the purpose of gifts? What about miraculous gifts like languages and healing—are they still in operation? What is the baptism of the Holy Spirit? Does every Christian possess the fullness of the Holy Spirit? Are all the gifts still in operation? If not, which ones still are, how did the others cease, and why? Can the gifts be counterfeited? What is the most important gift? All of these questions need to be dealt with in order to understand the subject.

B. The Background of the Corinthian Church

Now, an understanding of the situation in the Corinthian church is basic to an understanding of the whole picture regarding spiritual gifts. This is the normal process of historical, grammatical interpretation. We have to know what Paul said and we have to know what was meant by it in the time in which it was said. So, we have to reconstruct some history.

The Corinthian church was established by the apostle Paul during his second missionary journey (Acts 18). He spent eighteen

10

months there, and during that time he established the saints, built up the church, fought his enemies, and then at the end of that time he left. Later, they had other pastors who came to minister to them, with some distinction, but Paul's ministry was foundational.

1. The problems in Corinth

Not long after Paul left, several moral and spiritual problems developed in the Corinthian church. They were so severe in fact, that this first letter to the Corinthians deals exclusively with these problems.

a) The source of Paul's information

You say, "Where did Paul find out about the problems?" He had three basic sources:

(1) 1 Corinthians 1:11—Paul said that some of the household of Chloe came and told him about them.

(2) 1 Corinthians 16:17—"I am glad of the coming of Stephanas and Fortunatus and Achaicus; for that which was lacking on your part they have supplied." Here are three people who came from the Corinthian assembly with information regarding the church.

(3) 1 Corinthians 7:1a—"Now concerning the things about which ye wrote unto me." Apparently those three folks brought a letter, which asked further questions.

From these three particular sources the apostle Paul was informed about the problems that were occurring in this assembly. In response to the letter and the information from Chloe and the three others, he begins in the first chapter to write and solve these problems on paper, giving them the information for solving them in actuality.

b) The severity of their problems

Now, it is inconceivable that any one church could have manifested these problems to the degree that the Corinthian church did. For example:

(1) Their crimes against the Spirit

(a) Divisions (1:10-11)

(b) Human wisdom (1:18-25)

(c) Human personality cliques (1:12-17)

(d) Carnality (3:1-9)

11

(*e*) Sexual perversion—fornication and incest (5:1-8; 6:12-20)

(*f*) Worldliness (5:9-13)

(*g*) Lawsuits (6:1-8)

(*h*) Rebellion against apostolic authority (4:1-21)

(*i*) Marital conflict (7:1-40)

(*j*) Conflicts unmarried people have (7:1-40)

(*k*) Abuse of liberty (8:1-13; 10:23-33)

(*l*) Idolatry (8:4-13; 10:1-22)

(*m*) Pride (8:1-3; 10:12)

(*n*) Selfishness (11:17-22)

(*o*) Demon worship (10:19-22)

(*p*) Insubordinate women (11:2-16)

(*q*) Abuses of God's intended roles for men and women (11:2-16)

(*r*) Abuses of the Lord's Supper and love feast (11:17-34)

(*s*) Abuses and perversions of spiritual gifts (12:1—14:40)

Just as the Corinthians had perverted everything else in their assembly, they were perverting the dimension of spiritual gifts in their lives.

(2) Their corruption from society

They had managed to drag into their church life all of the features of their former pagan existence. They had not made a clear-cut separation—they had not come out from among the world to be separate. They had not ceased to handle unclean things but managed to drag them all into the assembly, even though they were rich in spiritual gifts. First Corinthians 1:7*a* says, "So that ye come behind in no gift." In other words, they had everything, they lacked nothing, they had a fullness of all the gifts. Yet, in spite of all that, with all the knowledge they should have had and with all the gifts they did have, they were ignorant of how they should function—especially regarding the gift of languages (called *tongues* in our day, but biblically the word is *languages*).

12

(3) Their confusion of the Spirit

Further, the concept of the Holy Spirit dominated their thinking, and they confused the manifestation of the Holy Spirit with ecstatic, enthusiastic activity.

(a) Their exploitation

For example, somebody who stood up in the congregation and gave an utterance (whether it was a language, prophecy, or an interpretation) seemed to them to be more godly the more wild and the more miraculous the utterance appeared. So, the gift of languages became the one that was exploited. The ecstatic speaking that occurred as if it were the true gift of languages was then given credence as the highest degree of spiritual maturity because it demonstrated the greatest manifestation of an outside power. It could not be identified with any normal faculty of man. They tended to lean toward that which was more bizarre and far out. This carnal concept was a remnant of their unsaved, idolatrous days when ecstatic utterances made by pagan priests and worshipers under the control of a demon were thought to be the highest level of religious experience. That is the kind of culture they lived in, and it had been dragged into the assembly.

(b) The extremism

Now, from the very start of His ministry, the Holy Spirit had been doing amazing things in their midst. The gifts were there in concert, ready for a divine symphony of body life to edify the church. They had seen Him manifest. But in that age in which they lived—an age when religion was connected with ecstasy, frenzy, and bizarre things—that kind of hysterical enthusiasm and extremism that existed in their pagan religion was dragged into the church and became a delusion regarding the work of the Spirit.

2. The prominence of the mystery religion

Now, in their culture they had a certain kind of religion that we call "the mystery religion." These mystery religions had, as a characteristic of their function, these kinds of frenzies, ecstasies, and enthusiasms.

a) Its infiltration of Corinth

When these things infiltrated the church, it was easy for the believers, in their carnal state, to confuse them with the true gifts of the Holy Spirit. It isn't surprising that this happened.

(1) Divisions

In their church there were divisions. Where did those divisions come from? They resulted from dragging in the things from the world that they held to before they were saved.

(*a*) Philosophers

The Corinthians were enamored with philosophers. They learned to have personality cults in their culture. They would worship one philosopher over another. So when they came into the church, they did the same thing, saying, "I am of Paul; or I, of Apollos; or I, of Cephas; or I, of Christ" (1 Cor. 1:12*b*). They created more personality cults.

(*b*) Philosophies

In their pagan life they also identified with different philosophies. It was a big thing in Greek culture to argue philosophy. When they entered the church they argued about the words of human wisdom. Paul said, "I didn't come to you with human wisdom. The natural man, with all his human wisdom, cannot understand the things of God" (1 Cor. 2:1, 14).

They dragged all of their human philosophies and their human personality cults into the church and polarized that mentality.

(2) Sex

The name of the city, Corinth, became a verb—"to Corinthianize." It meant "to go to bed with a prostitute." That is what others thought of Corinth, because that was the kind of culture it had. So, what happened in the church? They dragged that same morality into the church. According to chapter 5, a person was having sexual relations with his stepmother. In chapter 6 people are joining themselves to prostitutes. The same thing they had known in their pagan life they dragged into their church assembly.

14

(3) Lawsuits

According to 1 Corinthians 6:1-11, they loved to go to court. To them it was a sport to go to court and to dialogue. When they became Christians, they still sued each other, again dragging the same mentality from the world into the assembly of believers.

(4) Marital conflict

Another thing we see in their society was the terrible decline and fouling up of marriages. Chapter 7 deals with this problem, which they dragged in from the world.

(5) Abuse of liberty

According to chapters 8-10, they abused their liberty because they had come from an existential society where anything was all right. When they came into the church they started doing whatever they wanted, no matter how it affected anyone. Paul said, "You have to limit your liberty for the sake of another" (1 Cor. 8:9).

(6) Feminism

They even had a feminist revolution come into the church. Women wouldn't wear veils or allow themselves to be covered, which was a symbol of modesty.

Everything that was a part of their carnal lives manifested itself in their church. If all of this was present, we can assume that their pagan style of religion would also manifest itself in their assembly under the guise of their carnality. That is precisely what happened. The world's religion infiltrated the life of the church. They began to do things with new definitions and terms within the confines of Christianity, doing the same things they were doing before they ever knew Christ and calling them gifts of the Holy Spirit.

b) Its impact on the world

(1) The single origin

They worshiped under a system known as "the mystery religions." For over a thousand years these religions dominated Western culture. There were many forms of the mystery religions, but they can all be traced back to a single origin.

(a) The final form

In order to understand this, we need to look at Revelation 17:5. It discusses the final form of world religion. By the end of the Tribulation the true church is long gone, and the world begins to establish a form of religion. This composite form of world religion comes together under one heading called "MYSTERY, BABYLON THE GREAT, THE MOTHER OF HARLOTS AND ABOMINATIONS OF THE EARTH." The final form of world religion is called *Mystery Babylon*.

The mystery religions came out of Babylon. All false worship stems back to the Tower of Babel. So when this religion comes together at the end it is just a final form of the Babylonian false system. Notice that Mystery Babylon (i.e., the false religion that began at the Tower of Babel), is the mother of all other false systems. The true church is the bride, the false one is a harlot. The harlot religious systems were spawned and mothered by Babylon, and they will regroup again in the end time.

(*b*) The first form

The Tower of Babel was man's first sophisticated, organized counterfeit of true religion (Gen. 11:9). This tower was built to God, and Nimrod was the patriarchal apostate who set it all up. He was the grandson of Ham, who was the son of Noah. They established a false system of religion as a counterfeit to the truth. Every false system since then was spawned out of that. Why? When God judged those people He scattered them all over the world and they took with them the seeds of false religion begun at Babel. They adapted it, altered it, sophisticated it even more, changed it here and there, and added to it so that it became complex in various cultures. But the seeds of it all were at Babel, and that is why Mystery Babylon is called the mother of all false systems.

(2) The spawned network

Nimrod spawned a network of false religious systems. That is why there is so much similarity in these false systems around the world.

(*a*) Semiramis

Nimrod had a wife—a very evil person. Her name was Semiramis I. She was the first high priestess of the Tower of Babel religion. She founded what is known today as the mystery religions. She was the mother of it all.

Now, when God scattered these people, they took with them Semiramis's system. God not only scattered them, but He changed their languages. So, she received different names because different cultures have different languages, and that means different pronunciations. So, in Assyria she was called Ishtar, in Phoenicia her name was Ashtoreth, in Egypt her name was Isis, in Greece her name was Aphrodite, and in Rome her name was Venus. They are all names for Semiramis. They were worshiping Semiramis, the priestess that spawned false religion.

(b) Tammuz

Semiramis also gave birth to a son. His name was Tammuz. His name appears in the Bible in Ezekiel 8:14. In Phoenicia his name was Baal, in Egypt his name was Osiris, in Greece his name was Eros, and in Rome his name was cute, little, lovable Cupid. She said that he was conceived by a sunbeam. That is a counterfeit to the virgin birth. Supposedly he had no earthly father. Satan understood Genesis 3:15; he knew there would be a seed of a woman. Then, amazingly enough, Tammuz was killed by a wild boar and forty days later rose from the dead— another counterfeit.

(3) The sophisticated rites

Those in Greece would have known about this system of religion. They would have been worshiping the same system with some sophistication. They had all kinds of sophisticated rites and rituals. For example, they believed in:

(a) Baptismal regeneration—They believed that people were saved by being baptized in water, so they had systematic baptisms.

(b) Sacrificial systems—They mainly slaughtered pigs, lambs, dogs, and birds.

(c) Feasts and fasts

(d) Mutilations and flagellations—These came from the mystery system.

17

(4) The specifics of ecstasy

    (*a*) An explanation of its effect

> There was one thing that was characteristic about the mystery religions that found their way into Greece—they indulged in what they called *ecstasy.* Ecstasy is not what you feel when you kiss your girl friend. The word is *ecstasis* in the Greek and means to "cultivate a magical, sensuous communion with deity." In other words, they would do anything they could to get themselves into a semiconscious, hallucinatory, hypnotic spell in order to sensually commune with their deity and have a euphoric feeling. They assumed that this was a union with God.

A Historical Description of Ecstasy

I want to give you some quotes from S. Angus, who has a significant book entitled *The Mystery-Religions* (New York: Dover, 1975, pp. 100-101), in which he writes as a very objective historian. These are normal, routine, well-known facts about these systems. It is important to understand how these systems operated because they were the basis of the mess in Corinth.

"The *mystes* was brought into a mystic ineffable condition in which the normal functions of personality were in abeyance and the moral strivings which form character virtually ceased or were relaxed, while the emotional and intuitive were accentuated." Here is a situation in which a person enters into a condition where his personality becomes abnormal, where his normal morality is set aside so that he indulges in orgies, and where his brain goes into neutral and emotion takes over. This is ecstasy.

"These states were Ecstasy *(ecstasis)* and Enthusiasm *(enthousiasmos).* . . ." Enthusiasm, in our society, means something different. We define enthusiasm as "giving something your all," but that is not the Greek meaning. It is a state of euphoria induced in someone to make him semiconscious.

He goes on to say, "Both of which might be induced by vigil and fasting, tense religious expectancy, whirling dances, physical stimuli, the contemplation of the sacred objects, the effect of stirring music, inhalation of fumes, revivalistic contagion [such as happened in the church at Corinth], hallucination, suggestion, and all the other means belonging to the apparatus

18

of the Mysteries." They could induce this ecstasy through many ways: By vigil and fasting—that is contemplative; by tense religious expectancy—whipping people into some kind of anticipation; by the stirring effect of music; and by inhaling certain fumes such as incense. Some do that today in order to create a euphoric state.

"These two kindred abnormal states of consciousness, often indistinguishable, are united by Proclus when he speaks of men 'going out of themselves to be wholly established in the Divine and to be enraptured.'

"In ecstasy the devotee was lifted above the level of his ordinary experience into an abnormal consciousness of an exhilarating condition in which the body ceased to be a hindrance to the soul. Ecstasy might be of a passive character resembling a trance, or of an active orgiastic character of excitation resembling what Plato calls 'divine frenzy.' According to the means of induction, the temperament of the initiate, and his spiritual history, ecstasy might range anywhere from non-moral delirium to that consciousness of oneness with the Invisible and the dissolution of painful individuality which marks the mystics of all ages." He is saying that in ecstasy a person can go into all different kinds of responses in a trancelike way.

For example: the guru who sits and crosses his legs and goes into oblivion creates a form of ecstasy in his mind. The ultimate aim in life for the Buddhist is to enter nirvana—a state of total nothingness where he contemplates himself out of existence. Then there are the whirling dervishes and the mad, wild frenzies of ecstasy of other religions that end in orgies. This goes back to Baal. You see it even today. Some are "slain" in the spirit and fall into a trance. Others run wild and frenzied.

"In ecstasy, in the freeing of the soul from the hampering confinement of the body, in its communion with the deity, powers arise within it of which it knows nothing in the daily life hampered by the body. It now becomes free as spirit to hold communion with spirits: also released from transiency, it is endowed with capacities to behold what only the eyes of the spirit can behold, that which is removed beyond time and space." This euphoria creates a tremendously good feeling. People say, "This is fantastic! We have communed with the deity!" They conclude: "I felt so good! I never felt this way before. It has to be God." I know of people who can snort cocaine, smoke dope, shoot heroin, or get drunk and still feel better than the people who seek ecstasy. That is not the criteria. When this artificial euphoria is created, the assumption is made that they must have connected up with God.

"Physically the condition was one of anaesthesia, unconscious of pain or of anything hostile or disconcerting in the surroundings." Have you ever noticed that when someone goes to a healer with terrible pain and walks away feeling nothing, he is found to be in agony a day later because there was created a euphoric, anaesthetic response in the mind? "There is ample evidence that the Bacchae, for example, were insensate to pain and endued with preter-natural strength; so also were the priests of Cybele and the priests and priestesses of Ma. This anaesthesia to pain is a religious phenomenon known in all ages, especially in great revivals, and in many forms, from that of the Indian Yogi to the Christian martyr whose ecstasy took away the terrors of agonizing death by imparting miraculous fortitude. We may assume that this semi-physical, semi-psychic state was much coveted by the initiates. . . .

"Enthusiasm was the kindred state of communion often accompanying and confused with ecstasy. Under Enthusiasm were included by the Greeks all forms of Mantic, or prophecy and soothsaying, also revelations in dreams and visions, such revelations being the direct utterances of the deity." In all forms of enthusiasm there is the same underlying idea: God is involved.

Now, those two things (ecstasy and enthusiasm) made up the system of religion in which the Corinthians had lived and grown. When they became believers they stayed the same because they were not spiritual but carnal. They manifested the same type of religious behavior as they had every other dimension of the world by dragging this into their assembly. Their kind of religion was ecstatic, orgiastic frenzy. It was chaotic and confusing. Paul said, "Let all things be done decently and in order" (1 Cor. 14:40). In addition, he said, "Let all things be done unto edifying" (1 Cor. 14:26*b*).

(*b*) An example of its effect

Suppose that you were a visitor in Corinth and you said to your wife, "Let's go to church today. Let's attend the First Church of Corinth." So you go and arrive right on time at the place they meet, but all the rich people have already been there an hour and finished the love feast. There is nothing left for you

20

or the poor who are just arriving because they get there later from work. Then you notice that the rich are not only gluttonous but drunk, while all the poor people are sitting on the other side of the room with their stomachs gnawing. As a result, there is a great division.

Then somebody brings up a certain issue and they argue about it. The drunks are loud and obnoxious, and you are saying to yourself, "This is a funny church we are in." Then they abuse the Lord's Supper—drinking too much and eating it up. The Supper turns into a mockery. When that is ended, they begin the regular service and everyone stands up yelling and talking at the same time. People are speaking in ecstatic utterances, someone is trying to give a prophecy, and someone is singing a song. Then they give you a little brochure, "Welcome to the First Church of Corinth." If you happen to have an unbelieving guest with you he would go away saying, "These people are out of their minds!"

3. The perception of the source

This is exactly what was happening in Corinth. That is why Paul said, "That ye come together, not for the better but for the worse" (1 Cor. 11:17b). Paul has to try to straighten out their mess. One of the reasons I believe that the true gift of languages is simply languages, and not ecstatic babble, is that God would never give a gift that is the same as Satan uses. So, Greek religion invaded the Corinthian assembly, and they wrote the letter saying, "Would you please tell us how we can tell what is good and what is bad?"

a) The dilemma

I once read a book written by a writer who said that when someone stands up and gives a divine utterance we know one of two things: It is either of God or it is not. But that leaves you with a small dilemma, and it was exactly where the Corinthians were.

b) The declaration

So, Corinth was filled with priests, priestesses, soothsayers, and people in ecstasy and enthusiasm claiming divine power and divine inspiration. They were carnal and had dragged all this mess into the church. They expected the Holy Spirit to work because He had promised to work.

They knew that Joel 2:28*b* had begun to be fulfilled: "I will pour out my Spirit upon all flesh; and your sons and your daughters shall prophesy, your old men shall dream dreams, your young men shall see visions." They knew Jesus had told the disciples that when the Spirit came, amazing things would happen—people would speak with new languages (Mark 16:17). In John 14-16, Jesus promised to send the Spirit. In Acts 1:5*b*, before He ascended, He said, "Ye shall be baptized with the Holy Spirit not many days from now." They were expecting it, but when it did happen they were confused by Satan.

c) The delusion

Now, 1 Corinthians is one of the earliest written letters in the New Testament. It didn't take long for Satan to confuse the issues because he doesn't waste any time. When someone says to me, "Look what happened. It must be of the Spirit," they are assuming that Satan doesn't counterfeit. I talked with a leader in a modern movement who said to me, "You can't deny this experience." I said, "When that experience occurs, do you always, without question, know it is of God? Be honest." "No." "Could it be of Satan?" "Yes." "How do you tell the difference?" He had no answer. That is exactly the Corinthian situation.

d) The disclosure

Now, what was the question they asked Paul? They probably said something like this: "Paul, we have so many richly gifted people in our church, but the problem is, everyone wants to do everything at the same time. Then we have all kinds of wild things happening, and it's causing confusion. Could you help us solve our problem?" So he begins to solve their problem in verse one.

Lesson

I. THE IMPORTANCE OF SPIRITUAL GIFTS (vv. 1-3)

A. The Concern of Paul (v. 1)

"Now concerning spiritual gifts, brethren, I would not have you ignorant." Paul said, "I don't want you to be ignorant. I don't want you to be agnostics. I want you to understand this subject." Why? The church can't function without the operation of spiritual gifts—that is how the Holy Spirit operates and how the Body is built. In addition, Satan is counterfeiting it, so you can't be ignorant. But you cannot base your understanding on experience because you can't be that perceptive. The Corinthians admitted that they were not. The spiritual gifts in the Corinthian church were not being used in the way God intended. Instead of unifying the Body, they were splitting the Body.

1. An infallible source

   a) "Now concerning"

   Paul's first point is in 1 Corinthians 11:18, where he deals with abuses of the Lord's Supper. When he says, "Now," he uses the Greek particle *de* as a transition to his second point: "In the second place, you are abusing your fellowship concerning spiritual gifts, and I do not want you to be ignorant."

   b) "Spiritual gifts"

   The only word that appears in the actual text is *spiritual,* because *gifts* is implied. So the verse should read, "Now concerning spirituals, brethren, I would not have you ignorant."

   (1) The definition

   Now, *spirituals* is *pneumatikōn* in the Greek. This is a simple word. You can understand a lot about its meaning by understanding the word. *Pneuma* is "Spirit," and any time there is an *ikos* or *ika* or *ikōn* ending on a Greek word it means "characterized by" or "controlled by." So, *pneumatikōn* would be "characterized or controlled by the Spirit." The verse can now be translated, "Now concerning certain things characterized or controlled by the Spirit, brethren."

   (2) The determination

   What are these things? Some say he is talking about spiritual persons. In other words, the carnal people are the subjects of the first eleven chapters, whereas the spiritual people are the subjects of the remaining chapters. The spiritual people are the ones who speak in tongues and have the gifts. Does it mean spiritual people? The important question is: Is the word in the neuter or the masculine? We don't know; it is the same form for both. So, it could be spiritual persons if masculine, or spiritual things if neuter. How can we tell which one is correct?

The only way is to look at 1 Corinthians 14:1, where the same term is used in the same context. Paul says to follow after love and desire "spirituals." This time it is a distinct neuter form. So, the word here has to refer to spiritual things. Then he goes on to talk about prophesying and speaking in languages. The spiritual things he is talking about in chapter 14 are gifts. Therefore, we will assume that since the word is neuter in verse 1 of chapter 14, it is neuter in verse 1 of chapter 12 because the context is the same.

(3) The differences

What are these spiritual things? Verse 4 calls them "diversities of gifts." He is not referring to spiritual people, but to gifts. The word *pneumatikos* appears twenty-six times in the New Testament. Twenty-five of those times it means "characterized or controlled by the Holy Spirit." One time it is used in reference to Satan (Eph. 6:12).

You can learn a lot about spiritual gifts from that word because it tells you spiritual gifts are controlled by the Spirit. Paul's use of this word is one of five different terms he uses to refer to gifts. In verse 4 the word "gifts" is *charisma* in the Greek. It means that they are received by grace. You can't earn them. In verse 5 he uses the word "administrations." In the Greek it is *diakonia*, which means "serve." This word indicates that spiritual gifts are used to serve. In verse 6 he uses "operations." The Greek word, *energeō*, refers to energy, which means the gifts are energized by God. (The Greek word *phanerōsis* is "manifestation" in verse 7 and is the fifth word Paul uses).

So, spiritual gifts are controlled by the Spirit, given by grace from God, used to serve the Body, and empowered by the Lord. The different terms that he uses each have a different emphasis. In verse 1 they are simply spirituals—those things under the control of and characterized by the Spirit.

2. An intelligent understanding

"I would not have you ignorant." This verse is what we would call an idiom. It is a Greek idiom for something that is super emphatic. Paul reserved it for the times he wanted to say something very important like, "But I would not have you to be ignorant, brethren, concerning them who are asleep" (1 Thess. 4:13*a*). Here he is referring to the rapture. In Romans 1:13 he says, "Now I would not have you ignorant, brethren, that oftentimes I purposed to come unto you ... that I might have some fruit among you also, even as among other Gentiles." He did not want them ignorant about the impetus he had for preaching the gospel. In Romans 11:25 he did not want them ignorant about Israel and the plan God has for its restoration.

So, I want you to understand spiritual gifts. I don't want you to be ignorant about them. You say, "Why?" The church cannot mature or function without them. Satan will also try to counterfeit them—to confuse, cause chaos, and split the church. And this is exactly what has happened today. You must understand how to minister your gifts and to distinguish between what is and what isn't a gift.

There is a lot of ignorance today concerning spiritual gifts. It manifests itself in the abuse of gifts—ignoring them, neglecting them, overemphasizing the wrong ones, and confusing them with counterfeits. Paul says that this ignorance has to end. Hopefully the Spirit of God will direct us in the understanding of spiritual gifts so that the ignorance will come to an end.

Focusing on the Facts

1. What are some of the more common misconceptions regarding the church? What is the correct perspective? What does this tell us about the nature of the church (see pp. 9-10)?
2. How does the church manifest itself supernaturally (see p. 9)?
3. What is the function of spiritual gifts within the Body of Christ? Why does Satan try to counterfeit them (see pp. 9-10)?
4. How was the Corinthian church established (see pp. 10-11)?
5. What happened to the Corinthian church after Paul left? How was he able to find out about the problems (see p. 11)?
6. What were some of the problems within the Corinthian assembly (see pp. 11-12)?
7. How had the Corinthians managed to pervert spiritual gifts? Give two ways (see p. 12).
8. Why did the gift of languages become exploited (see pp. 12-13)?
9. What were some of the things from the world that infiltrated the Corinthian church? How did these manifest themselves (see pp. 12-15)?
10. What is the final form of world religion called? What was the source of this final form (see p. 16)?
11. Why has every false system of religion since the Tower of Babel been spawned out of that very first system (see pp. 16-17)?

12. Why is Semiramis I a very significant person in the development of false religious systems? why is Tammuz? What counterfeits of the truth involved Tammuz (see pp. 16-17)?
13. What were some of the sophisticated rites connected with Greek religion (see p. 17)?
14. What was the purpose of ecstasy in the mystery religions (see pp. 18-20)?
15. How was this ecstasy induced (see pp. 18-20)?
16. Why did the Corinthians manifest this kind of religious behavior in the assembly (see p. 20)?
17. What is one possible reason that the gift of languages is not ecstatic babble (see p. 21)?
18. What was the dilemma facing the Corinthians? What was the question that they asked Paul (see pp. 21-22)?
19. Why can't you base your understanding of how the Holy Spirit operates just on experience (see p. 22)?
20. What are *spirituals*? How are we able to determine what this word actually refers to (see p. 23)?
21. What are the five different terms Paul uses to describe spiritual gifts? What particular aspect of spiritual gifts does each describe (see p. 24)?
22. Why did Paul not want the Corinthians to be ignorant of spiritual gifts (see pp. 24-25)?

Pondering the Principles

1. What is your view of the church? How do you view your function within the church? Read Ephesians 4:11-16. What is the purpose for every member of the Body of Christ? What do you need to do in the areas of unity, Bible study, and speaking the truth in love in order to do your part in edifying the Body of Christ? Prayerfully consider the aspects of your life you would like to see changed as a result of this study of spiritual gifts.
2. Review the list of problems that were prevalent in the church at Corinth (see pp. 11-12). Of these problems, which ones are you aware of, or certain of, that are still a problem in the church today? Why are they still a problem? Why were they a problem in the Corinthian church? How can these problems be corrected? What part can you play in the correction of these problems? Ask God to give you wisdom in regards to your response to these problems. Remember, you are not the one responsible to make changes—God is—but your priority is to edify the Body of Christ.
3. Look up the following verses: Romans 1:11; 7:14; 15:27; 1 Corinthians 2:13, 15; 3:1; 9:11; 10:3-4; 12:1; 14:1, 37; 15:44, 46; Galatians 6:1; Ephesians 1:3; 5:19; Colossians 1:9; 3:16; 1 Peter 2:5. Each of these verses contain one of the uses of the word *spirituals*. In your

own words, what do each of these verses say, given the definition that *spiritual* means "characterized or controlled by the Holy Spirit"? Given this definition, what do you think *carnal* means? Examine your own life. Are you spiritual or carnal? Are you controlled by the Holy Spirit or not?

2

Concerning Spiritual Gifts—Part 2

Outline

Introduction
A. The Consideration of Christlikeness
  1. The purpose
  2. The plan
    a) Indwelling the individual
    b) Indwelling the church
  3. The process
    a) The spiritual endowment
    b) The spoils of the cross
    c) The special men
      (1) The positive result
      (2) The negative response
B. The Characteristics of Christ
  1. His example
  2. His enablement

Review
I. The Importance of Spiritual Gifts
A. The Concern of Paul

Lesson
B. The Counterfeit of Paganism
  1. The tradition
    a) The classification
    b) The characterization
      (1) "Carried away"
      (2) "Unto these dumb idols"
        (*a*) 1 Corinthians 10:19-20*a*
        (*b*) Galatians 4:8
        (*c*) Ephesians 4:17-18
        (*d*) Titus 3:3
        (*e*) 1 Peter 4:3
      (3) "Even as ye were led"
        (*a*) An irresistible leading

(b) An indistinguishable force
2. The tests
  a) The negative
    (1) The denouncement
    (2) The details
      (a) A professing Christian
      (b) A carry-over from the frenzy
      (c) A Jewish professing Christian
    (3) The deception
    (4) The defense
      (a) The support of Christ's deity
      (b) The significance of the death and resurrection
      (c) The simplicity of the true Christ
  b) The positive
    (1) The commitment
    (2) The confession

Introduction

Jesus has made clear that we who know God are salt and light in the world (Matt. 5:13-14). The Scripture also calls us ambassadors to the world (2 Cor. 5:20) and pilgrims in the world (1 Pet. 2:11). Paul told the Philippians that our citizenship is not here but in heaven (Phil. 3:20). And, we are sojourners in the world (1 Pet. 1:17). So, there is a purpose for our individual existence as believers in the society in which we live—to turn men to God through Christ. We are a witnessing community—a group of people placed in the world to draw the attention of the world to God.

A. The Consideration of Christlikeness

1. The purpose

Perhaps the most thrilling concept of all regarding our identity is found in Ephesians 4:13: "Till we all come in the unity of the faith, and of the knowledge of the Son of God, unto a perfect man, unto the measure of the stature of the fullness of Christ." The design of the church is to be brought into Christlikeness— till we all come to the full stature of Christ. God has given apostles, prophets, evangelists, and teaching pastors for the perfecting and the maturing of the saints for the work of the ministry that the Body might be built up. The ultimate goal of the building up is that we might come to a fullness of Christlikeness.

Not only are we to be salt and light, ambassadors, and pilgrims in the world, but we are to be Christ in the world. This is a

29

vital concept. The church is to be Christ in the world. I have chosen to call the church "Body II" and the incarnation "Body I"—Christ in a human body. We are "Body II"—Christ alive in the world in the church. This is a vital reality that we have to understand. The Lord Jesus wanted to remain in the world after the ascension by reproducing in us His very essence, life, personality, and character so that we might manifest Christ to the world.

2. The plan

How has God designed us to be Christ in the world? How can we literally represent Him and manifest His character to this world?

a) Indwelling the individual

The Bible says that He has planted within us the Spirit of Christ. Romans 8:9*b* says, "Now if any man have not the Spirit of Christ, he is none of his." But we have received the Spirit of Christ; therefore, Paul says, "The life I live is not my own, but it is Christ living in me" (Gal. 2:20). So Christ reproduces Himself in the world by living in the individual believer.

b) Indwelling the church

Now, Christ not only indwells every individual believer, but He indwells the corporate church. Ephesians 2:22 says that the entire church is built together as a habitation for the Spirit of Christ. Christ exists, not only in the individual life of a Christian but in the corporate life of the community of believers known as the Body of Christ. He produces His character in us first by dwelling in us.

3. The process

Ephesians 4:7-8, 11-13 contains the simplest explanation of how Christ reproduces Himself in the church. His presence is there, but His character becomes manifested in this way:

a) The spiritual endowment

"But unto every one of us is given grace according to the measure of the gift of Christ" (Eph. 4:7). By grace Christ has given the believer certain gifts—certain divine enablements. Not one Christian is excluded. We don't deserve it, we can't earn it, but these gifts of Christ are measured out individually and uniquely for every Christian. You say, "Why is 'gift' singular if some of us have more than one?" I think the plurality of our gifts can be expressed as our single

30

gift. My gift from God may be the gifts of preaching, teaching, and administration all combined into one gift. Sometimes you have opened one package and received three things in one box. But the design of the gift is to manifest His character. He gives us an aspect of His character.

b) The spoils of the cross

Verse 8 says, "Wherefore, he saith, When he ascended up on high, he led captivity captive, and gave gifts unto men." When Christ died on the cross He gathered some spoils— the spoils of the souls of the men and women that He won at the cross. He then gave them back to the church as gifts.

c) The special men

(1) The positive result

According to verse 11 He gave the gifts of apostles, prophets, evangelists, and teaching pastors. They are the gifted men given to the church. Verse 7 says that He has already given individual gifts to the believer, and it is the role of the gifted man to equip the gifted believers to use their gifts. Verse 12 says that the gifted men are given for the maturing of the saints for the work of the ministry.

The Lord Jesus Christ has given every believer a gift for the purpose of manifesting Christ in the church and ultimately in the world. In order to allow us the fullest use of those gifts and to bring them to maturity, God has also given to the church the gifted men. The result is in verses 12*b*-13—the edifying of the Body of Christ until the church together manifests the stature of the fullness of Christ. That is a great concept and very basic in identifying the church.

(2) The negative response

Now, if the gifted men do not perfect the saints or the saints do not minister their gifts, the Body will not be built up or manifest Christ. One of the difficulties in the church today is the fact that it is so fractured—Christians are disobedient in the area of gifts, and leaders are failing in perfecting the saints. The entire Body of Christ is crippled, distorted, and confused. The world cannot see the true manifestation of Jesus Christ. The gifts are given to the church to the ultimate end that the church is built up into the fullness of the stature of Jesus Christ. Individually and corporately we should represent Christ.

B. The Characteristics of Christ

Now, all of the spiritual gifts in their fullest sense are complete in Christ.

1. His example

There is the gift of prophecy, or preaching. Did Christ preach? Yes, He was the best. There is the gift of teaching. Did Christ teach? Yes, He was the best teacher. There is the gift of showing mercy. Did Christ show mercy? Yes, magnanimously, like no other person that ever lived. There are the gifts of ruling, helps, giving, and faith, each of which has its perfect example in Jesus Christ. He gave as nobody ever gave, ruled as nobody ever ruled, and had faith in the Father such as nobody has ever displayed. In other words, the spiritual gifts are characteristics of Christ that will be manifest through the Body corporate as they were manifest through the body incarnate. That is the purpose of spiritual gifts.

You say, "What about the miraculous gifts?" Christ had miraculous ability as confirmation of His identity. These gifts were also given in the early years of the church to confirm the message of God. So, all of the gifts find their perfection in Christ.

2. His enablement

Now, when we preach, teach, show mercy, help, lead, give, or have faith, we find that our gifts are a supernatural activity endowed and enabled by the Spirit of God. It manifests an attribute of Christ to the building of the Body. Thus Christ becomes evident in the world. The gifts are not random, but they specifically find their source in God, their channel in the Spirit, and their pattern, their example, and their completeness in the person of Jesus Christ. They are essential because they manifest Christ and build up the church.

Review

The amazing thing about the Corinthian church is that they had all the gifts. First Corinthians 1:7a says, "Ye come behind in no gift." They had been endowed with all spiritual gifts—they were fully equipped for maturing, they were fully equipped for ministering, and they were fully equipped to be Christlike. Instead, there was absolute chaos. There was a failure on the part of the gifted men to mature the saints. There was a failure on the part of the saints to minister the gifts they had been given. Instead, they were being counterfeited, exploited, neglected, abused, and confused, resulting in the terrible chaos that occurred relative to spiritual gifts. Paul wrote chapters 12-14 to deal with the urgent need for proper understanding and ministry of the gifts as spiritual endowments from God Himself.

Now, the Corinthian church was basically carnal and chaotic. There was little order. Every conceivable trial, turmoil, and sin was manifesting itself. They had managed to pervert the life of the church in every possible way, including spiritual gifts. Their society was drowning in the sea of mystery religions characterized by ecstasy and enthusiasm. This was a nonrational, ecstatic, orgiastic, trancelike activity that was supposedly the highest level of religious experience. As a result of this hysterical extremism, delusions regarding the true gifts had infiltrated the church at Corinth and they were now confused. Their public worship had turned into a disastrous exercise of selfishness, gluttony, drunkenness, and ecstatic, orgiastic frenzies as Satan busily counterfeited the gifts. These carnal people were left in confusion as to what was real. They had exalted the ecstatic and perverted the gift of languages. This became their major abuse.

As a result of all of this, some had written to Paul and asked him to help them to straighten out this mess. He wrote chapters 12-14 in response to the fearful marriage of the frenzy of the mystery religions with the truth of the grace gifts from the Spirit of God given to the Corinthian assembly. In chapter 12 he lays out basic theology; in chapter 13 he talks about love, the context in which all gifts operate; and in chapter 14 he directly deals with abuses. Three features are identified in Paul's basic presentation of the gifts: the importance of spiritual gifts, the source of spiritual gifts, and the kinds of spiritual gifts.

I. THE IMPORTANCE OF SPIRITUAL GIFTS

A. The Concern of Paul (v. 1; see pp. 22-25)

"Now concerning spiritual gifts, brethren, I would not have you ignorant."

Lesson

B. The Counterfeit of Paganism (vv. 2-3)

"Ye know that ye were Gentiles, carried away unto these dumb idols, even as ye were led. Wherefore, I give you to understand that no man speaking by the Spirit of God calleth Jesus accursed; and that no man can say that Jesus is the Lord, but by the Holy Spirit." These verses are tremendously critical in our understanding of the problems that were occurring in the Corinthian church and how we must deal with similar problems.

1. The tradition (v. 2)

   a) The classification (v. 2a)

   "Ye know that ye were Gentiles [heathen]." The word *Gentile,* in its technical sense, means "non-Jew." In its nontechnical sense it means "non-Christian." It can be translated "Gentile" or "heathen." A *heathen* is anyone who does not know God. For a comparison, 1 Thessalonians 4:5 uses the word in the same way.

   b) The characterization (v. 2b)

   "Carried away unto these dumb idols, even as ye were led." This is a picture of a victim of a system of religion who has little or no choice regarding his involvement. He is being led and carried away to dumb idols. He is strictly a victim.

   (1) "Carried away"

   The phrase "carried away" is a verb used frequently in the Bible to speak of leading a prisoner or a condemned person away to prison. In Mark 14:44 and 15:16 it is used with this meaning. In this context, the verb pictures someone caught, shackled, and dragged away to a dumb idol with no choice. The heathen are pictured not as being intelligent—choosing freely what their mind has concluded—but as helpless victims who know no better than to be led away by constraint to a dumb deity.

   I don't think that all people realize this. One particular individual has always said to me, "I would become a Christian, but I do not want to give up my freedom. I do not want to be restricted to having to do certain things. Right now I can choose whatever I want." I am reminded of many Scriptures, but of this one particularly. He is nothing but a pagan being carried away to a dumb deity. He is not free—he is a prisoner. According to Paul in Romans 6:17, he is a slave to sin.

   (2) "Unto these dumb idols"

   The ungodly man is led away to worship a nongod—a nondeity. Everyone worships somewhere. In the case of the Corinthian people, they had been led away to idolatry—gods who were dumb idols. Paul calls them "dumb"—dumb in the sense that they could not speak, answer, respond, give any direction or any revelation, and say anything authoritative. But that is the plight of the religious man without Christ—he is led away to a dumb deity and never knows the true freedom and the true dignity of a son of God.

Now, this is a biblical theme that occurs over and over again. Unregenerate people are hopelessly being led away to some stupid deity.

(a) 1 Corinthians 10:19-20a—"What say I, then? That the idol is anything, or that which is offered in sacrifice to idols is anything? But I say that the things which the Gentiles sacrifice, they sacrifice to demons."

(b) Galatians 4:8—"Nevertheless then, when ye knew not God, ye did service unto them which by nature are no gods."

(c) Ephesians 4:17-18—"This I say, therefore, and testify in the Lord, that ye henceforth walk not as other Gentiles walk, in the vanity of their mind, having the understanding darkened, being alienated from the life of God through the ignorance that is in them, because of the blindness of their heart." Darkness, blindness, alienation, and dumbness characterize the worship of an unregenerate individual.

(d) Titus 3:3—"For we ourselves also were once foolish, disobedient, deceived, serving various lusts and pleasures, living in malice and envy, hateful, and hating one another."

(e) 1 Peter 4:3—"For the time past of our life may suffice us to have wrought the will of the Gentiles, when we walked in lasciviousness, lusts, excess of wine, revelings, carousings, and abominable idolatries."

There is a tragic portrayal in the Scripture of an unregenerate man as being led as a victim into evil. His dumb deities can't respond, no matter how religious he might be. This is applicable to pagans around the world who do not worship the true God.

(3) "Even as ye were led"

Then you say, "What is the connection with this and spiritual gifts? First he was talking about spirituals, and now he is discussing the heathen." The connection comes in the last phrase in verse 2: "even as ye were led." The Greek verb *ago* implies being led away as a passive victim.

(*a*) An irresistible leading

In this passage, the verb has reference to an irresistible leading. The same verb appears in 2 Timothy 3:6: "For of this sort are they who creep into houses, and lead captive silly women laden with sins, led away with various lusts." It implies a leading away into sinfulnes. I think this is the application of verse 2: "You were victims, you were led away by demons to worship false gods. As a result, you got yourself into sinfulness. I think this is the application of verse to your society." Paul says, "You used to worship the way the pagans do—led away by demons to ecstasies and enthusiasm characteristic of the mystery religion. You have brought those old patterns into the church and are letting the demons invade your worship. You gave up your will to them."

(*b*) An indistinguishable force

They were unable to distinguish between the usual and the unusual, between the demonic and the divine. They could not distinguish what was from God and what was from Satan. There was intrusion, there was corruption, and there was chaos. They literally confused the work of Satan with the work of the Spirit.

So Paul was saying, "The truly spiritual people are not marked by being carried away—that is precisely the characteristic of your former kind of religion. You used to have a religion where the demons carried you away as victims into ecstatic, orgiastic kinds of activity. That was a former religion, but you have dragged your fanatical type of religion into the church and created chaos." The truly spiritual are not marked by being swept away into trances and ecstasies and emotional frenzies.

Out of Control!

Being out of control is never the Christian's use of his gift. When someone says, "I was slain in the Spirit," I say, "You have been slain, but it's not in the Spirit." You say, "Why are they slain?" I suppose that in many cases it is the thing to do,

36

so they do it. In other cases it may be a hypnotic or a demonic experience.

The Spirit of God does not operate the gifts of the Spirit when people are out of control. That is Paul's point in 1 Corinthians 14:

1. Verse 15—"What is it, then? I will pray with the spirit, and I will pray with the understanding also; I will sing with the spirit, and I will sing with the understanding also." I heard an album with some singing in the spirit, but it was just gibberish. It is fine to sing under the power of the Spirit as long as you sing with the understanding also.

2. Verse 33a—"For God is not the author of confusion."

3. Verse 40—"Let all things be done decently and in order." The Spirit of God does not operate the gifts of God when one is out of control or under some sort of supernatural seizure. When someone goes out of control—into a trance, faints, speaks ecstatic languages, or goes into frenzied behavior—that is never of God. That is reflecting a pagan style of religion that corrupted the Corinthian assembly, and which continues to do the same today. All spiritual gifts function in the full control and consciousness of the user.

Paul refers to the heathen ecstasies just to show how bizarre their behavior had become and how bold the demons had become when they knew they could get away with it in the church.

2. The tests (v. 3)

"Wherefore, I give you to understand that no man speaking by the Spirit of God calleth Jesus accursed; and that no man can say that Jesus is the Lord, but by the Holy Spirit."

Here Paul gives us the first principle by which we can determine the genuine spiritual gift. In light of the confusion and in light of the failure to distinguish the Holy Spirit's activity from heathen, demonic leading, Paul gives a basic test. It is both positive and negative.

a) The negative (v. 3a)

"No man speaking by the Spirit of God calleth Jesus accursed."

(1) The denouncement

Some people were actually standing up in the midst of the Corinthian assembly, supposedly manifesting the gifts of the Spirit, and cursing Jesus. You say, "How do you know that?" This is the very thing Paul was dealing with. He literally said: "No one speaking by the Spirit of God says, 'Jesus is *anathema.*' "

This is beyond belief to me. If someone stood up in Grace Church and said, "I have the gift of prophecy, and I would like to speak. Jesus is accursed," would you think that was of the Holy Spirit? I wouldn't have to think about it—I know it isn't of the Holy Spirit. But the Corinthians didn't know because they had made the judgment of the value of the gift on the basis of the experience rather than the content. If it was strange, ecstatic, and supernatural, they figured it had to be the Holy Spirit. After all, it was happening in the church. Someone had actually gone so far as to literally curse Jesus, and the people could not determine that it was not of the Holy Spirit. This is doubly unbelievable after their training under the apostle Paul.

This is perhaps how the scene would look: Everyone would be doing something at the same time—someone singing, someone speaking ecstatic speech, someone giving a prophecy, someone shouting out a word of wisdom, and someone in the middle of it all shouting, "Jesus is *anathema.*" They had no ability to distinguish the true from the false. You say, "How could they ever believe that was of the Holy Spirit?" Let me give you a little background.

(2) The details

(*a*) A professing Christian

First of all, it must have been a professing Christian who said this or they never would have believed it was of the Holy Spirit. They knew that the Holy Spirit only dwelt in Christians, so if they assumed that it was the Holy Spirit, they must have assumed this person to be a Christian. You and I would assume differently: "Here is a non-Christian." But they did not have enough sense to understand the difference or be open to it, so they figured that if he had the experience, he must be a Christian.

(*b*) A carry-over from the frenzy

When a person was beside himself with ecstasy, they said, "It is the Holy Spirit." Paul said, "It is not the

Holy Spirit! Just because this happens in the church doesn't make it of the Spirit." But those demons had free rein. They were actually saying in public, "Jesus is *anathema*," and getting away with it. That's how bad off this assembly was. Don't ever believe that just because something happens in the church it is of the Spirit. Satan spends much of his time in the church. In addition, just because someone in the church is under the control of outside forces, don't necessarily assume they are of God. It could be demons. So, the state of emotion and ecstasy lies behind the cursing of Jesus.

(c) A Jewish professing Christian

The word *anathema* is a common Greek word used in the vocabulary of a Jew to mean "devoted to destruction." In fact, it is the strongest Jewish word for "condemnation." It would be similar to one of us saying, "Jesus, be damned." You say, "Why would they say that about Jesus?" It no doubt was something that the Jews said frequently because Deuteronomy 21:23 says that whoever is hanged on a tree is accursed. Much of the Jewish criticism of Christianity might have been, "How could you claim that He was the Messiah when He was hanged on a tree. Cursed is such a one." So, it may have been a rather common statement by a Jew, "We don't accept a crucified Messiah—He is accursed." Perhaps it was not uncommon for them to pronounce curses on Jesus. It certainly was not uncommon for the apostle Paul, who tried to chase Christians down and make them curse Jesus (Acts 26:11). So this may have been a Jewish person professing to be a Christian, cursing Jesus in the church, and having that cursing accepted as from the Holy Spirit.

(3) The deception

You say, "But who would reason this way?" Let me give you the best explanation that I know. Already existing in the Corinthian assembly was a creeping heresy that became very prevalent in the New Testament era. It is the heresy that denies the deity of Jesus Christ and denies His sufficiency to save. It became known by the second century as Gnosticism. This was the basic formation of it, apparently growing in the Corinthian assembly—a nonloyalty to Jesus Christ.

Notice that it doesn't say, "Christ is accursed," but, "Jesus is accursed." Perhaps they were buying this heresy that separated the true Christ from the human Jesus. This was the Gnostic's view: the Christ's Spirit dwelt up in space and ruled the world. When the man Jesus (who was not the Christ) was baptized, the Christ's Spirit descended upon Him. In addition, just prior to His death, the Christ's Spirit left so that Jesus died as a cursed criminal. So, according to their view, the dying Jesus was just a man. That is why the Corinthians didn't understand that Jesus rose from the dead. Paul wrote the fifteenth chapter of 1 Corinthians to explain the resurrection. He said, "And if Christ be not risen, then . . . your faith is also vain" (v. 14). It is very likely that they were beginning to accept the belief that the Christ's Spirit and the human Jesus were separate. So they were cursing the human Jesus while supposedly acknowledging the glorified and divine Christ.

(4) The defense

(a) The support of Christ's deity

First Corinthians 16:22 supports this: "If any man love not the Lord Jesus Christ, let him be *Anathema Maranatha.*" You might curse Jesus, but Paul says, "If you don't acknowledge Him, curse you!" Paul is saying, "Look, you will be cursed unless you accept the Lord Jesus Christ." That is the fullness of His deity. If you say, "Well, I accept the Christ but deny the Jesus," curse you! If you say, "I accept Jesus but deny Christ," curse you! If you say, "I accept Jesus but deny His lordship," curse you! If you say, "I accept the lordship but deny the man Jesus," curse you! The Lord Jesus Christ is the incarnate God.

(b) The significance of the death and resurrection

This heresy (distinguishing the historical Jesus from the Spirit of Christ) had crept in to deny the incarnation. If the Christ left Jesus before the cross, then what is the significance of His death? There is no significance. What is the significance of His resurrection? Same thing—no significance. That is why Paul wrote 1 Corinthians 15. You can't just have a Jesus; there has to be Christ. They were hung up on the resurrection because they believed this lie. If you have a human Jesus, then you are going to have trouble getting Him out of the grave; and if He doesn't rise, then we are all hopeless. By believing this heresy, you destroy the significance of the cross and the resurrection, as well as the deity of Christ.

(c) The simplicity of the true Christ

A few months later, Paul writes this in 2 Corinthians 11:3: "But I fear, lest by any means, as the serpent beguiled Eve through his craftiness, so your minds should be corrupted from the simplicity that is in Christ." He says, "I'm afraid for you because there is a corrupting process going on in relation to your understanding of Christ." He continues, "For if he that cometh preacheth another Jesus, whom we have not preached, or if ye receive another spirit, which ye have not received, or another gospel, which ye have not accepted, ye might well bear with him" (v. 4). He is simply saying, "Avoid falling into the trap of believing in another Jesus. Don't let anyone corrupt your mind from the simplicity that is in the true Christ." What is this simplicity? It is the single identity of the true Christ. A simple thing is something that cannot be divided. The simple thing about Christ is that He is indivisible.

So, Paul is acknowledging in 1 Corinthians that they were separating the historical Jesus from the Spirit of Christ. He says, "This heresy has been tolerated so that someone saying, 'Jesus is accursed,' can be accepted in your community as having a gift from the Holy Spirit."

So, the doctrinal test is the first test of a gift. If anyone ministers a gift, what does he say about Jesus? What does he say about Christ? Anyone who says that Jesus is accursed is not speaking of the Holy Spirit. The first test of the operation of any gift is its connection with the authoritative, revealed Word of God. The reason they were out of line was that what they said did not agree with Scripture. When someone says, "I have a word from the Holy Spirit," if that word agrees with Scripture, it isn't necessary, and if it doesn't agree, then it isn't right.

b) The positive (v. 3b)

"And that no man can say that Jesus is the Lord, but by the Holy Spirit."

When someone comes into your midst and with all of his faculties, all of his mind, all of his heart, and all of his being, says, "Jesus is Lord," you know that is of the Holy Spirit.

(1) The commitment

Now, it isn't simply the words that are important; it is the commitment. The word "say" does not mean "to parrot." A skeptic can *say,* "Jesus is Lord." You can pay a man ten dollars to say, "Jesus is Lord." That isn't the point. No man can truly say, no man can truly confess, no man can truly acknowledge Jesus as the Lord except by the Holy Spirit. When that deep conviction of genuine understanding about who He is comes forth, it is of the Spirit. When someone curses Jesus, that is sufficient evidence that he is not of the Spirit. When somebody confesses Jesus, that is sufficient evidence that he is.

(2) The confession

It is very important that Paul says, "That no man can say that Jesus is the Lord." "Lord" is *kurios* in the Greek. It is the regular means in the New Testament for translating the tetragrammaton—the Old Testament name for God—*Yahweh.* The confession is that Jesus is God. When someone confesses that Jesus the man is in fact God, there is no separation, no Gnostic division— that is of the Holy Spirit. That leads me to believe they were separating the human Jesus from the divine Christ. So, the Spirit-prompted confession is distinguished from the counterfeit by the acknowledgment that Jesus the man is, in fact, God.

The test of anyone's gift or of the use of that gift is an accurate doctrine of the Lord Jesus Christ. The Holy Spirit always leads men to ascribe deity, lordship, and all-sufficiency to Christ.

Spiritual gifts are very important. They are important because verse 1 says not to be ignorant. If God feels that way—they are important! But, they are also important because Satan is busy counterfeiting them. If they are that much of a problem to him, then they must be important. My dad always used to say, "People don't counterfeit what isn't valuable." You don't ever hear about counterfeit brown paper. Nobody counterfeits sticks. People counterfeit money, diamonds, and whatever is valuable because the fact that these are valuable is the only reason for counterfeiting. If spiritual gifts are important for the life of the church in order that we might be built up to be like Jesus Christ, then we had better find out how we can use ours.

Focusing on the Facts

1. What is the purpose for each believer's individual existence in the world? What are some of the ways in which believers are characterized in the world (see pp. 29-30)?
2. What is the design for the church? Explain the concept of "Body I" and "Body II" (see p. 30).
3. In what two ways can believers manifest Christ to the world? How does Jesus Christ produce His character in us (see pp. 30-31)?
4. How does Jesus Christ manifest His character in believers (see pp. 30-31)?
5. Explain why Paul uses the singular form of the word "gift" in Ephesians 4:7 (see pp. 30-31).
6. Why did God give gifted men to the church? What is the ultimate result of their ministry, according to Ephesians 4:12-13? What happens if they fail in their ministry (see p. 31)?
7. In what ways do all of the spiritual gifts have their fullest completion in Christ? Give some examples (see p. 32).
8. How are Christians given the ability to manifest Christ in their lives (see p. 32)?
9. For what purpose did Paul write 1 Corinthians 12-14 (see p. 33)?
10. What does *Gentile* mean in its nontechnical sense (see p. 34)?
11. What does the phrase "carried away" refer to? How does Paul apply this to the heathen (1 Cor. 12:2; see p. 34)?
12. Why does Paul refer to the deities of the heathen as "dumb" (see p. 34)?
13. How does Scripture portray the unregenerate man? Give some examples (see p. 35).
14. What was characteristic of the heathen in their worship of false gods (see pp. 35-36)?
15. How does the Spirit of God operate the gifts of the Spirit in believers? Give some Scripture for support (see p. 37).
16. What totally unbelievable thing was actually occurring in the Corinthian church? Why were the Corinthians allowing this to happen (see pp. 37-38)?
17. Why did the Corinthians believe that what was happening in the church was from the Holy Spirit? Give the three reasons and explain each one (see pp. 38-39).
18. What does *anathema* mean? Why did Jews use this word in reference to Jesus (see p. 39)?
19. Explain the significance of the heresy that was beginning to creep into the Corinthian assembly. Give a summary of the basic doctrine that this heresy promoted (see pp. 39-40).
20. Why didn't the Corinthians understand the resurrection of Jesus from the dead (see p. 40)?

21. What is the fullness of Christ's deity? Why is the understanding of this significant for all believers (see p. 44)?
22. What is "the simplicity that is in Christ" (2 Cor. 11:3; see p. 41)?
23. What is the first test of a spiritual gift? Explain (see p. 41).
24. What is necessary to know when someone is speaking by the Holy Spirit? What is the confession that needs to be made (see pp. 41-42)?
25. How do we know spiritual gifts are important (see p. 42)?

Pondering the Principles

1. Look up the following verses: Matthew 11:29; 20:28; John 13:34; Romans 8:29; 15:2-3; 2 Corinthians 8:9; Galatians 6:2; Ephesians 5:2; Philippians 2:5-8; Colossians 3:13; Hebrews 12:2-4; 1 Peter 1:15; 2:21-24; 3:17-18; 1 John 3:1-3, 16. According to these verses, how are you to be Christlike? On a scale of 1-10, rate yourself in each of these areas. What are your strengths? What are your weaknesses? Which area do you want to improve in most? Ask God to give you the wisdom you need in applying His principles to this area of your life. Make it a goal this week to pursue changing those things in your life-style that have kept you from being Christlike. Remember, the Holy Spirit indwells you to give you the resources to accomplish this goal.
2. Meditate on the following verses: Ephesians 4:17-18; Titus 3:3; 1 Peter 4:3. Take this moment to thank God for saving you from such a life-style and bringing you into His glorious kingdom.
3. Look up the following verses: John 16:7-14; Romans 8:1-17; 1 Corinthians 2:10-14; 1 John 4:2-3, 15. What is one name for the Holy Spirit according to John 16:13? Why is this significant in terms of distinguishing what is of the Spirit and what is not? According to these verses, how does the Holy Spirit manifest truth through the believer? How can you tell when someone is truly manifesting the Spirit of Christ? In order to solidify the importance of the Holy Spirit's ministry in your own life, memorize Romans 8:14: "For as many as are led by the Spirit of God, they are the sons of God."

3

Concerning Spiritual Gifts—Part 3

Outline

Introduction
A. The Purpose of the Holy Spirit
   1. The conviction of nonbelievers
   2. The ministry to believers
     a) Individually
        (1) He regenerates
        (2) He assures
        (3) He adopts
        (4) He seals
        (5) He indwells
        (6) He frees
        (7) He empowers
        (8) He makes holy
        (9) He reveals truth
        (10) He guides
        (11) He prays
     b) Collectively
        (1) He creates fellowship
        (2) He assists worship
        (3) He inspires Scripture
        (4) He guides
        (5) He generates unity
           (*a*) The maintenance of genuine unity
           (*b*) The method of generating unity
B. The Purpose of Spiritual Gifts
   1. Their priority
     a) The definition
     b) The disclosure
     c) The distribution
   2. Their perversion
     a) The highest level
     b) The highest gift
        (1) The approval of Plato
        (2) The analysis by Greene

Review
I. The Importance of Spiritual Gifts

Lesson
II. The Source of Spiritual Gifts
   A. The Unity of Diversity
      1. The importance of varieties
      2. The implication of varieties
      a) Varieties of gifts
      b) Varieties of combinations
      c) Varieties of categories
      d) Varieties of power
         (1) The example
         (2) The equivalent
   B. The Uniqueness of Diversity
      1. The dimensions of spiritual enablement
      a) Spiritual
      b) Gifts
      c) Administrations
         (1) The purpose
         (2) The proof
            (*a*) 1 Peter 4:10*a*, 11*a*
            (*b*) Ephesians 4:12
      d) Operations
      e) Manifestation
         (1) For public display
         (2) For profitable declaration
      2. The dividing of spiritual enablements

Introduction

As Christians, we believe in God. We believe that God manifests His personality in three Persons: God the Father, God the Son, and God the Holy Spirit. Now, those three Persons work in total agreement, and yet God diversifies Himself. He is one, yet three. We want to concentrate on the ministry of the Holy Spirit in our continuing discussion of spiritual gifts.

A. The Purpose of the Holy Spirit

The Holy Spirit ministers to two categories of people: The people who know God and the people who don't.

1. The conviction of nonbelievers

To the people who do not know Christ, who do not know God, and who are not what we would call "born again," the

46

Spirit of God is involved in convicting. John 16:8 says that the Spirit of God convicts them of sin, righteousness, and judgment. His ministry is to bring them to God.

2. The ministry to believers

His ministry to believers is much more complex. Once we have come to know Jesus Christ, received Him as Savior, and been born into the family of God, the Spirit of God then begins to work in a multiplicity of ways in our lives. The Spirit of God ministers to believers individually and collectively.

a) Individually

What does the Spirit of God do for you as an individual?

(1) He regenerates

The Spirit of God caused you to be saved. In John 3:5 Jesus said that you must be born of the Spirit. It is the Spirit of God that works the transformation of salvation. And the Spirit of God, having worked the saving work, then continues to transform you into the image of Jesus Christ (2 Cor. 3:18). So, the Holy Spirit regenerates and transforms an individual.

(2) He assures

First John 4:13 says, "By this know we that we dwell in him, and he in us, because he hath given us of his Spirit." "The Spirit himself beareth witness with our spirit, that we are the children of God" (Rom. 8:16). God gives us an assurance. When you see someone who doesn't know if he knows God, who has no confidence in his redemption, and who has no security about the future, it may be that he is not a Christian and has no testimony in his heart from the Holy Spirit regarding this.

(3) He adopts

The Spirit of God adopts us as sons. He not only gives us the reality of sonship, but a sense of it. Galatians 4:6 says that the Spirit comes into our hearts causing us to cry, "Abba, Father." This is an endearing term that means "Daddy." So, the Spirit of God gives us a sense of being sons of God.

(4) He seals

When a king sent out a letter or decree in ancient times, he would pour some wax on it and stamp the wax with his seal. That made the document official. You and I have been given a stamp by God the Father—the Holy Spirit. By giving us the Spirit, He puts His stamp of authentication on us: "This is a bona fide child that belongs to Me."

(5) He indwells

First Corinthians 12:13 says that we all possess the same Spirit. Romans 8:9*b* says, "Now if any man have not the Spirit of Christ, he is none of his."

(6) He frees

Second Corinthians 3:17*b* says, "Where the Spirit of the Lord is, there is liberty." Freedom from law, freedom from having to please God by self-effort, freedom from the works-righteousness system that binds us, and freedom from sin and flesh and Satan are all ours in Christ.

(7) He empowers

Acts 1:8 says that after you receive the Spirit, you receive power.

(8) He makes holy

First Thessalonians 4:7-8 says that God has given us His Spirit to make us holy.

(9) He reveals truth

First Corinthians 2:9 says, "But as it is written, Eye hath not seen, nor ear heard [that's empiricism], neither have entered into the heart of man [that's philosophy], the things which God hath prepared for them that love him." In other words, man by empiricism and philosophy cannot discover God. Verse 10*a* says, "But God hath revealed them unto us by his Spirit." So, the Spirit of God in us teaches us and reveals truth to us.

(10) He guides

Romans 8:14 says, "For as many as are led by the Spirit of God, they are the sons of God."

(11) He prays

Romans 8:26*b* says, "The Spirit himself maketh intercession for us with groanings which cannot be uttered."

All of this the Holy Spirit does for the individual. You would be limping badly, spiritually, without the Holy Spirit. God gives us this fullness of the Spirit.

b) Collectively

You say, "I see what the Spirit does for me as an individual. But what is He doing for the church collectively? What is the Spirit of God doing in the midst of His church?" He indwells His total church. Ephesians 2:22 says that the church is the habitation of the Spirit. He is moving in His church.

(1) He creates fellowship

The Spirit of God is a catalyst who stimulates interaction in fellowship. Second Corinthians 13:14 talks about the fellowship of the Spirit. The Spirit of God generates fellowship. For example, in Acts 2 the Spirit of God descends and people begin to speak in other languages. Then Peter preaches and three thousand people are saved. Acts 2:42*a* says, "And they continued steadfastly in the apostles' doctrine and fellowship." The Spirit of God came and created fellowship.

(2) He assists worship

For example, when John goes to worship in Revelation 1:10 and 4:2, he says, "I was in the Spirit." The Spirit works in the act of worship. When believers come before God, the Spirit somehow draws out of us that worship toward God. So, He creates fellowship, He assists worship, and:

(3) He inspires Scripture

Whenever I open the Bible and teach the truths in the Word of God, or whenever you read them, remember that these things did not come by the will of men but by holy men of God who spoke as they were moved by the Holy Spirit (2 Pet. 1:21).

(4) He guides

In Acts 13:2 the Holy Spirit takes the collective body of people at Antioch and says, "Pick out Paul and Barnabas and send them off as missionaries." So, the Spirit of God directs the corporate life of the church.

(5) He generates unity

The Spirit of God generates unity in the church. Ephesians 4:3 says that we are to endeavor to keep the unity of the Spirit. The Spirit of God works for unity.

(*a*) The maintenance of genuine unity

We do not need to create unity in the church. We just need to stop creating division. Unity already exists. For example, in our house we have a basic corporate unity. My wife, our four kids, and myself are one. Genetically we are all out of the same, basic, common life stem. We share together. My wife and I become one in our children and our children are one with us. And there is also intellectual unity in our family. That doesn't mean that we are all of the same intelligence; it simply means that we all talk about the same things. We all come up together on the same intellectual plane. My kids will make value judgments based on what I think about issues. Your kids will do the same thing. There is also an emotional unity. All the members of our family respond the same way emotionally because we have learned to work together. In addition, there is volitional unity (i.e., we make similar choices).

Now, this is true in the church. The Spirit of God has created commonness in the church. It isn't up to us to create it; it is up to us to stop interrupting it. You don't have to create unity; you just need to stop creating division. The unity will take care of itself.

(*b*) The method of generating unity

Now, how does the Holy Spirit generate that unity? By giving everyone a mutual ministry to everyone else so that we begin to talk, think, feel, choose, have recreation, and socialize together. All of these dimensions of interaction create a basic unity generated from our common eternal life.

Now, it is critical that we minister to each other because that guards our unity. As soon as someone closes up and doesn't interact, share, or minister, then he becomes a point of isolation. But when there is a flow of ministry, there is going to be unity of the Spirit.

B. The Purpose of Spiritual Gifts

1. Their priority

The way in which we minister to each other is via our spiritual gifts. You say, "What is a spiritual gift?"

a) The definition

A spiritual gift is a God-given capacity through which the Holy Spirit supernaturally ministers to the Body. For example, I have the spiritual gift of teaching (or preaching). I minister to you as the Spirit of God energizes me. This is something that I can't do humanly, but something the Spirit of God must do through me. Your spiritual gift is not cooking—there are good cooks who don't even know God. It is a human ability. Your gift is not being a violin virtuoso. It is a terrific ability, but not a spiritual gift energized by the Holy Spirit. Your spiritual gift is a unique capacity to minister to the Body of Christ through the channel of the Spirit of God, who supernaturally touches the lives of other people.

b) The disclosure

This is critical: The Spirit of God has created corporate unity. To keep that unity we have to have mutual ministry where there is the interchange of all the dimensions of life—of thoughts and feelings and choices. This is why Paul was so upset with the Corinthians. In 1 Corinthians 12:1 he says, "Now concerning spiritual gifts, brethren, I would not have you ignorant." Why? If the gifts don't function, then the necessary spiritual unity will not exist in order for the church to be a corporate manifestation of Christ. There has to be the ministry of spiritual gifts occurring within the church.

c) The distribution

Then Paul says, "For to one is given, by the Spirit, the word of wisdom; to another, the word of knowledge by the same Spirit; to another, faith by the same Spirit; to another, the gifts of healing by the same Spirit; to another, the working of miracles; to another, prophecy; to another, discerning of spirits; to another, various kinds of tongues [languages]; to another, the interpretation of tongues [languages]" (1 Cor. 12:8-10). And, in verse 28, He "set some in the church: first apostles, second prophets, third teachers; after that miracles, then gifts of healings, helps, governments, diversities of tongues [languages]." Romans 12 has a similar list. These gifts are given to the individual believer through which the Spirit of God can minister to His church. They are very, very important.

Now, I don't want to ask how many of you know what your spiritual gift is, but I do want you to think about it. This is not something between you and me, but it is something between you and God. You are a steward. You don't own your spiritual gift; you manage it for Him. And it is either a case of good management or mismanagement. But if the unity is to be maintained, then the ministry of gifts is absolutely necessary.

2. Their perversion

The Corinthians had corrupted the whole system. They were not content with the gifts that God had given them—they wanted different ones. And they were perverting the ones they did have. This, then, became the point of pride: "Well, what gift do you have?" "I only have the gift of helps." "Sorry, too bad. I have the gift of prophecy." The eye was lording it over the ear (1 Cor. 12:16). The ear was saying, "I want to be an eye. I don't like being an ear. I want to be one of the more comely parts." This attitude was becoming a problem. They were a richly endowed church, but they had perverted everything.

a) The highest level

They lived in a society that was engulfed in the mystery religions. Their society expressed the highest level of religion as ecstasy. In other words, the more frenzied you were, the more you were in contact with the gods. You had connected up with God when you became hysterical. This had come into the church.

b) The highest gift

They took the gift of languages (the ability to speak in a language not learned) and made it the best gift. In the Greek culture, this kind of ecstatic confusion was a sign of their religion. They went into a frenzy in their festivals, and the result was orgies and wild, bizarre things such as demonic possession.

(1) The approval of Plato

For example, take a great intellectual like Plato and listen to what he said in the *Phaedrus:* "It is through mania [ecstasy due to divine possession] that the greatest blessings come to us." That is incredible! The more hysterical you are, the more spiritual blessing you are going to receive. Now, this is not an isolated statement by Plato. In *Timaeus* he also said, "No one in possession of his rational mind [Gk., *nous*] has reached divine and true exaltation." In other words, you can't ever touch deity until you are out of your mind. That is Plato's thought. The more nonrational the approach, the more the mark of divine inspiration. The more you were out of the spirit (Gk., *pneuma*), the less your mind (Gk., *nous*) was in it, and the more you were touching God.

(2) The analysis by Greene

Michael Greene, in his book *I Believe in the Holy Spirit* (Grand Rapids: Eerdmans, 1975), says, "The Corinthians would have rated in ascending order of value the teacher (in reliance on his rationality), the prophet (who spoke under divine inspiration intelligibly), and the man who spoke in tongues (whose inspiration was marked by unintelligibility)." Now, that is exactly what was going on in Corinth.

Further, Greene says, "To suppose that the more a man loses self-possession the more inspired by God he must be, is to deny God His place in the rational. To suppose that non-personal irruptions of *ruach* are the mark of inspiration is to forget that it is the Spirit of *Jesus* with whom we are dealing." The implication is that Jesus is not irrational. Greene continues, "Any such depersonalization of the Spirit is also disparagement of the ethical, as if it does not much matter how you behave so long as you have this mark of divine inspiration upon you." That is why somebody in a wild frenzy could say, "Jesus is accursed," and have others respond, "Oh, it's of the Holy Spirit." Why? They equated the experience with the Holy Spirit rather than the content. And this is what Paul corrects in 1 Corinthians 12:2-3. Further, Greene says, "If this particular gift is prized above all others, it easily leads to a cult of experience, and to excessive individualism (jealousy in those who have not got the gift, pride in those who have). In the midst of all this, Christian love can easily disappear." And, I might add, so will Christian unity.

So, the Corinthians had corrupted the gifts and Paul had to write chapters 12-14 of 1 Corinthians to straighten them out on the proper information and use of gifts.

Review

I. THE IMPORTANCE OF SPIRITUAL GIFTS (vv. 2-3; see pp. 22-54)

Gifts are vitally important. They are not to be confused with the work of demons, or the work of Satan, or the work of some frenzied pagans. They are divine marks of the Holy Spirit. Lucian, in *Dialogues of the Dead,* describing ecstatic activity, said, "A sort of god [lit., "demon"] carries us away wherever he wills, and it is impossible to resist him." Now that describes their pagan religion. But Paul says, "You used to be carried away" (1 Cor. 12:2). They needed to know the difference between the true and the counterfeit.

Lesson

II. THE SOURCE OF SPIRITUAL GIFTS (vv. 4-7, 11)

A. The Unity of Diversity

1. The importance of varieties

Verse 4 begins, "Now there are diversities of gifts, but the same Spirit. And there are differences of administrations, but the same Lord. And there are diversities of operations, but it is the same God who worketh all in all" (vv. 4-6). Now, you see in these verses a contrast: "the same Spirit," "the same Lord," "the same God." But on the other hand, there are varieties. One God, one Christ, and one Spirit means God has one will. He has built unity into His church, but it will only be maintained when there is a diversity of ministry.

I use the following illustration in my book on the subject (Body Dynamics [Glen Ellyn, Ill.: Victor, 1982]). A reporter comes to interview a quarterback and says, "You have a big game tomorrow. Are you ready for it?" "Oh, yeah! Really ready." "Do you really feel there is team unity?" "Oh, we've never had such unity. It is unbelievable." "Well, what do you mean?" "We are so united that all forty-four guys have decided to play quarterback." That is not unity! The only way unity functions is through diversity in teamwork. That is why the unity of the church is predicated on the ministry of our strengths to make each other strong. So there is the same

Spirit, same Lord, and same God working in all of us, but through diversities of ways.

2. The implication of varieties

The word *varieties* is interesting. It is a very broad word that literally means "distributions" in the Greek. God has distributed varieties of operations within His church. There are a variety of gifts. Some might have the gift of teaching, some might have the gift of giving, some might have the gift of helps, some might have the gift of administrations, the gift of governments, or the gift of giving. There are multiplicities of gifts within the framework of this distribution. And I am confident that most of us have more than one. One might be stronger in manifestation than another, but I think we all have a combination of them.

a) Varieties of gifts

This list in 1 Corinthians is not necessarily exhaustive. There is a different list in Romans 12, and there is a suggestion of a list in 1 Peter 4. There is no reason to assume that this is all there is. I read one book that said there were only four gifts. I read another one that said there were nine, another one that said there were eleven, another one fourteen, another one seventeen, another one nineteen. How many are there? I don't believe that is the point. I don't think we need to take a test on the gifts, put the results into a computer, and say, "I'm a _____ according to the computer."

b) Varieties of combinations

There are so many varieties of ways in which gifts function, that I'm not sure we can always catalog them in such an isolated fashion. Some of them overlap so much that you might have a mixture of gifts.

c) Varieties of categories

There may be thirty of us who have the gift of teaching, but all thirty of us may be manifesting it in entirely different ways, in entirely different styles, to entirely different groups of people, with entirely different objectives. But that is the beauty of diversity.

The word *varieties* is the best translation of the Greek word for "diversities" and "differences" in verses 4, 5, and 6 (see NASB*). I conclude that there are varieties.

*New American Standard Bible.

d) Varieties of power

Verse 6 refers to "operations" (i.e., energizing). There are different manifestations of divine power. Some gifts, manifested in certain ways, demand a different degree of power than others. Romans 12:3 talks about "the measure of faith" (cf. v. 6). God gives you gifts and measures out the exact amount of faith to make that gift operate.

(1) The example

For example, God gave me the spiritual gift, ability, and capacity to minister to a church. Since it is a large church, it requires a lot of responsibility. In a situation like this, there is a lot of anxiety because one has different people with different problems. It takes a certain kind of energizing by the Holy Spirit to handle this situation. If God gives me the capacity to teach, preach, and lead, but not the faith to believe that it's possible, I'm going to be a wreck. I am going to try to do something that I don't believe I can do. On the other hand, if God gives me the faith to believe that I can do this, but others keep telling me, "You can't do this. We need to get somebody else," I would be very frustrated. So, when God gives me the spiritual capacity, He measure out the faith equal to the task so I won't become frustrated.

(2) The equivalent

This means that the energizing is equivalent to whatever the gift might be. So, as the Spirit of God gifts you, He energizes you enough to operate the gift so that you have a sense of fulfillment. In all the varieties there are different manifestations of power.

B. The Uniqueness of Diversity

1. The dimensions of spiritual enablement (vv. 4-7)

There are five words in this chapter that are like five different facets of the diamond of spiritual enablement in the church.

a) Spiritual

In verse 1 the Greek word is *pneumatikos,* meaning that the source of spiritual enablement is the Holy Spirit.

b) Gifts

According to verse 4, there are "diversities of gifts." You have all heard the word *charismatic.* We may say that someone is *charismatic*. We mean that he has an electrifying, captivating, and charming personality. The word *charismatic* is from the Greek word *charis*, which means "grace." Grace is an undeserved gift. Remember this: your spiritual capacity—your *charisma*—is a gift of God's grace. You didn't deserve it. You can't say, "I am where I am today because of me." No, if you got where you are today because of you, then you don't belong in the church, and everyone else is paying the consequence. What you have is purely a gift of grace.

The word *charisma* is used seventeen times in the New Testament. Eleven times it refers to spiritual gifts, the other times to salvation. Is salvation a free gift? Yes. Did you deserve it or earn it? No. Spiritual gifts are free gifts, undeserved and unearned, granted by God's wonderful, loving, gracious kindness.

So, the first thing you learned about your capacity is that it is energized by the Holy Spirit (v. 1). Second, it is a gift that you didn't earn or deserve—given to you purely as a result of God's sovereign grace. That gives me a sense of responsibility. When someone gives me a gift and says, "Would you care for this?" I'm going to care for it! I want to be a steward; I want to make sure it's handled properly. The Spirit graciously gives out those grace gifts to all believers so that each of us can say with Paul, "By the grace of God I am what I am" (1 Cor. 15:10a). His grace was superabundant to me. The greatest mystery of my life, apart from God's saving me, is that God called me into the ministry. Why? It was His choice, and I thank Him for it.

c) Administrations

The word "administrations" (v. 5) in the Greek is *diakonion*. The similar word from our vocabulary is *deacon*. What does the word deacon mean? Servant. So, there are different grace gifts, different spirituals, different Holy-Spirit-energized enablements, and different services. Another word for spiritual gifts is *services*. It is not a different concept; it's just a different way to say the same thing.

(1) The purpose

The purpose of my gift is service. Jesus says, "For even the Son of man came, not to be ministered unto but to minister [Gk., *diakonos*, "to serve"]" (Mark 10:45a). Spiritual gifts are not designed as special privileges for the one who has them. My spiritual gift

57

is not for my edification. Now, I could pervert that. I could go into my office, study, write out all the things that I learned, preach a message into my tape recorder, and then turn it on and listen to it by myself. But that would prostitute my gift. When anyone says, "Well, I have this gift which I exercise only in private," that is self-edification. I say, "Well, it isn't a gift that the New Testament teaches, because the gifts are called services. That implies someone else is the object of your gift."

(2) The proof

(a) 1 Peter 4:10a, 11a—"As every man hath received the gift, even so minister [serve] the same one to another, as good stewards." Whatever your gift is, please serve somebody with it. Verse 11a says, "If any man speak, let him speak as the oracles of God; if any man minister [serve], let him do it as of the ability which God giveth." All the gifts are for others. Serve one another in divine energy.

(b) Ephesians 4:12—"For the perfecting of the saints for the work of the ministry [Gk., *diakonos*] for the edifying of the body of Christ." Beloved, your spiritual gifts are not for you.

Someone said to me, "Well, I believe that some of the gifts were for self-edification." You cannot find that anywhere. When the Corinthians perverted the gift of languages for self-edification, it was the same as my going into my office and teaching myself. That is not the intention of the gift—that is a perversion of it. That is why Paul says regarding spiritual gifts, "Seek that ye may excel to the edifying of the church" (1 Cor. 14:12). That is the right intention.

Not only are there these three terms: spirituals, gifts, and services, but there are:

d) Operations

There are a variety of energizings. The word comes from the Greek word *energeō*. God empowers each believer differently. Don't confuse this with natural talent—this is divine energizing. When we begin to function in the capacity that God has gifted us, there is a flow of divine energy that is thrilling. And it energizes the Word as it comes out of me to you. Once in a while I will listen to a tape on something I have taught in order to refresh my mind. After hearing it I have said to myself, "Did I say that? That's really terrific!" Then I realize the difference.

For example, one fellow said to me, "I have an observation to make. I just want you to know that you do not have the gift of counseling. I come to that conclusion based on having been counseled by you on several occasions." At first I thought he was wrong, based on my natural human reaction. But then I thought, "That's probably true." That is not what God has called me to do. I don't have an office as a marital counselor. I would probably be sitting there listening to somebody's problems week after week thinking, *"I wish they would leave so I could get back to my Bible."* So, I know the difference between what the Spirit of God has gifted and energized me to do and what I sometimes need to do although I may not have the sense of spiritual energy. So, you can see that the Spirit of God has this fantastic variety.

A Unique Snowflake

You are a snowflake. There are no two of you alike. God cannot trade you for anyone. If I said, "I have four nice kids, but I wouldn't mind a change. Maybe I'll give away one of my kids and get somebody else's kid," that would be wrong, because no child in the world would substitute for one of mine. You are a snowflake. The combination of gifts, energizings, and services that God has given you is unlike anything that He has given to someone else.

e) Manifestation

Verse 7 says, "But the manifestation of the Spirit is given to every man to profit." This is another word for spiritual gifts.

(1) For public display

"Manifestation" is a simple word that means "to make clear, to make visible, to make known, to make manifest." It means the very opposite of "to hide," or "to be private." Spiritual gifts are for manifestation. They are a visible, clear, manifest, public display. Again I say, when somebody says that he has a private gift, you ask, "How can it be private when all of the gifts are given to declare the working of the Spirit of God?"

(2) For profitable declaration

You say, "Well, maybe it is only to be manifest to him?" Verse 7 actually says, "The manifestation of the Spirit is given to every Christian for the common good." That is what the Greek word *sumpherō* ("profit") means. It isn't given for his good but for the good of all those who have been gathered together. It is a compound word and means "to gather together." Your spiritual gift is given to manifest the work of the Spirit to everyone that has been gathered together. My gifts are not intended for private purposes; my gifts are for the common good. Whatever the gift is, its purpose is to profit everybody.

What about the gift of languages? In chapter 14 Paul says not to use the gift of languages unless it is interpreted. Even though the gift was a sign to unbelieving Israel, it had to be interpreted in order to edify the church. No gift should be anything other than edifying to the people who are gathered together. So, when someone says that he has a private gift, it isn't true. It is to profit for the common good—to manifest the Spirit to all those gathered together.

2. The dividing of spiritual enablements (v. 11)

Verse 11 begins, "But all these worketh." This is the same word as in verse 6—energizing. He continues, "That one and the very same Spirit, dividing to every man" (v. 11*b*). How many Christians have gifts? All of them—not just a spiritual elite. You can't say, "The gifted ones are up on the podium." No, you are all the gifted ones. Mine is just different. You can do what I can't do in His energy.

Now, we all have them, but look at this beautiful thought: "dividing to every man," which is universality; and "severally," which is individuality (v. 11*c*). The word *severally* is a very interesting word in the Greek; it is *idios,* from which we get *idiot.* Do you know what an idiot is? He is someone who has no duplicate in the world. When we say, "He's an idiot," the word comes from an old word that means "peculiar." *Peculiar* originally meant "he's the only one." The Spirit of God universally gives the gifts, but to every individual He gives them peculiarly. Nobody has yours. You are a snowflake. It is not mass production; everybody is different. There are not forty-three teachers in one section, eighty-four givers over here, and forty-nine with faith over there. Everyone's uniqueness manifests itself in a unique way. So, the Spirit of God divides to every man severally and as He wills. Remember, you can't seek a gift. In the first place, gifts are from God, and in the second place, He is the one who wills what He gives.

Focusing on the Facts

1. What two categories of people does the Spirit of God minister to (see p. 46)?
2. What is the ministry of the Holy Spirit to unbelievers? In what two ways does the Spirit of God minister to believers (see p. 47)?
3. What is the ministry of the Holy Spirit to the individual Christian (see pp. 47-48)?
4. What is the ministry of the Holy Spirit in the midst of the collective church (see pp. 49-50)?
5. Why don't Christians have to create unity in the church? What do they have to stop doing (see p. 50)?
6. How does the Holy Spirit generate the unity in the church (see p. 50)?
7. Why is it critical for Christians to minister to each other (see p. 50)?
8. Give a definition of a spiritual gift (see p. 51).
9. What is a steward's function? How are you a steward of your spiritual gifts (see p. 52)?
10. How had the people of Corinth perverted this system? Explain (see p. 52).
11. Explain how unity functions when there is a diversity in teamwork (see p. 54).
12. What does *varieties* literally mean? Explain the importance of varieties in spiritual gifts (see pp. 55-56).
13. Why is there a need for a variety of energizings by the Holy Spirit? Explain what is meant by "the measure of faith" (Rom. 12:3; see p. 56).
14. What five words describe the different facets of spiritual gifts (see pp. 56-59)?
15. Explain why this spiritual capacity given to Christians by the Holy Spirit is called a gift (see p. 57).
16. What is the purpose of spiritual gifts (1 Cor. 12:5; see p. 57)?
17. Explain the need for the divine energizing of spiritual gifts (see p. 58).
18. What does *manifestation* mean? What purpose does this word have in defining spiritual gifts (see pp. 59-60)?
19. How many Christians have spiritual gifts? What word describes the uniqueness of each believer's gift (see p. 60)?

Pondering the Principles

1. List the eleven ways in which the Holy Spirit ministers to believers on an individual basis (see pp. 47-48). Next to each one, give an example of how the Holy Spirit has personally ministered to you in that area. Next, list the five ways in which the Holy Spirit ministers to the collective church (see pp. 49-50). In each case, how have you personally seen the Spirit minister? Take this moment to thank God for His gift of the Holy Spirit in your life.

2. Read Ephesians 4:1-6. According to verses 1-2, how must you live in order to preserve the unity of the Spirit? On a scale of 1-10, rate your life-style in the areas of lowliness, meekness, long-suffering, forbearance, and love. According to your life-style, are you mostly a positive influence on the preservation of unity, or are you mostly a positive influence on the creation of disunity? What changes do you feel are necessary in order for you to be a preserver of unity? Select the one you believe to be the most important, then make it your priority for this week. Ask God to give you the wisdom and spiritual guidance to make this a permanent change.

3. Spiritual gifts are a combination of five facets: first, their source is the Holy Spirit; second, they are gifts of God's grace; third, they are given for the purpose of providing service; fourth, they are energized by God for action in the believer's life; and fifth, they are given to publicly declare the work of the Spirit. Based on all these truths, why do you think so many Christians are not utilizing the gifts God has given them? Why do you have trouble exercising the gift God has given you? Be specific in your analysis. Is any of your trouble based on a misunderstanding of some of the above facts concerning spiritual gifts? If so, what? How can an accurate understanding of these truths help you in your practice? Commit yourself to God's control and seek to be a faithful steward of His gift to you. Memorize 1 Peter 4:10: "As every man hath received the gift, even so minister the same one to another, as good stewards of the manifold grace of God."

4

The Gifted Men—Part 1

Outline

Introduction
A. The Body Principle of Spiritual Gifts
    1. The manifestation of the Body
    2. The members of the Body
       a) Maturing
       b) Mastering
B. The Basic Principles of Spiritual Gifts
    1. They are essential
    2. They are counterfeited
       a) Fleshly counterfeits
       b) Satanic counterfeits
    3. The Holy Spirit is the source
    4. They will always unite
    5. They are not a sign of spirituality
    6. They are not for the possessor, but the other members of the Body
    7. They have the promise of divine energy
    8. They come in varieties
       a) A unique position
       b) A unique composition
          (1) The illustrations
          (2) The increase
          (3) The irresponsibility
    9. You can have a gift and not be using it
   10. There are several terms to describe these divine enablements
   11. The list is not exhaustive
   12. All gifts are to build the Body
   13. Some gifts are also sign gifts
   14. The gifts are distinct from the fruit of the Spirit

Lesson
I. A Focal Position
A. A Distinct Approach
    1. The gifts

Introduction

A. The Body Principle of Spiritual Gifts

  1. The manifestation of the Body

Jesus Christ, in His incarnation, revealed Himself in a human body. Through that body all of the attributes of deity were made manifest, and God became visible in human history. God has revealed Himself a second time—in "Body II," the church. The corporate assembly of believers is indwelt by God in order to make God visible to the world and apparent in human history.

  2. The members of the Body

Each one of us who knows the Lord Jesus Christ is an individual and vital member of that Body. And, like members of a human body, we must work together in order to bring about a full, functioning body. The church, in the same way, must have a mutual ministering and working interdependence for the purpose of unity in Body II. God would then be visible through the manifestation of Christ in the corporate life of the church.

a) Maturing

As we function, work, minister, and build each other up, Christ becomes manifest, to the glory of God. That is the design of spiritual gifts (i.e., spirituals, the divine enablements, the endowments, the energizing, the services, the *charismaton;* 1 Cor. 12:1, 4-7). Paul uses five different words for them (see p. 25). As we minister, the Holy Spirit energizes us, and we build each other up. For example, as I minister to you, you are built up. As everyone else ministers to you, you are built up. The purpose of this ministry is for you to come to maturity and be like Christ. As we all individually become like Christ, then corporately we become like Christ. It is God's design for the church to be a corporate manifestation of Christ to the world.

b) Mastering

There is another benefit. As we minister our gifts, not only do we build each other up, but we help each other to understand how to better minister in a given area.

For example, you may not have the gift of preaching, but as I preach to you, you are being built up and learning how to better communicate your faith. I may not have the gift of mercy, but as you show mercy to me I will learn how to be merciful to someone else from having seen you in action.

So, this beautiful, mutual interdependence not only builds us up to Christlikeness, but it helps us to better minister to each other in all areas and in all dimensions. The Spirit of God has designed this network of mutual ministry in the church. It is vital to the Christlikeness of both the individual and the Body in order to manifest God in the world. When a Christian is not functioning as he should, he is crippling other Christians and consequently the total manifestation of Christ in the world, to say nothing of forfeiting the blessing and reward that comes through his own obedient life.

B. The Basic Principles of Spiritual Gifts

Now, I have been giving you some of the basic principles on which the whole subject of spiritual gifts must be built. Many people don't have this foundation of basic principles in order to govern the true and the false. What are the basic principles? Let me give you fourteen basic principles on which spiritual gifts operate:

1. They are essential

Paul says, "I would not have you ignorant" (1 Cor. 12:1*b*). The gifts are essential for the life of the Body. Ephesians 4:12 says that the saints must minister in order that the Body might be built up.

2. They are counterfeited

Anything that God does, Satan counterfeits. So, the spiritual gifts are counterfeited. First Corinthians 12:2-3 explains in detail the fact of this counterfeiting. We know tht they are counterfeited all the time. There are two basic counterfeits: fleshly counterfeits and satanic counterfeits.

a) Fleshly counterfeits

For example, Paul had the gift of preaching, but he could have preached in the flesh. To the Corinthians he said, "And I . . . came not with excellency of speech or of wisdom" (1 Cor. 2:1*a*, cf. v. 4). In other words, "I didn't let my spiritual gift become a counterfeit. I didn't come to you appealing with human wisdom, speech, and oratory." So, it is possible to have a fleshly counterfeit.

b) Satanic counterfeits

These satanic counterfeits, such as the false prophets, the false proclaimers, and false teachers, who are really mouthpieces for Satan, are also possible.

Be aware that the gifts are going to be counterfeited today as they have always been.

3. The Holy Spirit is the source

All spiritual gifts are supernaturally empowered, energized, and given by the Holy Spirit. They are beyond the natural. It is not like singing, playing an instrument, or being clever with a certain art; they are supernatural enablements. First Corinthians 12:1 calls them "spirituals." They are characterized and controlled by the Holy Spirit. They are manifestations and workings of the Spirit (1 Cor. 12:7, 11).

4. They will always unite

Spiritual gifts will always unite the Body; they will never divide it. First Corinthians 12:4 says, "The same Spirit." Verse 5 says, "The same Lord." Verse 6 says, "The same God who worketh all in all." Verse 11 says, "But all these worketh that one and the very same Spirit." If the same Spirit, the same Lord, and the same God operate the gifts, then there cannot be disunity. So, whenever spiritual gifts create division, they are not spiritual, but counterfeit. True gifts will always unite.

5. They are not a sign of spirituality

Someone might say, "Well, I am spiritual because I have the gift of _____." No. Spiritual gifts have absolutely no relation to spirituality. The Corinthians had spiritual gifts, but they were not spiritual. First Corinthians 1:7a says, "Ye come behind in no gift." Paul also said to the Corinthians, "You are carnal" (1 Cor. 3:1). They were carnal, but they did have spiritual gifts. Spiritual gifts belong to all Christians, carnal or spiritual. So, when someone says he has a certain gift, it doesn't mean a thing in relation to his spirituality.

6. They are not for the possessor, but for the other members of the Body

According to 1 Corinthians 12:5, the gifts are called "services." All service is something I do for you. In verse 7 they are called "manifestations." A manifestation is something that is made public. And they are "given to every man to profit" (v. 7b). The Greek literally says, "For the good of those gathered together." In other words, they are all given for the good of others. It does no good for anyone to operate a spiritual gift independent of other people. No gift is given for self-edification as its intent and purpose. None of them are.

7. They have the promise of divine energy

We can find this in several verses of 1 Corinthians 12: they are "spiritual" (v. 1), they are of "the same Spirit" (v. 4), they are of "the same Lord" (v. 5), "it is the same God who worketh all in all" (v. 6), and "all these worketh that one and the very same Spirit" (v. 11). There is an energizing by God in all these things. It is fantastic to realize that we become channels through which the power of God comes to touch the lives of other people. That is why 1 Peter 4:10-11a says, "As every man hath received the gift, even so minister the same one to another, as good stewards of the manifold grace of God. If any man speak, let him speak as the oracles of God; if any man minister, let him do it as of the ability which God giveth." In other words, minister your gifts in the divine energy; don't counterfeit them. Why would you even want to when they have the promise of divine power?

8. They come in varieties

   a) A unique position

   There are varieties of gifts (v. 4), varieties of services (v. 5), varieties of operations (or energizings; v. 6), and verse 11 says, "Dividing to every man severally [uniquely, particularly]." No two Christians are alike. Every Christian has his own unique place and position in the Body, from which he can minister in a way no other Christian can duplicate. That is why all of you are vital. There are no unessential people—no bench warmers in God's design. Now, there are people who have put themselves on the bench, but that was not God's intention.

   Now, the varieties of gifts indicate the uniqueness of every individual's ministry. I don't believe that each of us has only one area of ministry. I don't believe that you can divide everyone up and say, "You only have one gift—either teaching, exhortation, helps, governments, or wisdom." I don't believe that this is the intention of the Spirit of God. When He says there are varieties, there is an interchange of gifts.

   b) A unique composition

   Some people ask me, "Do you believe that a Christian has only one gift?" In a sense, yes. That is what is implied in 1 Peter 4:10: "As every man has received a gift." Ephesians 4:7 says, "According to the measure of the gift of Christ." So in two places Scripture refers to a singular gift. Now, some people say, "This means that all of us have only one area of ministry." I believe the Bible shows us that we have one gift, but that one gift is a composite of various kinds of enablements. These all come together to make that one unique gift that is ours, and ours alone.

   (1) The illustrations

   Someone asked me, "Well, what about Timothy? In 1 Timothy 4:14 Paul says to Timothy, 'Neglect not the gift that is in thee.' And in 2 Timothy 1:6 he says, 'stir up the gift.' Doesn't this mean that Timothy had only one gift?" Yes. "Well, what was that one gift?" Now here you have problems. If you say Timothy had only one thing that he could do, what was it? Paul said to him, "Preach the word" (2 Tim. 4:2*a*). Oh, he had the gift of preaching. But Paul also said, "Do the work of an evangelist" (2 Tim. 4:5*b*). Oh, he was an evangelist. Paul said, "Teach faithful men" (2 Tim. 2:2*b*). Oh, he had the gift of teaching. Paul said, "Exhort with all long-suffering and doctrine" (2 Tim. 4:2*b*). Oh, he had the gift of exhortation. You say, "Which one did he have?" Not any one of them, but a composite of ministry capabilities that the Spirit of God had given him in one package. For example, you may have had a birthday on which you received many things in one box. This is the way God works and the way the Spirit of God has put the varieties together.

If someone were to say to me, "John, what do you feel your gift is?" I could ask ten different people on the staff of Grace Church, and they would tell me different things. Someone would say that I have the gift of preaching. Someone would say that I have the gift of teaching. Someone told me that he felt I had the gift of wisdom. Someone told me a long time ago that he felt I had the ability to lead. Well, what does this mean? I can't say that I only have the ability to minister to the Body in one little way. I'm convinced that the Spirit of God has stirred some gifts together and said, "Here, MacArthur, this is yours." I believe this based on the patterns you can see in the gifted men of the New Testament. They were always doing a multiplicity of things.

(2) The increase

When God puts you in the Body, He gives you what you need to minister based on your personality. The Spirit of God pours in a multiplicity of ministries through which He wants you to minister to the Body. Some of us have more than others; some may have a combination of two, three, four, five, six, or more. That is the beauty of variety.

Don't put the Holy Spirit in a box! We have no right to put an end to all the variety and classify everyone in one specific category. According to the Greek word *charisma,* we have received grace gifts. Paul uses the word sixteen times and to speak of all kinds of things in the New Testament. So don't become too classified.

(3) The irresponsibility

Some people say, "I only have one area in which I have been gifted, so I don't have the responsibility in the other areas. I might know someone has a problem, but since I don't have the gift of mercy I don't need to become too involved." That is a copout! One of the reasons that some of us are gifted in one area is to help the people who are not gifted in that area to know how to minister.

For example, I am sure that I am not gifted in certain areas. This is confirmed to me both by my own attitude and other people. But that doesn't mean I want to be irresponsible. God may not have called me to the Body of Christ to minister with the gift of helps, but that doesn't mean that when somebody asks me for help I say, "I'm sorry, I'm a leader." That is ridiculous—ludicrous! I want to learn how to help. I want someone who has the gift to show me the pattern so I can learn from him and minister.

It is only a question of emphasis. We are to minister in all areas. I could say, "Well, I don't have the gift of giving. Hallelujah! I have the gift of receiving. So, lay it on me." Wait a minute. We are all called upon to give: "Let every one of you lay by him in store, as God hath prospered him" (1 Cor. 16:2b). Let every one of you exhort one another (Heb. 3:13). We are all to build up one another in all areas (1 Thess. 5:11). We are all to show love (Rom. 13:8). If you see that your brother has a need, how can you shut up your emotions to him and not meet his need? (1 John 3:17). So, all these areas are areas of responsibility, but some of us have a greater responsibility in them because we have a supernatural energizing to minister in that area to the total Body. So, don't catalog the gifts and separate them into little boxes. There are varieties.

9. You can have a gift and not be using it

We can all testify to this from personal experience. Paul says to Timothy, "Stir up the gift" (2 Tim. 1:6b). This tells me that Timothy became discouraged very easily. When things didn't go well, he stopped ministering. Many Christians are

70

like that, and there are others who never get started ministering.

10. There are several terms to describe these divine enablements

They are called energizings, services, manifestations, grace gifts, and spirituals (1 Cor. 12:1, 4-7).

11. The list is not exhaustive

I thought I had read everybody's list until I was in a bookstore and picked up another book on the charismatic gifts that listed twenty-three different gifts. That is the biggest list I have ever seen. It just proved to me again that when you try to isolate the gifts, you get yourself in trouble. The list in 1 Corinthians 12:8-10 contains the word of wisdom, the word of knowledge, faith, healing, the working of miracles, prophecies, discerning of spirits, languages, and the interpretation of languages. Romans 12:6-8 has another list of the enablements that is completely different: prophecy, ministry, teaching, exhortation, giving, ruling, and showing mercy. What does it mean when there are two completely different lists? There is flexibility. Even the term *charisma* is too broad to be confined to a small list. It refers to anything God has given.

The Issue of Good Words

I resent being called a "noncharismatic." I am not a noncharismatic; I am a charismatic Christian. I mean that I have received grace from God. Do you know a Christian who isn't a charismatic? Do you know any Christian at all who didn't receive grace from God? I don't know any. I am saved by grace, equipped by grace, kept in grace, and I will be glorified by grace. There are not charismatic Christians and noncharismatic Christians; there are only true charismatics and counterfeit charismatics. We need to keep the terminology clear.

We usually have to give up good words because people use them to refer to movements. We used to have a good word, *fundamentalist.* But a movement was made out of it, and then people said, "I don't want to be a fundamentalist." People made a movement out of a word, so now we are afraid to use a good word. I am not ready to give up on the word *charismatic.* I'm as charismatic as a Christian can be. The word *charismatic* comes from the Greek word *charis,* meaning "grace gift." Everything I have is a gift of God's grace. So, I am not ready to give the word up; I just want to be careful that people understand its use.

71

12. All gifts are to build the Body

Ephesians 4:12 says, "For the work of the ministry for the edifying of the body of Christ." First Corinthians 12:7 indicates that the gifts are for the profit or the benefit of those gathered together.

13. Some gifts are also sign gifts

Sign gifts were given for the apostolic age. First Corinthians 14:22 says, "Wherefore, tongues [languages] are for a sign, not to them that believe, but to them that believe not." There Paul says very clearly that the gift of languages was given as a sign for unbelievers. Yet, 1 Corinthians 14:5 says, "You should never speak in languages except you interpret in order that the church may receive edifying." Even though it was a sign gift, it was also to have a capacity for edification. So, all gifts were given to build the church, even the sign gifts.

14. The gifts are distinct from the fruit of the Spirit

Don't confuse the fruit of the Spirit with the gifts of the Spirit. Galatians 5:22-23 says, "But the fruit of the Spirit is love, joy, peace, long-suffering, gentleness, goodness, faith, meekness, self-control." The gifts are activities—action ministries. However, the fruit must be behind the action. When the action operates without the fruit, the gift is being operated in the flesh.

There are the principles. Now, there are basically three categories essential to the understanding of spiritual gifts: One, the gifted men; two, the permanent edifying gifts; and three, the temporary sign gifts. Now, as a beginning point, 1 Corinthians 12:28 says, "And God hath set some in the church: first apostles, second prophets, third teachers; after that miracles, then gifts of healing, helps, governments, diversities of tongues [languages]." Ephesians 4:11-12 says, "And he gave some, apostles; and some, prophets; and some, evangelists; and some, pastors and teachers; for the perfecting of the saints for the work of the ministry for the edifying of the body of Christ." Now, let's look at the gifted men.

Lesson

I. A FOCAL POSITION

A. A Distinct Approach

In Ephesians 4:11, the first two positions that Paul names are apostles and prophets. Now, what are apostles and prophets?

Some people say that they are gifts. They are not gifts! That is not the correct and precise way to treat them. There is not a gift of apostleship or a gift of a prophet. They are gifted men. They are official titles—special ministries.

1. The gifts

   a) Their nature

   Ephesians 4:7 says, "But unto every one of us is given grace according to the measure of the gift of Christ." Every one of us has received the gift, the divine enablement, the divine endowment, the divine capacity to minister to the Body in a unique way commensurate with our personality. We all have the gift. The Greek word for "gift" is *dorea*. It refers to a free gift, with the stress on "free." It is not emphasizng so much the quality or the character of the gift as it is its gratuitous nature. We have all received a supernatural, spiritual, free gift.

   b) Their character

   Now, Ephesians 4:8 says, "Wherefore, he saith, When he ascended up on high, he led captivity captive, and gave gifts unto men." In this verse Paul uses a completely different Greek word for gift—*dogma*. This word does not refer to the free, gratuitous nature, but the character of the gift. He is referring to the very special quality of the gift.

2. The gifted men

   Ephesians 4:9-10 are a parenthesis. So, if you skip over verses 9-10, verses 8 and 11 read this way: "He gave gifts unto men, and He gave apostles and prophets, evangelists and teaching pastors." Verse 11 refers to the gifts that He gave in verse 8. What are those gifts? Apostles and prophets. According to verse 7, all Christians receive spiritual gifts. But in verses 8 and 11, He gives gifted men. Whom does He give them to? To the church. Ephesians 4:12 says, "For the perfecting of the saints." So, a distinction needs to be made between spiritual gifts and gifted men.

   To illustrate from my own life, the Spirit of God has given me a gift to minister to the Body. He has also given me as a gift to the local assembly. All of us have received gifts, but some of us (in God's grace) become gifted men given to the church. I am a teaching pastor. I am not an apostle, I am not a prophet, and I am not an evangelist. I have been given to the church as a gifted man, and that is different from my gift.

I have been given to teach others how to minister their gifts and to build them up so that the church might be built up. This is the difference between the gift and the gifted men.

B. A Divine Appointment

Now, 1 Corinthians 12 aids us in understanding this distinction. Verse 28 says, "And God hath set [lit., "appointed"]." God has appointed. It isn't a grace gift; it's a divine appointment—like an ambassador's being appointed to a post in Italy, France, England, or any other country. God has appointed apostles, prophets, and teachers. In addition, He has given gifts such as miracles, healing, helps, governments, and languages. There are men appointed to office as well as gifts given to believers. The distinction between the two is made in the word *appointed* and the phrase "after that," found in the middle of verse 28.

Now, there are five offices of gifted men. Ephesians 4:11 gives four, whereas 1 Corinthians 12:28 repeats apostles and prophets and adds a fifth—teachers. The gifted people given to the church are apostles, prophets, evangelists, teaching pastors, and teachers. The question is: Are they all given to the church for the entire duration of the church? In other words, does the church always have to have apostles, prophets, evangelists, teaching pastors, and teachers? Was there a time when the church didn't have all five? Does the church have all five now?

II. THE FOUNDATIONAL POSITIONS

A. Apostles

1. Their unique apostleship

The apostle was the primary gifted man in the history of the church. The Greek word *apostolos,* from which we get *apostle,* is the simple, common, everyday word for messenger. Now, some people are confused when they see that word appearing in the New Testament. They want to elevate everyone who is a messenger to someone with an official title. So we have to be careful to make a distinction between the official apostles and the simple messengers.

a) The primary apostles

There are a few men in the New Testament who fall into a very special category of apostles.

(1) Their identity

(*a*) The Lord Jesus Christ

74

Hebrews 3:1 says, "The Apostle and High Priest of our profession, Christ Jesus." He is the first Messenger—the first Sent One. He is the Apostle!

(b) The twelve

The twelve are called apostles. There are lists of them in Matthew 10:2-4 and Luke 6:13-16. In Acts 1:25-26 they chose one to take the place of Judas. The lot fell to Matthias, and he was numbered with the eleven apostles. Here the word *messenger* takes on a technical meaning. Before, it had a general meaning. Christ gave it a very special technical meaning; the twelve gave it a technical meaning as an official title. When someone says, "Who is an apostle?" the twelve are referred to.

You say, "Is that the limit of its official use?" No. One other man in the New Testament falls into the category of an official apostle.

(c) Paul

Romans 1:1 says, "Paul, a servant of Jesus Christ, called to be an apostle, separated unto the gospel of God." Galatians 1:1 says the same thing.

These thirteen are the official apostles.

Throne, Throne, Who's Got the Throne?

Some people will say, "Well, how come there are only twelve thrones? Who isn't going to sit on one of the thrones in the kingdom?" Of course the argument is: "Matthias shouldn't have been chosen. The Spirit of God wanted Paul to be the twelfth. They simply were out of line when they chose Matthias." Well, people only come to that conclusion based on sentiment for Paul. Don't worry about Paul. He is probably going to receive more reward than anyone. He was the most faithful man in recorded history. I don't know who won't sit on a throne. But the Bible doesn't say they were wrong in choosing Matthias.

(2) Their importance

What was their duty? First John 1:1-3 says, "That which was from the beginning [Christ], which we have heard, which we have seen with our eyes, which

75

we have looked upon, and our hands have handled, of the Word of life (For the life was manifested, and we have seen it, and bear witness, and show unto you that eternal life, which was with the Father, and was manifested unto us)—That which we have seen and heard declare we unto you." Who is this collective "we" that John is talking about? It is the apostles. He is speaking as an apostle, saying that an apostle is someone who heard and saw the manifestation of Jesus Christ and declares Him to others.

There are no apostles today because no one sees Jesus Christ today. First Peter 1:8 says, "Whom, having not seen, ye love." When someone says that he saw Jesus the other day, remember this verse. The apostle had to be those who had seen, heard, and had a vital personal relationship with Jesus Christ. They had to see the resurrected Christ. When choosing Matthias (Acts 1:22), Peter said, "Must one be ordained to be a witness with us of his resurrection." They had to see the resurrected Christ. You say, "What about Paul?" He saw the resurrected Christ (Acts 9:5; 18:9-10; 22:17-18; 23:11).

b) The secondary apostles

You say, "Well, what about the other uses of the term *apostle?*" The other uses are far more general. It was a very common word.

Laying the Foundation

The apostles had no successors. W. A. Criswell aptly says, "Like the delegates to a constitutional convention, when their work was done, the office ceased." In fact, after Acts 1 they are rarely mentioned. If we need apostles and prophets today, why are they never mentioned in the epistles to the founding churches (i.e., 1 and 2 Timothy and Titus)? In all of the instruction to the church—how it is to be run, governed, and operated, and who is to lead and serve the church—there is never a word about an apostle or prophet. After Acts 15, the last time we know they ever met together, they are scattered all over the world and never appear again. Why? When they were gone, they were gone—period.

Ephesians 2:20 says that the church is built on the foundation of the apostles and prophets. Once the foundation is laid, the building goes up. So I believe apostles and prophets have ceased and their ministry has been taken over by evangelists, teaching pastors, and teachers.

To illustrate how quickly the apostles faded away, by the time the Jerusalem council met in Acts 15, James the Lord's brother, who was called a messenger (an apostle in the secondary sense), presided over the council, not one of the official twelve or Paul. The church had already been founded. The design of God was for the apostles to lay down the solid doctrine and the pattern for the church's founding, then turn over to the elders and deacons the actual running of the church while they faded away.

There were others who were called "messengers." In Romans 16:7 Andronicus and Junias are called messengers. James, the Lord's brother, is called "a sent one" (Gal. 1:19). Second Corinthians 8:23 says that certain messengers accompanied Titus. Epaphroditus is even called a messenger in Philippians 2:25. But these are more general uses. The official category has passed away. If you want to use *apostle* in its very general sense, all of us are messengers today because we carry the good news to a needy world.

2. Their unique abilities

   a) 2 Corinthians 12:12—"Truly the signs of an apostle were wrought among you in all patience, in signs, and wonders, and mighty deeds [miracles]."

   b) Hebrews 2:3-4—"How shall we escape, if we neglect so great salvation, which at the first began to be spoken by the Lord, and was confirmed unto us by them that heard him." Who were the ones that heard the Lord? The apostles. Verse 4 continues, "God also bearing them witness, both with signs and wonders, and with diverse miracles and gifts of the Holy Spirit."

They had unique abilities and miraculous powers. According to Acts 5:15-16, whenever Peter's shadow fell on people, they were healed. They were a unique group for a unique period of history to lay down a doctrinal foundation and to establish a pattern. The only church the apostles ever collectively founded was the church at Jerusalem. And they set it forth as the model. Of course, Paul individually established churches, but the collective apostles established a church and worked and ministered in just that one area of Jerusalem.

Now, we don't need apostles today because we already have doctrine. Do we need new doctrine? Do we need new truth?

Do we need a new pattern for the church? No. Some people say, "Well, what about the missionary today? Isn't he a 'sent one'?" Yes, he is an apostle in the general sense of the word. Others want to say, "The modern apostle is the theologian. That is easy to explain: He simply has the gift of knowledge. You don't need to make him an apostle. He is just someone who is studying what the apostles have already said.

Now, the second foundational office of gifted men is the office of:

B. Prophets

1. The definition

Who are the prophets? The Greek word *prophētes* means "one who speaks out." We think of a prophet as somebody who says, "In three weeks the sky is going to fall." It actually wasn't until medieval times that the word *prophet* even came to be connected with the idea of prediction in the English language. It was always connected with the idea of speaking forth. The prophet was someone who gave God a voice in the world.

2. The difference

You say, "What was the difference between a prophet and an apostle?" In some cases, there wasn't a difference. Paul was both. Peter was both. We know Paul was both because Acts 13:1 calls him a prophet, while everywhere else he is called an apostle. There really isn't much difference between the two, but there is some. Prophets:

a) Remained in a local ministry

The apostle had a broad-base ministry to the worldwide church. The prophet had a ministry to a local congregation. The only time Paul was ever called a prophet was when he was one of the five pastors at the church at Antioch (Acts 13:1). The prophet apparently stayed in a more localized ministry.

b) Spoke revelation from God

The prophets were a distinct, unique group. Their message was revelation from God. In the Old Testament, the prophet spoke revelation from God. In the pages of the New Testament, Paul, Peter, John the Baptist, and Agabus, to name a few, spoke revelation from God (John 3:27-36; Acts 2:14-40; 11:27-28; 13:1). They spoke the word of God.

c) Taught apostles' doctrine

Every time they opened their mouths, it wasn't always revelation. They might preach and proclaim as did the five pastors in Antioch (Acts 13:1). They didn't necessarily predict the future every time they opened their mouths, and they didn't just give revelation every time they opened their mouths. They spoke for God sometimes by direct revelation and sometimes based on what they had learned from the apostles.

This is an office, not the gift. The office has passed away, but the gift of proclamation is still here.

3. The duty

What was the prophets' function? Their function was to give revelation to a local group of believers. That is why the pastors at Antioch were called prophets. That is why Agabus had the unique ministry of prophecy concerning what was going to happen to the church in Jerusalem. Acts 15:32 says, "And Judas and Silas, being prophets also themselves, exhorted the brethren with many words, and confirmed them." So they had a ministry of exhortation as well. "Confirmed them" probably means that they confirmed their word with miracles.

4. The distinction

A prophet was geared to a local congregation. First Corinthians 14:29 says, "Let the prophets speak two or three, and let the others judge." Verse 32 says, "And the spirits of the prophets are subject to the prophets." There is no indication of apostles in Corinth, but there were prophets. This, again, corroborates the idea of a localized ministry. So, the apostles had a general, broad, widespread responsibility; the prophets had a localized responsibility.

a) Regarding revelation

Revelation given to the apostles was doctrinal; revelation given to the prophets was practical. That is a general distinction. The apostles laid the doctrinal basis—the Word of God—whereas the prophets gave practical advice to the church. Why?

The church was an infant church. They didn't have the composite Word needed to extract practical principles. They didn't know what was coming in the future. They were little babies. The prophets had the vital ministry of communicating God's truth to them, in order to preserve the church in its infancy, until such a time as the Word of God was finished and they had their standards. Once that was accomplished, the apostles and prophets ceased to have any purpose.

b) Regarding subjection

One more distinction is found in 1 Corinthians 14:37: "If any man think himself to be a prophet, or spiritual, let him acknowledge that the things that I write unto you are the commandments of the Lord." Paul says, "If anyone claims to be a prophet, make sure that what he says agrees with what the apostles wrote." So, the prophets were subject to the apostles.

The prophets were a temporary group. They were around only until the close of the Old Testament canon. Then the prophets don't appear in the four-hundred-year period after the Old Testament. When the New Testament was to be written, prophets appeared again. But as soon as the New Testament was completed, the prophets disappeared. There aren't any prophets today because the Word of God gives us all we need.

The Functions of the Apostles and Prophets

The apostles and prophets had three functions.

1. Foundation

Ephesians 2:20 says that the church is "built upon the foundation of the apostles and prophets, Jesus Christ himself being the chief corner stone." They had the responsibility of laying the foundation.

2. Revelation

They were God's mouthpiece to reveal His truth—both doctrinally and practically. Ephesians 3:5 says, "Which in other ages was not made known unto the sons of men, as it is now revealed unto his holy apostles and prophets by the Spirit."

3. Confirmation

They had gifts and abilities to do miracles to confirm their revelation.

Now, if revelation is complete, then that part of their function is finished. If that part of their function is finished, then there is no need for any confirming signs. And if the church founda-

80

tion is already laid, it doesn't have to be laid again. So, the ministry of laying the foundation is gone, the ministry of revelation is gone, and the confirmation of that revelation is gone. When those ministries ceased, the apostles and prophets ceased with them.

Focusing on the Facts

1. Why does God indwell the corporate assembly of believers (see p. 64)?
2. What are two benefits of the believers' mutual ministry to each other (see p. 65)?
3. What is the result when a Christian is not functioning as he should (see p. 65)?
4. What are the fourteen basic principles that make spiritual gifts (see pp. 66-72)?
5. What are the two basic ways in which spiritual gifts are counterfeited? How is the counterfeit manifested (see p. 66)?
6. What is meant by the fact that spiritual gifts are "given to every man to profit" (1 Cor. 12:7; see pp. 66-67)?
7. What do the varieties of gifts indicate? Does each Christian have only one gift? Explain (see p. 68).
8. What was Timothy's gift? Support your answer (see p. 69).
9. How many areas are believers responsible to minister in? Why is a believer who is gifted in one area more responsible to minister than a believer who is not gifted in that area (see p. 70)?
10. What are the three categories essential to an understanding of spiritual gifts (see p. 72)?
11. What is the difference between spiritual gifts and the gifted men (see p. 73)?
12. What are the five offices of gifted men (see p. 74)?
13. What is the general definition of *apostle* (see p. 74)?
14. Who were the official apostles? What was their duty (see pp. 74-75)?
15. Why are there no apostles today? What happened to them (see pp. 76-77)?
16. What unique abilities belonged to the apostles (see p. 77)?
17. Give a definition of a prophet (see p. 78).
18. What are the differences between a prophet and an apostle? Explain the importance of these differences (see pp. 78-79).
19. What were the three functions of the apostles and prophets? Why are these functions no longer necessary (see pp. 79-80)?

Pondering the Principles

1. Do you think that you have only one gift, or do you believe that you have a blending of several gifts? Why? Review the lists in Romans

12:6-8 and 1 Corinthians 12:8-10, 28. What do you normally find yourself doing when you are around Christians and controlled by the Spirit? A comparison of what the Spirit consistently does through you, with the biblical references to spiritual gifts, will probably give you a good idea of what your blending of spiritual gifts is.

2. Do you often say, "I only have one area in which I have been gifted, so I don't have responsibility to minister in other areas"? Look up the following verses: Romans 12:5, 10; 13:8; 15:5, 7, 14; 16:16; Galatians 5:13; 6:2; Ephesians 4:2; 5:21; 1 Thessalonians 5:11; Hebrews 3:13. What areas of ministry do you have responsibility in as a Christian? If you are not gifted in an area, how can you learn to minister in that area? Pick a particular area of ministry that you would like to be more effective in, then seek out God to help you to find those people who can help you grow in that area.

3. Based on the teaching in this lesson, how would you respond to someone who told you that there were still apostles and prophets today?

5

The Gifted Men—Part 2

Outline

Introduction
A. The Context of Redemptive History
   1. Act I
   2. Act II
   3. Act III
B. The Church in Redemptive History

Review
 I. The Focal Position
 II. The Foundational Positions
   A. Apostles
      1. Their unique apostleship
         a) The primary apostles
         b) The secondary apostles
      2. Their unique abilities
   B. Prophets

Lesson
III. The Fundamental Positions
   A. Evangelists
      1. The special proclamation
      2. The supporting passages
         a) Ephesians 4:11
         b) Acts 21:8
         c) 2 Timothy 4:5
      3. The subordinate position
         a) Their association with the apostles
         b) The affirmation by the church
      4. The specific purpose
         a) Plants churches
         b) Preaches and teaches the Word
   B. Pastor-Teachers
      1. A caring ministry
         a) Applying doctrine

b) Protecting and feeding
   2. A complementary ministry
C. Teachers

Introduction

A. The Context of Redemptive History

To begin this study, let's back up all the way to the beginning of the Bible—all the way to Genesis. This should put our study in its total context.

  1. Act I

Act I of redemptive history was very long. It lasted from Eden to Bethlehem—from the birth of the world to the birth of the world's Savior. Included in this history is the preparation of the coming of Messiah to Israel. The record of Act I is the Old Testament. It teaches only one primary truth: There is one God and there are no runners up. "The Lord our God is one Lord" (Deut. 6:4*b*) is the primary thrust of the entire Old Testament. That is the one message that God wanted to put forth to society.

Abraham was the first to be taught this when he still lived in Ur of the Chaldees (Acts 7:2-3; Heb. 11:8). And it was for this reason that he moved out in faith. But this truth had to be relearned by his descendents again and again over the next twenty centuries. The Lord alone is God, and there is no other. In the intertestamental period—the four hundred years between the end of the Old Testament and the beginning of the New—there was a tremendous attempt on the part of the Greeks, led by Antiochus, to make Israel worship idols. The Temple was desecrated, and the Greeks made an effort to overcome their religion and shatter their belief, but it failed. The Maccabeans then led a revolution that enabled the people to hold onto their commitment.

Following this, in the early years of the New Testament and just prior to its writing, the Romans occupied Palestine. With their polytheism, they inundated the land with all of their gods, but Israel refused to fall into that worship. They demanded that the Romans remove their standards with Caesar's picture on them. They also demanded that Rome mint special coins without the image of Caesar, because that constituted idolatry and they wanted no part of it. And it was the Jewish belief in the one God that so alienated them from their Roman counterparts and finally led to the destruction of the Temple in 70 A.D. Israel established God's message for the rest of the world: The Lord is the only God.

2. Act II

Act II in redemptive history covered the period from Bethlehem to Pentecost. God, having established that He was the only God, then invaded history and entered the world. In the Old Testament, God is there; in the New Testament, God is here. That is the difference. God became visible in man's world. Jesus brought God into the realm of human touch. That is why Paul said, "For in him dwelleth all the fullness of the Godhead bodily" (Col. 2:9). That is also why "they shall call his name Immanuel, which, being interpreted, is God with us" (Matt. 1:23b). There is one true God. Now, He is not only before us as Creator, above us as Sovereign, but beside us as Savior.

3. Act III

Act III was even more incredible because God is not there or here, but in us. An even greater dimension is the fact that God comes to dwell in us. Act III covers the period from Pentecost to the rapture. That is the age in which we now live.

You can see the revelation of the Trinity in these three acts: God the Father, revealed as one God; God the Son, revealing Himself in human history; and God the Spirit, God in us in this age. God testified in the Old Testament through His word, in the New Testament through His incarnation, and now God speaks to the world through His church. We are the Body of Christ. We are God in the world. In Act I, God is one; in Act II, God is man; and in Act III, God is in man. That is redemptive history. Act IV will be the blazing return of Jesus Christ when He comes in glory to reveal Himself, manifest God, and take over the world.

B. The Church in Redemptive History

Today God lives in His church. The Holy Spirit lives in His Body—in you and me who are Christians. You say, "Why do you say all this?" In Act I God wanted to manifest Himself; in Act II God wanted to manifest Himself; and in Act IV Jesus Christ will manifest Himself. What do you think God wants to do in Act III? Manifest Himself. How? Through you and through me. It is only when the church is visibly Christlike that Christ is seen in the world.

How can we manifest God in the world? Only by obeying what God has given us to do: By the mutual, interdependent network of spiritual ministries within the Body. The result is that the Body is built up and Christ is made manifest (Eph. 4:12). If we are to manifest Christ in the world, we have to minister to each other in order to build up each other to be like Christ. To do that He has given each of us spiritual gifts—capacities, capabilities, and avenues of ministry. Every believer is called and gifted for a ministry to equip, to energize, to build up, and to serve in order that the Body may grow and that Christ may be made visible by the collective church.

How is He going to do this? He has given us gifts. There are three categories: Gifted men, permanent edifying gifts, and temporary sign gifts for the New Testament age. We will continue our look at the gifted men.

Review

I. THE FOCAL POSITION (see pp. 72-74)

The Lord knows that if the church is to radiate Christ, someone has to lead it and take charge! There are five categories that constitute the gifted men given for the building of the church: apostles, prophets, evangelists, teaching pastors, and teachers. There are not gifts but gifted people given as gifts to the church.

II. THE FOUNDATIONAL POSITIONS (see pp. 74-81)

A. Apostles (see pp. 74-78)

Who were the apostles?

1. Their unique apostleship (see pp. 74-77)

   a) The primary apostles (see pp. 74-76)

      Mark 3:13-14 says, "And he goeth up into a mountain, and calleth unto Him whom he would: and they came unto him. And he appointed twelve, that they should be with him, and that he might send them forth to preach." The next phrase recorded in the King James Version does not appear in the better manuscripts, so verse 15 should continue: "and to cast out demons." Verses 16-19 go on to name these men. They were the apostles—the official group of apostles. They were to preach and cast out demons—proclaiming the gospel and invading the kingdom of Satan. They had an official title: the twelve. Later on, when Judas was gone, they were called the eleven, to whom Matthias was added.

They were an official group with a basic task. Preach the gospel. They bore an authoritative and original witness. They preached a message no one in history had ever preached before. When they were finished, they vanished. There were only twelve. But in addition to the eleven plus Matthias, there was one other called an apostle. Second Corinthians 11:5 says that he "was not a whit behind the very chiefest apostles." He was no less than Peter, James, and John. Who was he? Paul. He fit into that category, giving a total of thirteen apostles. Their ministry was the giving of an original, authoritative, miraculous testimony to the gospel.

b) The secondary apostles (see pp. 76-77)

Now, there were others in the New Testament also called apostles. Second Corinthians 8:23 sheds some light on the two different categories of apostles: "Whether any do inquire of Titus, he is my partner and fellow worker concerning you; or our brethren be inquired of, they are the messengers [apostles] of the churches." The apostles of the Lord (Paul always said, "An apostle of the Lord Jesus Christ") and the apostles of the churches are the two categories of apostles. The apostles of the churches would be men like Andronicus and Junias (Rom. 16:7), James, the brother of our Lord (Gal. 1:19), Barnabas (Acts 14:14), and perhaps Titus. These men were not personally commissioned by the Lord Jesus Christ, and they had not personally seen the resurrected Christ as had the twelve and Paul. They were a different group—simply "messengers." They are the apostles of the churches. Their ministry was unofficial compared to that of the apostles of the Lord Jesus Christ. But they were called by God for a very special purpose and unique mission in the infant church: To proclaim truth, to proclaim doctrine, to teach the Word, and to lay the foundation.

There were also counterfeit, false apostles. Second Corinthians 11:13 says that there are false apostles. If there are false apostles, we know that they are not counterfeits of the thirteen apostles because everyone knew there were only thirteen. You could not say, "I am apostle Ephraim." People would say, "I'm sorry, we know who the thirteen are." But the second category could be counterfeited. You could lay a claim to be an apostle of Christ in the sense that you are an apostle of the churches. This is where Satan sowed in the false apostles.

So, there are the two categories of apostles. God gave divine revelation to the official men. The apostles of the churches were messengers of the churches. They moved around, preaching the gospel in those early years and perhaps had miraculous capabilities given to them by the Holy Spirit to confirm their ministry (2 Cor. 12:12).

The apostles were not a self-perpetuating group. In fact, when James was beheaded, nobody was chosen to take his place. The only reason someone took Judas's place was to complete the twelve. But when the twelve true apostles died, no one took their places, because there was no apostolic succession. Consequently, there is no succession of apostolic gifts. They had a nontransferable commission given them directly by Jesus Christ. When they died, it was over. They had no permanent activity in the life of the church. They belonged only to the church's infancy. They were used to teach doctrine and to basically form the patterns of the church. And they were mobile—always moving around. They ceased when the New Testament was finished and the pattern of the church established.

2. Their unique abilities (see p. 77)

B. Prophets (see pp. 78-81)

The prophets, in a similar way to the apostles, spoke for God during the foundation years of the church. A prophet did not move in an itinerant manner like an apostle but remained localized. They are found in local congregations in the New Testament. Rather than being sources of divine, doctrinal revelation, they gave practical wisdom to the church. They would warn the church about coming problems. They would try to give God's special message to a local congregation regarding His will for their lives. In addition, since the apostles were authoritative, the prophets had to be subject to the apostles' teaching (1 Cor. 14:37).

Now, the Lord Jesus Christ gave apostles and prophets to the church. Their purpose was threefold: foundation—Ephesians 2:20 says that they are the foundation of the church; revelation—Ephesians 3:5 says that they were to make known that which was hidden in the past; and then confirmation—the ability to do miracles to prove that they were speaking for God. Their purpose: Establish the church with solid doctrine. When they passed from the scene, their ministry was taken over by another group.

III. THE FUNDAMENTAL POSITIONS

This group consists of evangelists, teaching pastors, and teachers.

A. Evangelists

Ephesians 4:11 says, "And he gave some, apostles; and some, prophets; and some, evangelists."

1. The special proclamation

   We think of an evangelist as someone who travels around preaching the gospel. Some say that the derivation of the word comes from soap sellers. These men used to market the soap after they had made it. They would go downtown, find a dirty guy, haul him out on the street corner, and wash him. Then they would say, "That's what the product can do." So, those who preached the gospel were called "soap sellers" because they were cleaning up the insides of people. That basically is what an evangelist is: One who proclaims good news—a preacher of the gospel.

2. The supporting passages

   This term occurs only three times in the New Testament.

   a) Ephesians 4:11—Here they are referred to as a collective group given to the church after the apostles and prophets. I am convinced that the evangelists have taken over the role of the apostles. They are involved in the more itinerant ministry. This doesn't mean that they are always on the move. Paul would stay in one place for three years if he had to (Acts 20:31). And Timothy stayed in many places for different lengths of time. Their ministry is a moving ministry—an itinerant ministry.

   b) Acts 21:8—"And the next day we that were of Paul's company departed, and came unto Caesarea; and we entered into the house of Philip, the evangelist, who was one of the seven, and abode with him." Philip was originally a deacon, one of the seven chosen in Acts 6:5. Now we find that he was called Philip, the evangelist. Here, we meet an evangelist.

On the Trail of an Evangelist

If we want to know what an evangelist is like, we ought to follow one around. So let's follow Philip and find out just exactly what he was involved in. Acts 8:4 says, "Therefore, they that were scattered abroad went everywhere preaching the word." Now that is what an evangelist does—preach the Word. It is important to remind many evangelists that it is important for them to preach the Word and not just read the text, depart from the text, tell ten stories, and give an invitation.

Verse 5 continues, "Then Philip went down to the city of Samaria, and preached Christ unto them." There is an example of an evangelist at work—he is a preacher of Christ. He is endeavoring to win people: "And the people with one accord gave heed unto those things which Philip spoke" (v. 6a). That is the basic identity of an evangelist. Now, Philip had the ability also to do miracles in order to confirm to the people that what he was saying was true. God gave those evangelists in that day miraculous ability since the written New Testament was not yet available.

Verse 35 presents a totally different situation for Philip: "Then Philip opened his mouth, and began at the same scripture, and preached unto him Jesus." In the first part of Acts 8, Philip is preaching Jesus to a crowd; at the end of Acts 8, he is preaching Jesus to one man. It needs to be stressed that an evangelist can be equally effective with groups and individuals. The evangelist is given to the church and energized for the purpose of winning people to Jesus Christ. Incidentally, verse 40 says, "But Philip was found at Azotus; and, passing through, he preached in all the cities, till he came to Caesarea." An itinerant preacher of the gospel can be an evangelist.

    c) 2 Timothy 4:5—"But watch thou in all things, endure afflictions, do the work of an evangelist, make full proof of thy ministry." Paul was saying, "Timothy, in order to make full proof of your ministry, you need to do the work of an evangelist." This leads me to believe that Timothy was an evangelist.

So, there is a collective group of evangelists, and Philip and Timothy as examples of evangelists. Surely, there were many more. And there have been many more throughout the history of the church. We even have evangelists today. The New Testament evangelist proclaims the good news.

3. The subordinate position

One of the most scholarly works that has ever been written, translated from German, is the *Theological Dictionary of the New Testament,* edited by Gerhard Kittel. It is a series of word studies on New Testament words. This is what is said

90

regarding the word *evangelist:* "There can have been little difference between an apostle and an evangelist, all the apostles being evangelists. On the other hand, not all evangelists were apostles, for direct calling from the risen Lord was an essential aspect of the apostolate. In all three New Testament passages the evangelists are subordinate to the apostles."

a) Their association with the apostles

Not all the evangelists were apostles, but all the apostles were evangelists. This is important—that the work of preaching the gospel, which belonged to the apostles, is now the work of the evangelists. Apostles are not needed anymore because they laid down the doctrine; now, the evangelists continue their work. They are not equal to the apostles, but they do the same work as the apostles.

For example, Philip, the evangelist, was definitely not an apostle. According to Acts 8:5-12, he preached in Samaria, the people believed, and he baptized them. But none of them received the Holy Spirit. They had to wait until Peter and John arrived (Acts 8:14-15). In those beginning days of the church, the Holy Spirit was imparted to new believers only through the ministry of the apostles. Philip was not able to impart the Holy Spirit to them. He is seen as a subordinate to the apostles, yet he preached the gospel. Today, people who preach the gospel are not apostles; they are evangelists.

In addition, Timothy (an evangelist and proclaimer of the gospel) was a pupil of an apostle, but not an apostle. And in the list in Ephesians 4:11, apostles come first and evangelists come third. So, evangelists are always seen in a subordinate role. Yet it is clear that they continue the proclaiming ministry of the apostles.

b) The affirmation by the church

In the first century, the early church Fathers knew there was no apostolic succession. A study of the first-century church provides helpful information in understanding the New Testament. The things that they believed are indicative of what the New Testament writers meant because there was such a short time span between them. Eusebius, a fourth-century historian, reported that the first-century church Fathers said evangelists were the successors to the apostles, who died. They saw the evangelist as the continuum of proclamation.

4. The specific purpose

What does an evangelist do? His primary task is to preach the gospel. Philip is an example of an evangelist who preached the gospel in brand new territory where Christ was not named, and then started a church. Timothy is an example of an evangelist who went to established assemblies and mobilized the people to evangelize their city. There were evangelists who traveled as missionaries, founding and planting churches; and there were evangelists who went to local assemblies when they were small, mobilizing the people to reach out, proclaim Christ, and capture the community for Jesus.

Some of you may have had the experience of being in a church where a man came but never got past the stage of evangelizing. Maybe it would have been wiser for him to go to a new territory so that a pastor-teacher could come in and continue the work of maturing the saints on a long-range basis. This is the work of winning people to Christ and building them up. It isn't just floating in for a week and then leaving. Paul said to Timothy, "Do the work of an evangelist" (2 Tim. 4:5b). You say, "Well, what does an evangelist do?"

a) Plants churches

He wins people to Christ and plants churches. It may well be that Titus was also an evangelist. Paul said to him, "Ordain elders in each city" (Titus 1:5). He would go in, build up the saints to maturity, and even appoint the elders. This means he would have to stay until they were mature enough to rule themselves.

b) Preaches and teaches the Word

In 1 Timothy 4:13, Paul says to Timothy, "Till I come, give attendance to reading, to exhortation, to doctrine." In other words, "Timothy, until I get there, read the text, explain the text, and apply the text. Be an expository preacher and teacher." In verse 15 Paul says "Give thyself wholly to them." In verse 16 he says, "Take heed unto thyself and unto the doctrine." In verse 6 he says, "Nourished up in the words of faith and of good doctrine." Then in 2 Timothy 2:2 he says to teach "faithful men, who shall be able to teach others also."

What does an evangelist do? He teaches and preaches. An evangelist is not someone who can just preach sermons and get people to respond. One evangelist said, "I am nothing but a motivator. I don't expect to teach anybody." That doesn't make any sense. What does he use to motivate people—truth or falsehood? If he uses truth, then he is a teacher. If he uses falsehood, then he is a phony. I think he uses truth; I just think he ought to recognize that he does.

So, evangelistic work can be carried on in places where Christ is not named, or it can be carried on in places where there is an established group of believers trying to win a city for Christ. Evangelism is a ministry of preaching the gospel and teaching the Word of God. Teaching is no less a part of the work than any of the other offices. The ministry of apostles, prophets, evangelists, and teaching pastors is for the perfecting of the saints (Eph. 4:11-12a).

B. Pastor-Teachers

Ephesians 4:11 mentions apostles, prophets, evangelists, and teaching pastors. That is only one office, not pastors and teachers. The Greek is clear on that. Now, this is the office that fills up the void of the prophets. When the New Testament prophets all died off, the teaching pastor then had the local ministry to a body of believers. Now, what is a teaching pastor's job?

1. A caring ministry

a) Applying doctrine

He is given to the church to remain in a local congregation and minister to its practical needs by applying doctrine. He is doing what the prophet did in a revelatory sense but using God's Word. He is shepherding the church—guarding, defending, warning, challenging, instructing, building walls around it for its protection, and motivating it on a long-term basis.

Now, I don't know about other men, but that's where I'm at. That is my environment—I love it. I know in my heart that that is what God has called me to do. I used to travel around the country and preach. But that was frustrating to me because I wanted so much to land someplace. Finally, God opened the opportunity at Grace Community Church. I know what it is to have the heart of a teaching pastor.

b) Protecting and feeding

What does the teaching pastor do? He is called a teaching pastor, so he is to do two things: pastor and teach. You say,

"Well, what does pastor mean?" Protect the flock. "What does teach mean?" Feed the flock. Protect and feed. That is the basic ministry. Paul's message in Acts 20:28-31 is "Feed and warn, teach and warn. Teach them with tremendous conviction, and warn them with tears." That is a teaching pastor. Sometimes, in the New Testament, he is called an elder, sometimes an overseer. He is a teaching shepherd. He stays in one place in order to mature the people. He protects the flock, builds safeguards for them, and warns them.

People say, "Why do you say certain things against certain groups?" I want to warn you about them. Sometimes I will get a call from someone, telling me that he has discovered some significant thing to be true. He will say, "I don't think you believe that." It is my privilege to say, "I want to show you why that isn't true" (or why we "don't believe that"). I am trying to build some safeguards into his own thinking. Pastor-teachers teach, lead, warn, rule, shepherd—that sounds like my week. One day I will spend the whole day studying the Bible. The next day I might have to go somewhere and teach. The next day I might have to make five phone calls to people who are fooling around with something they shouldn't, such as false doctrine, or someone has left his wife, or something else. I do whatever I can to try to keep the flock in tow. That is the role of the shepherd.

2. A complementary ministry

There are other men given to the Body of Christ whose only vision is the world of lost people. God has designed it that way. The teaching shepherd doesn't sit back and criticize the evangelist, nor does the evangelist criticize the teaching shepherd. If both are operating in a biblical fashion, then they complement each other according to God's design. God needs men in America, in Canada, in Mexico, and across the sea because that is how He builds His church in any land. You say, "Well, what category do the missionaries fall into?" They fall into both categories. Some are teaching pastors, some are evangelists.

So, Christ gives to the church apostles and prophets for foundation, revelation, and confirmation, in order to establish the early church with solid doctrine. Then He gives to the church (from the early church right up to today) evangelists and pastor-teachers for evangelism, edification, exhortation, and equipping the church for effective ministry. These are the gifted people Christ has given to His church.

That is God's design. The exciting thing about this is that some of you are called to this ministry. People say to me, "When were you called to the ministry?" My mother says, "Oh, when he was five he used to stand on a box in the back yard and preach. I knew then he was called to the ministry." She may have known, but what else did I know? I was in church four days a week, I heard my dad preach all the time—that's all I ever knew. It wasn't until later in my life that I sensed God's tremendous call, after I had been to college. Some of you may be at a different point in your life, but God may be reaching out to touch your life to give you to His church as an evangelist or a teaching pastor.

C. Teachers

The category of teachers is mentioned in 1 Corinthians 12:28. Some people want to combine that with pastor-teachers and say that it is the same gift. They might be right. According to Acts 13:1, the pastors in Antioch were called prophets and teachers, so there exists that parallel. But I tend to think that it is a separate category because it is a different term than pastor-teacher. For our discussion, we will assume that it is different so that we can obtain the widest possible interpretation.

Who would these teachers be? Just that—teachers. One of the riches of Grace Community Church is the teachers God has given it. I don't mean people with the gift of teaching, I mean gifted people with a unique teaching ministry. I owe much of the growth in my life to men who were neither evangelists nor pastor-teachers. They are teachers and seminary professors— men who have spent their lives studying. In some cases they have written books that changed my thinking. You go to conferences in the summer to hear Bible teachers. God has given teachers to His church in order to supplement, undergird, and add to the ministries of evangelists and teaching pastors. They all work together to build the Body. And that is our commitment at Grace Community Church.

Training Camp

The local church is essentially a training place to equip Christians. Out of this training place should come evangelists, teaching pastors, and teachers for the church of Jesus Christ around the world. Nothing thrills me more than to see somebody go off to seminary, take on a pastorate, or go to the mission field. It is thrilling to have someone say, "John, I feel called by God to the pastorate," or, "I feel called by God to win people to Christ in evangelism," or, "I sense God speaking to me about studying the Bible that I might be a teacher in a Bible college, Christian college, school, or seminary."

How Can You Know if You Are Called?

You say, "But John, how do you know if you fit the bill? How do you know if you are called?"

1. The call of Moses

   a) The call

   Exodus 3:1-4 says, "Now Moses kept the flock of Jethro, his father-in-law, the priest of Midian; and he led the flock to the west side of the desert, and came to the mountain of God, even to Horeb. And the angel of the Lord appeared unto him in a flame of fire out of the midst of a bush; and he looked, and, behold, the bush burned with fire, and the bush was not consumed. And Moses said, I will now turn aside and see this great sight, why the bush is not burnt. And when the Lord saw that he turned aside to see, God called unto him out of the midst of the bush, and said, Moses, Moses. And he said, Here am I." Here is the first principle of a call. God wanted Moses to lead Israel out of Egypt, and God took the initiative. He set a bush on fire and said, "Moses, Moses." Moses said, "Yes." God does not say, "Oh, I certainly hope MacArthur goes into the ministry. I wish he would find out that I want him there." If He wants you there, you will hear the call. God takes the initiative. That is the first thing to learn. God will call you.

   How will God call? In different ways, with a tremendous, overwhelming sense of responsibility in your heart toward a particular ministry. God will reveal His will. God will call you. For example:

   (1) Psalm 32:8—"I will instruct thee and teach thee in the way which thou shalt go; I will guide thee with mine eye."

   (2) Psalm 48:14—"For this God is our God forever and ever; he will be our guide even unto death." The psalmist knew God would guide.

b) Burden

So God gave a call to Moses, and verse 7 continues, "And the Lord said, I have surely seen the affliction of my people who are in Egypt, and have heard their cry by reason of their taskmasters; for I know their sorrows." For years Moses had a deep burden in his heart for his people, Israel. He even murdered an Egyptian, and that is why he was in the wilderness (Ex. 2:11-15). He wanted his people out, and now God said to him, "Moses, I have the same burden you have." Here is the second part of knowing your call: Sensing that you carry a divine burden.

I remember when I used to think of nothing else than, "God, can You ever use me to help teach Your church to grow?" I used to be appalled at the ignorance of Christians. I used to speak on it wherever I went. I used to carry this burden for the maturing of the saints. I had a call from God, and I had a divine burden.

c) The goal

Now, in verse 8, God gives Moses a plan—a goal: "And I am come down to deliver them out of the hand of the Egyptians, and to bring them up out of that land unto a large and good land, unto a land flowing with milk and honey" (cf. vv. 9-10). God says, "I'm going to deliver them; I'm going to take them to Canaan." The third thing that is a part of the call into the ministry is a knowledge of the result. Moses says, "I have a call from God, a divine burden, and now I have heard about the result. If I do this, we are going to go to Canaan." Going into the ministry excited me because I said, "God, just think of what will happen if we can teach people Your Word! Think of how they will grow, and how they will get excited, and how they will be blessed!" When you have the call, feel the burden, and see the goal, it is time to move out.

d) The inadequacy

But Moses felt inadequate. Verse 11 says, "And Moses said unto God, Who am I, that I should go unto Pharaoh, and that I should bring forth the children of Israel out of Egypt?" God could have said to him, "Moses, you are somebody. I have some material on self-image that you have to read. It is ridiculous for you to feel this way. Moses, you were the son of Pharaoh's daughter; you were raised in the courts. You are hot stuff, Moses!" Do you think God said that to him? No. Moses said, "Who am I?" and God ignored his statement because it was irrelevant.

God's answer is in verse 12: "And he said, Certainly I will be with thee." In other words, "It isn't who you are, Moses; it is who I am that matters." God is not looking for those who feel sufficient. There are plenty of people in the spiritual world who offer themselves because of their adequacy. In 2 Corinthians 3:5, the apostle Paul says, "Not that we are sufficient of ourselves to think anything as of ourselves, but our sufficiency is of God." God says that it is irrelevant who you are; it is who He is that matters.

So, there are four ingredients involved in a call to the ministry: the call, the burden, the goal, and the inadequacy. I have never yet felt adequate. I have never yet felt sufficient. The ministry scares me every day, even though I have done it for years. God says, "I'm going to take care of you." When Moses said, "What am I going to say when I face the people of Israel?" God said to say, "I AM hath sent me unto you" (Ex. 3:14b). What does it matter whether I am sufficient or adequate? God is.

You say, "That is an isolated illustration." Well, what about:

2. The call of Gideon

God does not want you to analyze how well you speak, how handsome you are, how clever you are, and how smart you are. The Lord had to deliver Israel into the hand of the Midianites because they were sinning. Later, the Lord decided to rescue them, so He chose Gideon. In Judges 6:15, Gideon says, "Oh my Lord, wherewith shall I save Israel? Behold, my family is poor in Manasseh, and I am the least in my father's house." Now the Lord didn't say, "Now, Gideon, you have a fine family and a wonderful upbringing." Instead, He said, "Surely I will be with thee" (v. 16a). Gideon's statement was irrelevant.

3. The call of Jeremiah

God wanted another leader. Jeremiah 1:4-8 says, "Then the word of the Lord came unto me, saying, Before I formed thee in the womb, I knew thee; and before thou camest forth out of the womb, I sanctified thee, and I ordained thee a prophet unto the nations. Then said I, Ah, Lord God!

> Behold, I cannot speak; for I am a child. But the Lord said unto me, Say not, I am a child; for thou shalt go to all that I shall send thee, and whatsoever I command thee thou shalt speak. Be not afraid of their faces; for I am with thee."

When God calls you to a task, and you have an overpowering sense of weakness, an overpowering sense of need, and an overpowering sense of inadequacy, then you have cause to rejoice because you are in good company. Men of God throughout the centuries have felt the same way. But those same men of God who believed themselves inadequate, believed God was adequate. That is the challenge.

Focusing on the Facts

1. What is the one primary truth that is taught throughout the entire Old Testament (see p. 84)?
2. What was the opposition that Israel faced in holding to their belief in one God (see p. 84)?
3. What is the main difference in God's relationship with man between Act I and Act II of redemptive history? Between Act II and Act III (see p. 85)?
4. What is Act IV of redemptive history (see p. 85)?
5. How can Christians manifest God in the world (see p. 86)?
6. What was the responsibility of the unofficial apostles? How are they different from the official apostles (see p. 87)?
7. What does an evangelist do? How is the function of an evangelist related to soap sellers (see p. 89)?
8. Based on Philip's example, what does an evangelist do (see pp. 89-90)?
9. Explain the similarities and differences of roles between the apostle and the evangelist. Support your answer (see p. 91).
10. Why is apostolic succession not necessary (see p. 91)?
11. Describe the two different ways in which the primary task of the evangelist is accomplished (see p. 92).
12. What is the twofold ministry of the evangelist concerning the Word of God? Why are both necessary (see p. 93)?
13. What office filled up the void of the prophets after they had died out (see p. 93)?
14. What is the basic ministry of the teaching pastor (see p. 93)?
15. Who are the teachers that God has given to the church? What is their function (see pp. 93-94)?
16. What are the four ingredients involved in a call to the ministry (see pp. 96-98)?
17. How does God call someone into the ministry (see p. 96)?
18. Why is it important to feel inadequate in yourself to accomplish the ministry that God has called you to (see p. 98)?

Pondering the Principles

1. How do you manifest God in your life as the one God? What activities do you participate in that would lead someone to believe that you do not believe in one God? Read Numbers 15:37-41; Deuteronomy 6:4-9; 11:13-21. In your own words, give a summary of what God is teaching in these verses. Based on this study, how do you believe God wants you to respond to His Word? How do you respond to His Word now? What kind of changes would you like to see occur in your life, your response, and commitment to God's Word? Ask God to help you to make the daily commitment to respond to His Word in an obedient and practical manner.

2. Have you ever wondered if God has called you to a particular ministry, yet you are not certain how to know for sure? Review the four ingredients that make up a true call of God (see pp. 96-98). Compare these ingredients with your present situation. Do you feel a tremendous, overwhelming responsibility in your heart for a particular ministry? Do you sense a deep burden in your heart for the people involved? Can you see a goal on the horizon that might be accomplished by your participation in this ministry? Perhaps what is holding you back is a tremendous sense of inadequacy on your part—feeling that there is no way that you could help in this area. But remember, this is precisely the attitude that God desires in His servants. If you feel and have the desire in all these areas, God may be calling you to be involved in a particular ministry. Remember, no ministry is too small to reap eternal benefits. To help you to have the right attitude, memorize 2 Corinthians 3:5: "Not that we are sufficient of ourselves to think anything as of ourselves, but our sufficiency is of God."

6

The Permanent Edifying Gifts—Part 1

Outline

Introduction

Review

Lesson
I. The Speaking Gifts
   A. Prophecy (Rom. 12:6; 1 Cor. 12:10)
      1. The proclamation of prophecy
      2. The priority of prophecy
         a) In time
            (1) The past
               (*a*) The Old Testament
               (*b*) The New Testament
            (2) The present
               (*a*) 1 Corinthians 14:1
               (*b*) 1 Corinthians 14:39
         b) In ministry
            (1) To believers
            (2) To unbelievers
      3. The presentation of prophecy
         a) Revelation
            (1) The definition disclosed
            (2) The delivery demonstrated
               (*a*) In the Old Testament
               (*b*) In the New Testament
         b) Reiteration
            (1) The point of prophecy
            (2) The proof of prophecy
               (*a*) 1 Thessalonians 5:16-21
               (*b*) 1 Corinthians 14:37
               (*c*) Romans 12:6
   B. The Word of Knowledge (1 Cor. 12:8*b*)
      1. Understanding the Bible
      2. Utilizing the gift

Introduction

Spiritual gifts are vital. If the purpose of the Body of Christ is to honor Christ, it will only occur when we are a complete, functional, maximized body—ministering the gifts that the Spirit of God has so graciously given to believers.

The Benefits of Exercise

When the Body functions as it should, there are four basic results. These are important because all of us are result oriented.

1. The people receive the blessing

You will be blessed when you minister and see the fruit of your labor. God never intended the ministry to be carried on by professionals, while everyone else watched. God intends all of us to minister, so that all of us see God at work, see fruit, and understand the joy and blessing. So, one of the benefits of the functioning Body is that you receive the fullness of what God intended.

2. The witness is dynamic

A fully functioning, redeemed community, in the midst of a nonredeemed community, is dynamic. When Peter exercised his gift of prophecy on the Day of Pentecost, three thousand people were saved (Acts 2:14-41). When other believers exercised the gift of giving and shared what they had, the Lord added daily to the church those people who saw that kind of love and wanted to be a part of it (Acts 2:44-47). The early church in Jerusalem, throughout the book of Acts, illustrates how the ministry of the gifts of believers created a response in the unredeemed community.

3. Leaders are made apparent

In a full functioning body of believers, leadership rises to the top. There is a lot of material on leadership available to the church today because there is a need for leadership. The people won't do what they ought to do unless there is someone to help them and work with them. Leadership is a priority.

The church tries to find its leaders in amazing ways. There are seminars and books on leadership. There is a great amount of material that is simply an adaptation of the world's system for finding leaders. It is the old SNL syndrome—The Strong Natural Leader. Find the guy with all the psychological qualifications. As the church has become more like the world, it has tended to opt for the world's standards. So, when the church says, "We have to educate our people," they want a man with an education or a man with a degree in education. The church might also say, "We have a lot of problems; we'd better get someone with some psychological training to handle those problems," or, "We have a lot of young people with needs; we'd better find an expert in the youth area," or, "The world ought to hear about us; let's hire a PR guy," or, "Our worship services are rather dull; let's get a lot of musicians and have some creative worship."

So, the church opts for the stylized leadership that is characteristic of the world. But the truth is, all God ever expected from His leaders was that they have certain gifts of the Holy Spirit and certain moral and spiritual qualifications. These qualifications become manifest in the ministering community. As people minister, they simply will emerge as leaders. Spirit-filled leadership always emerges rapidly when God is freely at work in His Body.

4. Unity develops

When unity develops, there is a beautiful love and a wonderful fellowship. This fulfills our needs and reaches out to touch the lives of those who would like to have their needs met.

These benefits result when the Body truly functions. And the key to making it function is the use of these spiritual gifts.

Review

We have been discussing the three categories that come under the heading of spiritual gifts. The first category was the gifted men: the apostle, prophet, evangelist, teaching pastor, and teacher. Those five individuals are the gifted men given to the church to lead, direct, and perfect the church (1 Cor. 12:28a; Eph. 4:11-12).

The next category is the permanent edifying gifts. There are some gifts that the Spirit of God has given to the church for the duration of the church's ministry. These gifts are to be ministered at all times in the life of the church. There are other gifts in the third category, the temporary sign gifts, given only for a special period of time and for a very specific purpose.

Now, there are two categories of permanent edifying gifts. First Peter 4:10 says, "As every man hath received the gift, even so minister the same one to another, as good stewards of the manifold [lit., "multicolored"] grace of God." You are a steward; minister your gift. Then Peter divides the gifts into two categories: "If any man speak, let him speak as the oracles of God; if any man minister [serve], let him do it as of the ability which God giveth" (v. 11a). There are two kinds of gifts: speaking gifts and serving gifts. All gifts serve in a sense, and the service gifts may involve communication, but Peter's terminology helps us distinguish between these two categories.

Lesson

I. THE SPEAKING GIFTS

There are five speaking gifts mentioned in Romans 12:6-8 and 1 Corinthians 12:8-10.

A. Prophecy (Rom. 12:6; 1 Cor. 12:10)

There is a big debate today about whether the gift of prophecy still exists. There are people who want to say that prophecy has passed away, based on 1 Corinthians 13:8. They say that prophecy has been done away because the perfect thing has come (i.e., the Bible). When the Bible was finished, prophecy, tongues, and knowledge passed away. Now, that is usually a viewpoint given in order to eliminate tongues. But when they have eliminated tongues, they also have to eliminate prophecy and knowledge because they are in the same verse. I believe that poses some very serious problems. However, we will assume that prophecy has not been done away with.

1. The proclamation of prophecy

The Greek word for prophecy is *prophēteia,* ˙from the verb *prophēteuō*. It is a basic word coming from *pro* ("before") and *phēmi* ("to speak"). It means "to speak before." It does not mean "to speak before" in terms of time but "to speak before" in terms of an audience (i.e., "to speak in public, to publicly proclaim"). That is the gift of prophecy. It is not necessarily revelatory (i.e., revelation direct from God) or nonrevelatory (i.e., proclaiming something God already revealed in the past). It is simply a communicative gift. The idea of predicting the future was only an English addition to the word from the Middle Ages. A Greek or a Hebrew knew that prophecy simply meant "to speak publicly."

Now, what is the gift of prophecy? It is the ability given by the Spirit of God to a person to proclaim God's truth to others. First Corinthians 14:3 says, "But he that prophesieth speaketh unto men." There, in very simple terms, is a definition of the gift: He speaks unto men God's word. I wish that the Bible translated the word *prophecy* "proclaiming." It is the gift of proclaiming, the gift of speaking before men.

2. The priority of prophecy

  a) In time

    There has never been a time in the history of God's dealing with men that someone hasn't had this gift, because at all times God had someone speaking His word.

  (1) The past

    (*a*) The Old Testament

      For example, the Old Testament abounds with uses of the enablement to prophesy. The primary function of the Old Testament prophets was to proclaim God's word. Some of it was future proclamation, and some of it was present proclamation, and some of it was reiteration of past proclamation. Very often the prophets would speak about what God had done. Prophecy was not just prediction—that was only one-third of its capacity. It was simply the gift of proclaiming God's truth and speaking God's word.

      I am confident that prophets and the gift of prophecy ranked number one in the Old Testament. It was the most critical aspect because the Old Testament was the composite of that prophecy. It is what God proclaimed that was recorded. In fact, Peter comments regarding the Old Testament: "For the prophecy came not at any time by the will of man, but holy men of God spoke as they were moved by the Holy Spirit" (2 Pet. 1:21). The entire Old Testament is a proclamation of God.

(*b*) The New Testament

In the New Testament, prophecy was just as vital because God was not through revealing Himself. He disclosed all of the mysteries (Eph. 1:9), He made known to the apostles His will (Col. 1:9), and the Spirit of God brought to their remembrance all that Jesus told them so that they could write it down (John 14:26). The New Testament writers claimed they were inspired by God. When the whole of the New Testament was complete, it too was a proclamation from God. In fact, in Revelation 1:3 John says, "Blessed is he that readeth, and they that hear the words of this prophecy." What does that mean? Simply, the proclaiming of God's truth.

So, in the Old Testament, the most vital thing was that people proclaim God's truth. In the New Testament, the most vital thing was that the people proclaim God's truth.

(2) The present

In addition, I believe in this post-New Testament age, the most vital thing is that people proclaim God's truth. I don't think it has changed at all—that is still what God desires.

(*a*) 1 Corinthians 14:1—"Follow after love, and desire spiritual gifts, but rather that ye may prophesy." This is vital. When you come together as a congregation, desire for prophecy to be the gift that is used.

(*b*) 1 Corinthians 14:39—"Wherefore, brethren, covet to prophesy, and forbid not to speak with tongues." When they came together, all that they were doing was speaking with tongues. Tongues had a place, but they needed to quit doing that all the time and desire to exercise prophecy. Why? It is the most vital gift because it is a proclamation of God's truth.

b) In ministry

Prophecy is also vital because it ministers:

(1) To believers

First Corinthians 14:3 says, "But he that prophesieth speaketh unto men to edification, and exhortation, and comfort." Prophecy ministers to believers in those three ways.

(2) To unbelievers

First Corinthians 14:24-25 says, "But if all prophesy, and there come in one that believeth not, or one unlearned, he is convicted of all, he is judged of all. And thus are the secrets of his heart made manifest; and so falling down on his face he will worship God, and report that God is in you of a truth." Paul is saying, "When you all come together and babble in these tongues, the people who come into your midst think you have lost your minds. But if you will prophesy, when they come in, they will listen and be convicted. As a result, they will fall on their faces, repent, and believe."

Prophecy, then, ministers to believers and unbelievers. That is why Paul encourages them to be exercising that gift.

3. The presentation of prophecy

Now, I don't feel that we can restrict this only to revelation. Sometimes, when the people spoke proclamation, they were reiterating something already revealed. They certainly couldn't preach the gospel as direct revelation—it had already been given. If they were giving the gospel to unbelievers, as indicated in 1 Corinthians 14:24-25, they would simply have been reiterating something God had already revealed. So, we conclude that prophecy can fall into one of two categories: revelation or reiteration.

a) Revelation

(1) The definition disclosed

What is revelation? It is disclosing something never before disclosed, saying something never said, knowing something never known. Sometimes a prophet opened his mouth and spoke something never said before. It came right out of the mind of God—divine revelation that became Scripture. And what the prophets said could also have been a practical word from God that isn't recorded in Scripture.

(2) The delivery demonstrated

(a) In the Old Testament

Here is the common Old Testament usage: Ezekiel said, "Moreover, the word of the Lord came unto me, saying" (Ezek. 7:1). When the word of the Lord came to Amos, he said, "The lion hath roared; who will not fear? The Lord God hath spoken; who can but prophesy?" (Amos 3:8). Jeremiah said, "But his word was in mine heart like a burning fire shut up in my bones" (Jer. 20:9*b*). This was revelation—God pouring His word through the prophet. But, there were other times when a prophet preached a message that God had already given. There were occasions in the Old Testament when the prophets simply reiterated something that was common knowledge.

(*b*) In the New Testament

Sometimes, the New Testament prophet or apostle exercised the gift of prophecy. He might receive divine revelation and speak something for the first time. Other times he would repeat something that had been said. Sometimes the prophecy was doctrinal; sometimes it was practical.

For example, a group of elders came together to set apart Timothy for the ministry and laid their hands on him (1 Tim. 1:18; 4:14). Paul said, "Neglect not the gift that is in thee, which was given thee by prophecy, with the laying on of the hands" (1 Tim. 4:14). On that occasion, when they commissioned Timothy, someone probably received a prophecy from God. There were multiple prophecies regarding his life (1 Tim. 1:18). That is another case of direct revelation. Some of that direct revelation then was scriptural, some of it was practical. Some of it was also practical for a believing community. In Acts 11:27-30, a prophet named Agabus prophesied a famine. As a result, some Christians sent relief to those who would be oppressed by the famine.

So prophecy is revelatory. There were times, during the era of the writing of Scripture, when God spoke directly through the prophet His word. There was no way that these prophecies could ever have been known because they had never yet been said.

b) Reiteration

(1) The point of prophecy

Prophecy can also be reiteration, I don't think anyone can say that no one has the gift of speaking before people. If they insist, then what do you call my gift? We would have to come up with a new name for it. Proclamation is as good a word as any. The point of prophecy is not that it is always revelatory; the point of prophecy is given in Revelation 19:10: "For the testimony of Jesus is the spirit of prophecy." In other words, the heart of all proclamation is Christ. Someone who proclaims or gives testimony for Christ is fulfilling the spirit of prophecy.

(2) The proof of prophecy

Now, there are some people who insist that prophecy has ceased. The word itself means "to speak before." This is still going on. There are still people today who have the ability to speak before others to proclaim God's Word. By its very simplicity, prophecy has the possibility of broad implications. For example:

(a) 1 Thessalonians 5:16-21—The last few verses of 1 Thessalonians 5 have been done a terrible injustice because of the way it is organized. It consists of short phrases with seemingly no connection: "Rejoice evermore. Pray without ceasing. In everything give thanks" (vv. 16-18a). We don't connect them, but they are connected. In the original writings of the New Testament there were no paragraphs or verses, and there wasn't much punctuation. So, we can read verses 19-21 this way, "Quench not the Spirit, despise not prophesyings, prove all things; hold fast that which is good." This is very interesting. He says, "Don't hate prophesyings." Why? If you do, you will quench the Spirit (v. 19). Why? The Spirit has given prophecy. Don't just throw it out, but test it and hold on to what is good (v. 21). The Spirit has given to the church people who proclaim. Don't quench the Spirit by despising the gift; just examine the prophecy and hold on to what is good.

You say, "But, how do we examine a prophecy?"

(b) 1 Corinthians 14:37—"If any man think himself to be a prophet, or spiritual, let him acknowledge that the things that I write unto you are the commandments of the Lord." What are the things that Paul has written? The commandments of the Lord—the New Testament epistles. So he says, "If anybody claims to be a prophet, and he prophesies, judge him by the written Word." Don't despise prophesying; that would quench the Spirit. Simply test it; find out what is good. And what is the test? How can you know if a prophet is right or wrong? If he agrees with the Bible, he is right; if he doesn't, he is wrong. That is the test.

(c) Romans 12:6—"Having then gifts differing according to the grace that is given to us, whether prophecy, let us prophesy according to the proportion of faith." Other gifts are mentioned in the following verses. Interestingly enough, not one of the gifts mentioned is miraculous in nature. But prophecy is included with this list. All of the gifts that are miraculous in nature are listed in 1 Corinthians 12. None of those listed in Romans 12 are miraculous in nature, yet prophecy is included here also. This shows me that prophecy can be miraculous in the revelatory sense or in the sense of proclaiming what has already been revealed. So, prophecy is included in both groups.

Notice that verse 6 says, "Let us prophesy according to the proportion of faith." The word "proportion" means "the measured out, the limit." In other words, that is all there is; there isn't any more. It is the proper proportion.

Notice that verse 6 says, "Let us prophesy according to the proportion of faith." The word "proportion" means "the measured out, the limit." In other words, that is all there is; there isn't any more. It is the proper proportion.

Now, many people think that "according to the proportion of faith" means "whatever proportion of faith God has given—the ability to believe God." No. The definite article is present in the Greek, so the verse says, "According to the measured out amount of faith." If you are going to prophesy, be sure your prophecy agrees with the already revealed body of truth called "the faith."

So, the nonrevelatory aspect of prophecy is seen in a list of gifts that are nonmiraculous, although they are supernatural as energized by the Spirit. Paul is saying that if you have the gift of prophecy, then be sure you prophesy according to the proportion of the faith that has already been revealed (i.e., the Word of God). The exact same construction of faith is used in Jude 3: "Contend for the faith which was once delivered unto the saints." "The faith" is the revealed truth—not our subjective faith, but objective faith—that is to be the criteria upon which the gift of prophecy, in its nonrevelatory sense, functions.

Prophecy is proclaiming. It was revelatory at one period of time, but when the Bible is finished, Revelation 22:18 says, "If any man shall add unto these things [the words of this book], God shall add unto him the plagues that are written in this book." The revelatory aspect is finished. It belonged to the infancy of the church and concluded at the closing of the canon of Scripture. It ceased at that point. The nonrevelatory reiteration continues. And we can thank God that throughout the history of the church, there have been great proclaimers of Christ—and there still are today.

B. The Word of Knowledge (1 Cor. 12:8b)

First Corinthians 12:8 lists two gifts: "For to one is given, by the Spirit, the word of wisdom; to another, the word of knowledge." Let's look first at "the word of knowledge."

1. Understanding the Bible

The word *knowledge* is so broad that it defies a closed definition. It is very hard to be specific about what it means. The phrase is "the word of knowledge," and that indicates to me a speaking gift—the utterance of knowledge. The Greek word for "word" is *logos* and can mean "written on a page, spoken to a crowd, spoken privately to individuals." It is speaking knowledge. This is a special gift. You say, "Well, what is it?" It is the Spirit-given ability to observe biblical facts and make conclusions. In other words, it is the ability to understand the Bible. I praise God for people with this gift. I don't have the gift of knowledge. I have to read what has been written by those who have the gift in order to help me to understand biblical truth. Then I can take it and apply it. The gift of knowledge is the ability to observe biblical facts and make conclusions.

For example, you may go to the bookstore and buy a book that has been written by someone with the gift of knowledge. He will take different biblical truths, put them together, and come up with a fantastic conclusion about some truth. This is the basic gift for biblical interpretation. These are the people who continue their training, perhaps obtaining Ph.D. degrees in cuneiform and Sanskrit, so they can read the ancient characters in caves. Out of this they begin to collect biblical facts and come to conclusions, which, later on, could be translated into practical insights and information. The ability to understand the Bible is a vital area.

2. Utilizing the gift

There are different ways that this gift is manifest. It can belong to people who have never been to college or seminary, but they have an ability to study the Bible, draw out facts, and make conclusions by observation. It is energized in different ways. A hundred people might have it, yet it might work differently with each one. It might be in combination with wisdom. Sometimes I feel I have one tenth of the gift of knowledge and nine-tenths of the gift of wisdom.

a) Revelation

Now, at one time the word of knowledge was surely revelatory. In the cases where the word of knowledge would come to someone, God had given His will to that individual, who would say, "Here is a divine truth." He would utter it direct from God. I believe that Paul received that kind of knowledge (Eph. 3:3-5; Col. 1:25-27). God would directly give him a particular word of knowledge, and he would proclaim that word. So, it was revelatory on occasion.

b) Reiteration

Other times it was not revelatory, but simply taking what was already written and expanding on it. The Greek word for *knowledge* is used over three hundred times in the New Testament, with so much variation that there is no way it can be isolated only to revelation. Some people want to say that it is never used outside of revelation. That is not possible; it is used for many things. The Bible even says that the Christian is to be filled with knowledge (Col. 1:9-10).

The best definition of the gift of the word of knowledge is in 1 Corinthians 13:2: "And though I have the gift of prophecy, and understand all mysteries, and all knowledge." This is the gift of understanding the mysteries that have been revealed. The people with this gift are the writers, scholars, teachers, professors, and researchers. I know some people who do nothing but research; they are available to be hired by a writer, an author, or an institution to research a given area of biblical truth and to draw out of it all the basic conclusions as a basis for someone's book, course, or whatever the group wants accomplished.

The third speaking gift is:

C. The Word of Wisdom (1 Cor. 12:8*a*)

This gift was used in a revelatory sense in the early church when God would give someone special wisdom. Incidentally, the word *wisdom* is *sophia* in the Greek. It is used in so many ways in the New Testament that it is impossible to isolate it only to revelation.

1. The skillful application

What is this gift? It differs from knowledge in this way: The emphasis is on the skill of application rather than the knowledge of facts. Wisdom is the ability to take the facts that the gift of knowledge has brought out and make a skillful application of it. It could belong to a Christian counselor, who identifies a problem and then by his knowledge of the Word of God draws out the principles that can be practically applied to solve the problem. It is the gift of the expositor, who can take the Word of God, study the commentaries, read from all those who have the gift of knowledge, and out of that draw the applicable principles to living. It can also be a gift that a believer ministers to another believer, by assisting him in his practical life.

The gifts of knowledge and wisdom are also very different. Many of you know people who have much Bible knowledge but virtually no wisdom, so that they are ridiculous when it comes to application. They are the absent-minded professor type. They have all this knowledge in their minds, but they can't seem to make it work in their lives.

Wisdom, then, is the skill to apply the facts that have been discovered by someone with the gift of knowledge. Now, someone might have both knowledge and wisdom equally or a lopsided combination of them.

2. The scopious categories

Since wisdom (Gk., *sophia*) is such a broad word, don't confine it only to revelation. In fact, in the New Testament, twelve of the twenty-seven books use the word *sophia*. It is used in five categories.

a) An attribute of God (Rev. 7:12)

b) Intellectual ability (Matt. 12:42)

c) The person of Jesus Christ, who is called the wisdom of God (1 Cor. 1:24)

d) Proud human wisdom opposed to God (James 3:15-17)

e) Spiritual understanding of God's will

This is the primary use of *sophia*. I believe this is exactly what the gift is—the ability to understand God's will and make an application to obedience. And this is the way it is used most often in the New Testament (Matt. 11:19; 13:54; Mark 6:2; Luke 7:35; 21:15; Acts 6:10; James 1:5; 3:13, 17; 2 Pet. 3:15). Those passages incorporate the main use of wisdom—that we know and behave in accord with God's will.

What is the gift of wisdom? The Spirit-given ability to show us the principles that we need to know and obey to fulfill God's will. It had a revelatory aspect, but that was not its exclusive use. Godet says, "Knowledge makes the teacher, wisdom the preacher and pastor." But I would go even further than that and say, "Knowledge is the collecting of facts; wisdom is the application."

The Attempt to Eliminate Gifts

There are people who want to eliminate knowledge, wisdom, and prophecy as still existing today. They have a problem, because if they eliminate prophecy, then what do they say the people are doing who proclaim the Word? If they eliminate knowledge, what are the theologians and the people who dig out deep truth with their skill doing? And if they eliminate wisdom, what are they going to call the gift of taking the truth and applying it to life? They will have to come up with new names because God is still doing these things, and there are people still ministering in these ways.

Now, the fourth speaking gift is the gift of:

D. Teaching (Rom. 12:7)

Romans 12:7 says, "Or ministry, let us wait on our ministering; or he that teacheth, on [the] teaching." Again, the definite article is present in the Greek. In other words, whatever you teach, let it be consistent with the teaching of the Word.

1. The distinction

What is the gift of teaching? First, we should distinguish between the gift and the office. You can be a teacher in the church, and that is an official position. If you were a teacher, you certainly would have the gift of teaching. But not all who have the gift of teaching are recognized as official teachers because the gift can be exercised in so many ways.

2. The definition

a) Passing on truth

The gift of teaching is the ability, in the Holy Spirit, to pass on truth to someone else. Prophecy is proclaiming Christ to an audience; teaching is passing on truth to others so that they receive it and implement it. It is a communicative ability. People say, "Well, what is the gift that enables a person to share one on one with someone and build him up?" Maybe it is the gift of teaching, because they are passing on truth to others so they will receive it and implement it in their lives.

b) Systematic teaching

There are many forms of the basic word *teach* in the Greek—*didaskalos, didasko, didaktikos.* In all the various forms, the root meaning carries with it the idea of systematic teaching or systematic training. It is the word that is used to refer to a choir director who trains a choir over a long period of rehearsals until they are able to perform. The gift of prophecy could be a one-time proclamation of Christ, but the gift of teaching is a systematic training problem to take a person from one point to another. What is the curriculum for the teacher? The Bible, the Word of God. The gift is to teach systematically the truth of God.

It can be used with men—one on one, one on two, one on three, one on five thousand. It can be used with women—one on one, one on two, one on three, one on five thousand. It can be used by a lady in a little group of children. It can be used by a mother to a son. It can be used by a husband to his wife. It can be used in any conceivable way that the Spirit of God desires. It is the ability to pass on truth in a systematic progression so that someone receives it, implements it, and a change of behavior takes place. In fact, it is a gift that belongs to a lot more of us than we realize.

E. Exhortation (Rom. 12:8)

Romans 12:8 says, "Or he that exhorteth, on exhortation." This is the revealed exhortation of God to man. What is exhortation? The Greek word is *parakaleō. Paraklētos* is "comforter." The word means "to comfort, help, advise, or strengthen." It is the gift of strengthening. God has given some people to the Body whose job is not necessarily to proclaim, or to dig out the facts, or to figure out the principles and apply them in wisdom, or to systematically teach. It is simply to strengthen people. These people encourage, they help, they advise, they strengthen. It is the ability to provide comfort, courage, help, and strength to someone who needs it. It can come through the pulpit because prophecy is exhortation. It can come through teaching. It can come through counseling. It can come in many ways. It is the ability to get alongside someone who has a problem and build him, encourage him, strengthen him, and bear his load.

People say, "It's the gift of counseling." That's wrong. Counseling is not a gift; counseling is a process. I am quite confident that there are some counselors who exercise the gift of teaching, some who exercise the gift of strengthening, and some, like me, who exercise the gift of proclaiming. Now, that doesn't always work in a counseling situation. But there is no gift of counseling. The gift can be used in counseling, in teaching, and in informal conversation. Luther said, "Teaching is directed to the ignorant, exhortation to those who know better."

I want you to notice a beautiful progression in these gifts. This is how God ministers to His Body: Prophecy proclaims the truth. Knowledge clarifies the truth. Wisdom applies the truth. Teaching imparts the truth to someone else. And exhortation demands that it be obeyed. All of them come together as we minister to each other so that the Body might be built up.

Focusing on the Facts

1. What are the four results that occur when the Body functions as it should (see pp. 102-3)?
2. How can witnessing be dynamic? Give some examples (see p. 102).
3. How does the world find its leaders? How does the church? What kind of qualifications are necessary for leadership in the church (see p. 103)?
4. What is the basic difference between the permanent edifying gifts and the temporary sign gifts (see p. 104)?
5. What are the two categories of permanent edifying gifts (see p. 104)?
6. Why does a debate exist today about the existence of prophecy (see p. 104)?
7. Define prophecy. What is the gift of prophecy (see pp. 104-5)?
8. How was prophecy utilized in the Old Testament? in the New Testament (see pp. 105-6)?

9. Why is prophecy vital in our day (see p. 106)?
10. How is the gift of prophecy able to minister to both believers and unbelievers (see pp. 106-7)?
11. What two categories make up the gift of prophecy (see p. 107)?
12. What is revelation? How was it manifested in both the Old and New Testaments (see pp. 107-8)?
13. What is the point of prophecy? Why shouldn't prophecy always be revelatory (see p. 109)?
14. Why should we not hate prophesyings, according to 1 Thessalonians 5:19-21? What one thing should be done to prophecy (see p. 109)?
15. How is prophecy to be examined? What is the basis for this examination (Rom. 12:6; 1 Cor. 14:37; see p. 110)?
16. Explain what is meant by "the faith" (Rom. 12:6; Jude 3; see p. 111).
17. Define the gift of the word of knowledge (see p. 111).
18. How is the gift of the word of knowledge manifested (see p. 112)?
19. What is the difference between the word of wisdom and the word of knowledge? Who can minister the gift of the word of wisdom (see p. 113)?
20. Wisdom falls under what five categories? Which one is the primary use of the word (see pp. 113-15)?
21. "Knowledge makes the _____ , wisdom the _____ and _____" (see p. 114).
22. What is the gift of teaching? What is the difference between the gift and the office (see pp. 114-15)?
23. What one word describes the process that teaching goes through to take an individual from one point to another (see p. 115)?
24. What is the curriculum for the teacher (see p. 115)?
25. What does *exhortation* mean? How does exhortation reach the individual (see pp. 115-16)?
26. What is the difference between the ability to counsel and the gift of exhortation (see p. 116)?
27. "_____ is directed to the ignorant, _____ to those who know better" (see p. 116).
28. What are the five ways that these gifts minister to the Body (see p. 116)?

Pondering the Principles

1. Review the four results of a truly functioning body (see pp. 102-3). On a scale of one to ten, how does the local body you are a part of manifest these results? Which one is manifest most often? Why? Which one is manifest least? Why? Do you pray for your brothers and sisters in Christ to manifest their gifts? In what ways do you

think you could help your local body to manifest any one of these results? Pray that God would help you to determine how you might be most effective in helping the body to truly function as it should.

2. Where do you think the Bible came from? Look up the following verses: Isaiah 16:13; 24:3; Jeremiah 1:9; Ezekiel 2:7; Hosea 1:1; Joel 1:1; Micah 1:1; Zephaniah 1:1; Haggai 1:1; Zechariah 1:1. In order to have the proper understanding of the source of Scripture, memorize 2 Peter 1:21: "For the prophecy came not at any time by the will of man, but holy men of God spoke as they were moved by the Holy Spirit."

3. Review the five speaking gifts. Do you find yourself with the great desire to proclaim Christ, and do you follow through in that desire? Then you may be gifted in the area of prophecy. Do you find that you have the ability to observe biblical facts and make conclusions from those facts? Then you may be gifted in the area of the word of knowledge. Do you find that you have the ability to understand God's will and make application of it towards obedience? Then you may be gifted in the area of the word of wisdom. Do you find yourself with the desire and ability to pass on the truths of the Bible to someone to help him grow? Then you may be gifted in the area of teaching. Do you find that you have the desire and ability to strengthen someone in his walk with God? Then you may be gifted in the area of exhortation. Perhaps you do not know if you have the ability in one of these areas, but you certainly have the desire. Ask God to help you to determine how you might begin to step out and exercise that desire. Remember, whether or not you are truly gifted in one of these areas is not the issue, but that you are ministering to the Body of Christ.

7

The Permanent Edifying Gifts—Part 2

Outline

Introduction
A. Determining Your Behavior
   1. The requirement of the Spirit's control
   2. The results of the Spirit's control
     a) Holiness
     b) Joy
     c) Liberty
     d) Confidence
     e) Victory
     f) Ministry
B. Defining Your Gift
   1. The issue: walk in the Spirit
   2. The problem: many colors

Review
 I. The Speaking Gifts

Lesson
II. The Serving Gifts
   A. Leadership (Rom. 12:8; 1 Cor. 12:28)
     1. The definition of terms
       a) Management
       b) Mobilization
         (1) Revelation 18:17
         (2) Acts 27:11
     2. The distinction from wisdom
       a) The comparison
       b) The contrast
     3. The direction in trials
     4. The dimension of leadership
       a) Among church leaders
       b) Among the laity
     5. The diligence to act
     6. The decency of order

B. Serving (Rom. 12:7; 1 Cor. 12:28)
  1. Loving support
    a) Acts 6:1-3
    b) 1 Timothy 6:2
    c) Romans 16:3, 9
    d) Philippians 2:25-30
  2. Loving service
C. Giving (Rom. 12:8)
  1. Super giving
  2. Simple giving
    a) Singleness of motive
    b) Sincerity of sacrifice
      (1) Mary
      (2) The church
      (3) The Macedonians
      (4) The Philippians
      (5) The Salt Shakers
      (6) C. T. Studd

Introduction

A. Determining Your Behavior

  1. The requirement of the Spirit's control

Every Christian is given a marvelous gift the moment he becomes a Christian. The moment that we believe, we receive the Holy Spirit. He is God, the third Person of the Trinity, who takes up residence in our lives. From the moment that you believed, the Spirit of God came to live within you. He became your guide, your truth-teacher, and your power supply in order to do all for the glory of God. As a result, the New Testament urges us to behave in a certain way relative to the Spirit. For example, we are to walk in the Spirit (Rom. 8:4), live in the Spirit (1 Pet. 4:6), be filled with the Spirit (Eph. 5:18), pray in the Spirit (Eph. 6:18), manifest the fruit of the Spirit (Gal. 5:22), and to exercise the gifts of the Spirit (1 Cor. 12:11). On the negative side, we are warned not to grieve the Spirit (Eph. 4:30), resist the Spirit (Acts 7:51), or quench the Spirit (1 Thess. 5:19).

All of this shows us how vitally important it is that we operate in the sphere of the Holy Spirit. The Christian life is a Spirit-dominated, Spirit-directed, and Spirit-controlled existence.

2. The results of the Spirit's control

When we allow the Spirit of God to reign in our lives—to have control and give direction—some marvelous results always occur:

a) Holiness—Under the direction, control, and complete domination of the Spirit of God, our life pattern results in a constant sanctification.

b) Joy—A constant satisfaction occurs when we walk and live in the Spirit.

c) Liberty—"Where the Spirit of the Lord is, there is liberty" (2 Cor. 3:17b). There is a constant sense of freedom.

d) Confidence—A constant security occurs when we walk in the Spirit.

e) Victory—There exists a constant strength against the adversary.

f) Ministry—There is a constant service to the Body of Christ. So, when we walk in the Spirit, not only are there personal results, but there is another result—we are able to minister to others and to build them up in Christ. As I walk in the Spirit, my gift is ministered to you. As you walk in the Spirit, your gifts are ministered to one another. As we live, move, walk, and are filled with the Spirit, He operates through us via the spiritual gifts we have been given to minister to other believers.

B. Defining Your Gift

1. The issue: walk in the Spirit

People often ask me, "How can you know your spiritual gift?" I reply, "That isn't the issue." It doesn't really matter if I have defined my gift. In the first place, it is elusive—I can't always pinpoint it. The issue is: Walk in the Spirit. If I walk, live, and am filled with the Spirit, it is not too important for me to understand the definition of my gift. It isn't an academic issue; it's a matter of getting on your knees and asking the Spirit of God to dominate and control your life. As you yield to Him, the Spirit of God operates through you. And that will be your area of ministry. So, the best way to know your gifted area is not to figure it out and then do it but to walk in the Spirit and then look back and say, "So that's what I do." Don't worry about definitions. It doesn't matter to me that I have a definition; it only matters that I walk in the Spirit so He can minister through me.

2. The problem: many colors

Now remember, when you try to define your gift, you will run into some problems because there is so much overlapping of the gifts. When I was in high school, a lady wanted to paint my portrait. I remember that she held a palette in her hand and painted with a palette knife. On the palette she had some primary colors, which she had squirted out of some tubes. Then she began to mix all of those colors together. It was amazing to see the various combinations of colors that came out of those primary colors. Finally, she began to paint them on the canvas.

This is exactly how spiritual gifts function. The Holy Spirit has a palette. On it are some primary gifts. They are the gifts that are listed in Scripture. But by the time they are spread around, there is a mixture. Each one of you becomes a very stylized, individual, particular, peculiar, unique portrait.

When we study the five speaking gifts and the six serving gifts that make up the permanent edifying gifts, we are simply studying the primary colors. And the Holy Spirit will mix them and put them on you as He has on no one else. The combination is unique. That is why you will have trouble finding definitions.

Review

In our last lesson we began a study of the permanent edifying gifts, after studying the gifted men. There are two general categories for these gifts, as illustrated in 1 Peter 4:10-11: The speaking gifts and the serving gifts.

I. THE SPEAKING GIFTS (see pp. 104-22)

In the last lesson we looked at the five speaking gifts. They are five of the primary colors, any of which can be mixed in with any of the others. The five speaking gifts are: prophecy, knowledge, wisdom, teaching, and exhortation. They are all related to speaking the Word of God. Prophecy proclaims God's Word; knowledge clarifies God's Word; wisdom applies God's Word; teaching imparts God's Word; and exhortation demands God's Word be obeyed. All five are related to speaking in relationship to God's revelation.

Lesson

II. THE SERVING GIFTS

Now, the second category of permanent edifying gifts is the serving gifts. The serving gifts are geared for service. The issue is not to proclaim the Word of God; the issue is to serve someone's needs. And these six serving gifts are also primary colors that can be mixed with the speaking gifts and with each other to turn out unique combinations in the case of every individual Christian. These gifts appear in two passages: 1 Corinthians 12:28 and Romans 12:6-8.

A. Leadership (Rom. 12:8; 1 Cor. 12:28)

First Corinthians 12:28 says, "And God hath set some in the church: first apostles, second prophets, third teachers; after that miracles, then gifts of healings, helps, governments, diversities of tongues [languages]." Notice the word "governments." That introduces us to the gift of leadership. Also, Romans 12:8 says, "He that ruleth, with diligence."

1. The definition of terms

The word is *ruling* in Romans 12:8 and "governments" in 1 Corinthians 12:28. Both refer to leadership—they are synonymous.

a) Management

The word *ruling* means "to lead, to manage, to have charge of, to oversee, to rule." That is leadership.

b) Mobilization

The word "governments" basically means the same thing, but it also has a unique literal meaning: "to steer a ship." It is the Greek word *kubernēsis*. It refers to the skill of piloting a ship—to the one who is at the helm of the ship, who charts the course, who knows the destination, and who is able to keep the ship on course.

Leadership is the ability to see an objective, formalize it, mobilize a group of people, and then get them to reach that objective. It is not the ability to push paper around a desk. It is not the person who has the most pencils who has the gift of leadership. And it is not necessarily sitting in an administrative seat of responsibility, because that person could also have the gift of serving or helps. But it is the ability to make decisions and determine direction—mobilizing people to reach an objective. The pastor doesn't own the ship; he simply is responsible for piloting it. Christ says to the pastor, "Here is the goal, here are the people. Now mobilize them and move them there!" That is leadership.

(1) Revelation 18:17—Here is a part of the account of the fall of the world's system of economy during the Tribulation: "For in one hour so great riches are come to nothing. And every shipmaster, and all the company in ships, and sailors, and as many as trade by sea, stood afar off, and cried when they saw the smoke of her burning, saying, What city is like unto this great city?" That describes the destruction of the Babylonian economic system during the Tribulation as relative to the people involved in the shipping trade. The word "shipmaster" is *kubernēsis,* the very same word translated "governments" in 1 Corinthians 12:28. So, the word can refer to someone who pilots a ship or to someone who has responsibility for leadership.

(2) Acts 27:11—In Acts 27, the apostle Paul is on his journey to Rome by ship, and the ship encounters trouble from a storm. The word used in verse 11 for the pilot of the ship is the very same Greek word— someone who charts the course and takes the people to the goal, a mobilizer and mover of people.

The Pilot Brain

The word *kubernēsis* is interesting because we get an English word from it: *cybernetics.* Some of you may have heard of or read the book *Psycho-Cybernetics.* Cybernetics is a science that studies the brain relative to its governing of the body. So, cybernetics still refers to ruling—to piloting a ship—only here to how the brain makes the body respond.

2. The distinction from wisdom

In the Greek translation of the Old Testament (the Septuagint), there are four places where *kubernēsis* is used. In these four places we find that it is used in connection with wisdom. In Proverbs 12:5 it is translated "counsels." *Kubernēsis* assumes the leader has wisdom—the practical ability to reach a goal.

a) The comparison

There is an interesting comparison of the use of *kubernēsis* in the Greek Old Testament (the translation of the original

Hebrew). Ezekiel 27:8 says, "The inhabitants of Sidon and Arvad were thy mariners; thy wise men, O Tyre, that were in thee, were thy pilots." The word "pilots" is *kubernēsis* (cf. vv. 27, 28). Notice that Ezekiel says that the pilots were their wise men. So, piloting a ship was connected with wisdom.

b) The contrast

As we learned in our study of wisdom, it is the ability to solve a problem by making practical application of a principle to life. But there is a difference between someone who has wisdom in leadership and someone who has the gift of the word of wisdom. The word of wisdom is speaking out the practical truths of the Word of God. The wisdom in leadership is an enablement for someone to wisely approach and reach an objective. One is an exhibited speaking gift relative to proclaiming the Word, while the other is more of an obscure directive by which some person reaches a goal. I want you to make that distinction so you don't think that just because someone is a leader he has the word of wisdom. There are many people with wisdom in leadership who do not have the verbal, proclaiming wisdom that is given by God.

3. The direction in trials

Some within the Body of Christ have the ability of leadership. They know how to form objectives and directives to reach a goal. They know how to mobilize people. Two words define the gift of leadership: direction and decision making. A true leader is like the true shipmaster in the storm—when the going gets rough, he hangs on, and everyone reaches the destination. He has the ability to keep the ship on course during the storm.

4. The dimension of leadership

a) Among church leaders

Some people have the thought that the gift of leadership is one that is synonymous with pastors, elders, and bishops (i.e., it doesn't belong to the general population of the church, only to the people who are the pastors). I would say that pastors normally have this gift. It would be hard to rule a church if you didn't have the ability to lead. First Timothy 5:17 refers to the elders that rule well. The fact that elders and pastors rule in the church assumes that God would give them the gift of leadership. In fact, Hebrews 13:7, 17, and 24 says that the elders have the oversight of the church. So, we believe that the gift of leadership should belong to the pastoral staff and the elders that lead the church. But does it end there? There are some who would have us believe it does. I say it doesn't.

b) Among the laity

There are many ways in which the gift of leadership is used by the laity. The church is far too complex to function with everyone serving and no one leading at all the levels. There are some churches with the philosophy that one man rules the entire church. We call them "monolithic monsters." One man rules, and that is it. Organizations exist that are like that. But even in those kind of situations, there have to be other people who are able to implement certain ideas into action. I am convinced that the gift of leadership can belong to the laity. It has always been God's plan that out of the laity would come other leaders (Ex. 18). Some of you have responsibility for a group of people—coordinating a Bible study toward an objective, mobilizing them, and then helping them reach that goal.

That is leadership. There are many possible manifestations and energizings of it. It has to go beyond the pastor-teacher, the evangelist, the apostle, and prophet; it has to extend throughout the Body of Christ.

5. The diligence to act

Romans 12:8 gives us another aspect of the gift of leadership: "He that ruleth, with diligence." The word "diligence" basically means "speed," or "haste." Who is a good leader? Someone who recognizes a need and acts quickly. If you are in a position of leadership and see a need, meet it now. One of the things I believe and try to teach others is never to let a problem or a need go on any longer than it already has. Solve it today, not tomorrow. That is a hard lesson to learn because we all tend to procrastinate. One of the hardest disciplines I have had to face was forcing myself to deal with issues the moment I became aware of them. When you see the need, meet the need.

6. The decency of order

Now, some of the Corinthians had the gift of leadership, but they weren't using it because it wasn't showy or ecstatic enough. They were so busy falling all over each other in frenzies, and so busy jabbering in ecstatic languages, that they didn't have time to bother to lead. That is why 1 Corinthians 14:33 says, "For God is not the author of confusion but of peace." And in verse 40 Paul says, "Let all things be done decently and in order." In other words, "Instead of everyone doing what's spectacular, somebody organize. Get some objectives, some directives, make some decisions, and mobilize the people to fulfill the will of God."

This gift is a great need—the ability to see an objective and to mobilize a group of people to reach that objective. It involves decision-making ability. God knows how we need these people. If you have this ability, use it with haste because leaders are desperately needed to resolve issues in the church.

So, God has given leaders to His church. Leadership is not an easy responsibility because there are people who react negatively to what you do or say. Sometimes you have to stand all alone in making decisions. Sometimes you alienate people and create hard feelings. Don't try to be a leader unless God has gifted you in that area. And remember, all the gifts operate in the atmosphere of love (1 Cor. 13:1-7).

B. Serving (Rom. 12:7; 1 Cor. 12:28)

All gifts are service, according to 1 Corinthians 12:5, but out of all of these gifts there is one that is very specialized in terms of service. In 1 Corinthians 12:28 is the little word "helps." In Acts 20:35 the same Greek word is translated "support." It is a supporting gift, a helping gift. In Romans 12:7 it is called the gift of "ministry." It is the same gift.

1. Loving support

The word *helps* literally means "to take a burden off of someone else and place it on yourself." It is the gift that comes alongside leadership. I believe that the secretaries who are part of the staff of Grace Church must have the gift of helps. They have the responsibility of implementing all of the things that the leadership is doing. Believe me, if it were not for the Spirit of God's energizing them, they would wind up in a mental institution due to the volume of work. The gift of helps is the gift that allows everything to occur. The people who have this gift are able to help in any conceivable way.

a) Acts 6:1-3—The apostles said, "We can't wait on tables; we have to teach the Word and pray. Get some people who can wait on tables." They called them servers—deacons. Originally the word referred to waiting on tables. For the people with this gift, their greatest joy and labor of love is to serve other people. There is no glory, no fanfare, and no acclaim, just serving.

b) 1 Timothy 6:2—"And they that have believing masters, let them not despise them because they are brethren but, rather, do them service." You can use the gift of helps if you work for a Christian employer by supporting him, helping him, and fulfilling your required task with joy. All the gifts should be ministered in love and joy.

c) Romans 16:3, 9—In this portion, Paul gives a catalog of all the people who have helped him. In verse 3 he says, "Greet Priscilla and Aquila, my helpers in Christ Jesus." What did Aquila and Priscilla do for him? Maybe they made some sandals for him. Maybe Priscilla stitched up a torn tunic. Maybe they gave him a bed. Maybe they gave him some food. I don't know what they did, but they helped him. The same thought is in verse 9. "Greet Urbanus, our helper in Christ." What did Urbanus do for him? Who knows? Maybe he marketed some of those tents Paul made. I don't know what he did, but he helped Paul.

Help!

I believe the most needed and therefore the most common gift the Spirit of God gives is the gift of helps. We have to have it. We can't accomplish anything if we don't have cooperation and help. Maybe you can't preach, can't teach, can't sing, but you can clean, you can take a meal to someone, you can fix something for someone, you can mow the neighbor's lawn because he isn't feeling well—you can do most anything.

d) Philippians 2:25-30—In this passage, Paul talks about Epaphroditus, who was his helper. He says he was "my brother and companion in labor, and fellow soldier, but your messenger, and he that ministered to my need" (v. 25b). He also says, "He was near unto death, not regarding his life, to supply your lack of service toward me" (v. 30b). Epaphroditus served Paul to the point that he even gambled with his life. He nearly died, but he wouldn't stop serving Paul's needs.

2. Loving service

The gift of helps is a beautiful and marvelous gift that is absolutely necessary for the progress of the Body of Christ. It doesn't attract a lot of attention, and since it doesn't, nobody in Corinth was practicing it. There were no leaders and no helpers. They were all given over to ecstatic, wild, and frenzied behavior because it was glamorous. So, no one was helping.

The list of gifted men and gifts from 1 Corinthians 12:28 really puts the gift of helps in perspective: "First apostles, second prophets, third teachers; after that miracles, then gifts of healings, helps, governments, diversities of tongues [languages]." Right in the midst of all these grandiose gifts, Paul interjects helps. Why? He wants the Corinthians to know that this gift flows with the others. The gift of helps—no public recognition, just loving service. So, God has gifted us in the areas of leadership and helps (service).

C. Giving (Rom. 12:8)

Romans 12:8 is the only verse where this gift is mentioned. Now, verse 6 says, "Having then gifts differing according to the grace that is given to us." Verse 8 says, "He that giveth, let him do it with liberality."

1. Super giving

The word "giveth" is a compound Greek word. The normal Greek word for *give* is *didomi* and just means "give." But this compound word is *metadidomi,* which means "super give." All of us are called upon by the Spirit of God to give. All of us are to invest. The Bible tells us that we are to sow bountifully in order to reap bountifully (2 Cor. 9:6). All of us are to lay by in store the first day of the week as God has prospered each one of us (1 Cor. 16:2). All of these things are commanded very clearly in terms of our giving. But there are some of us who are to be super givers—who are to go beyond the normal because we are gifted in that way.

2. Simple giving

a) Singleness of motive

Verse 8 adds "with liberality." The literal root meaning for "liberality" is "simplicity." Kittel *(Theological Dictionary of the New Testament)* says it means "sacrificial liberality." Now, what does *simplicity* mean? When you give with simplicity you give with one single motive. If there is a need, I give. Most people give with two motives—meet the need but make sure there is enough left for us. Most of us usually calculate how much we will give this way: "Now how much should we give to the Lord?" "Well, how much will we have left if we give that much?" But the gift of giving enables someone to give with only one motive—the need. Nothing else enters his mind. Singleness of mind and singleness of heart translate into an undivided motive. Godet says, "According to its etymological meaning, the word signifies: the disposition not to turn back on oneself; and it is obvious that from this first meaning there may follow either that of generosity, when man gives without letting himself be arrested by any selfish calculation, or that of simplicity, when he gives without his left hand knowing what his right does—that is to say, without any vain going back on himself and without any aim of pride." The gift of giving is to be exercised with singleness of mind and with no consideration of self.

b) Sincerity of sacrifice

The gift of giving is not a public gift. Giving with pretension and public display is not a gift; it's hypocrisy. I don't believe that the gift of giving even relates to how much someone has. Some people who don't have very much have the gift of giving away all they have. Other people who have a lot don't have the gift, whereas others who have a lot have the gift. All of us need to invest in the Lord, but the gift is the desire to give when a need arises. And this is illustrated in so many beautiful ways in the New Testament.

(1) Mary

John 12:3-5 says, "Then took Mary a pound of ointment of spikenard, very costly, and anointed the feet of Jesus, and wiped his feet with her hair; and the house was filled with the odor of the ointment. Then saith one of his disciples, Judas Iscariot, Simon's son, who should betray him, Why was not this ointment sold for three hundred denarii, and given to the poor?" A denarius was one day's wages for one day's hard work. Mary poured three hundred day's work on His feet in one act of love. That is how costly that ointment was. Now that is the gift of giving—magnanimous, knowing no bounds, with no thought of the absence of that possession once it has been given.

(2) The church

The believers in the early church held all things in common (Acts 2:44-45). When someone had a need, someone would sell his property or some possession and give the money to the person who had the need.

130

(3) The Macedonians

The Macedonians had the gift of giving. In 2 Corinthians 8:2 Paul says, "Their deep poverty abounded unto the riches of their liberality." They didn't have much, but they gave everything they had.

(4) The Philippians

Some of the Philippians had the gift of giving. In Philippians 4:18 Paul tells them that they have given him too much. But that is how the gift works.

(5) The Salt Shakers

Some years ago, a group of people in our church got together. They all believed that they had the gift of giving. They started a little fellowship called "Salt Shakers." Various people who had needs would get checks in the mail. It could be in the amount of $100, $200, $300, $50, $75—any amount that would help. Only the return address of "Salt Shakers" would appear. They were just some people who wanted to minister their gift to those who had need. That is the gift of giving—meeting needs, without any show.

(6) C. T. Studd

One man who had this gift was C. T. Studd. His biography contains a beautiful story. His father was extremely wealthy. He was to inherit a substantial amount of money—several hundred thousand dollars. This took place in the 1880s, and at that time it amounted to more than £29,000. The following is what the biography says:

"So far as he could judge, his inheritance was £29,000. But in order to leave margin for error, he decided to start by giving £25,000. One memorable day, January 13, 1887, he sent off four cheques of £5,000 each, and five of £1,000. As cooly and deliberately as a business man invests in some 'gilt-edged' securities, as being both safe and yielding good interest, so C. T. invested in the Bank of Heaven. This was no fool's plunge on his part. It was his public testimony before God and man that he believed God's Word to be the surest thing on earth, and that the hundredfold interest which God has promised in this life, not to speak of the next, is an actual reality for those who believe it and act on it.

"He sent £5,000 to Mr. Moody, expressing the hope that he would be able to start some Gospel work at Tirhoot in North India, where his father had made his fortune. Moody hoped to carry this out, but was unable to, and instead used the money to start the famous Moody Bible Intitute in Chicago, writing, 'I will do the next best thing and open a Training School with it, from which men and women will go to all parts of the world to evangelize.'

"£5,000 he sent to Mr. George Muller, £4,000 to be used on missionary work, and £1,000 among the orphans; £5,000 to George Holland, in Whitechapel, 'to be used for the Lord among His poor in London,' asking for the receipt to be made out in his father's name, because of the spiritual help Mr. Holland had been to his father; and £5,000 to Commissioner Booth Tucker for the Salvation Army in India. This £5,000 arrived just after they had had a night of prayer for reinforcements vitally needed. It was used to send out a party of fifty new officers.

"To Miss McPherson for her work in London, to Miss Ellen Smyly in Dublin, General Booth of the Salvation Army, Rev. Archibald Brown in the East End of London, and Dr. Barnardo's Home, he sent £1,000 each.

"In a few months he was able to discover the exact amount of his inheritance. He then gave some further thousands, mainly to the C.I.M. [China Inland Mission], leaving another £3,400 still in his possession. . . . Just before the wedding he presented his bride with this money. She, not to be outdone, said, 'Charlie, what did the Lord tell the rich young man to do?' 'Sell all.' 'Well then, we will start clear with the Lord at our wedding.' " They then wrote the following letter to General Booth on July 3, 1888:

" 'My dear General, We are so sorry last mail to hear of Mrs. Booth's serious illness, our hearts do go out in deep sympathy to you both. I cannot tell you how many times the Lord has blessed me through reading your and Mrs. Booth's addresses in *The War Cry* and your books. And now we want to enclose a cheque for £1,500. The other 500 has gone to Commissioner Tucker for his wedding present. Besides this I am instructing our Bankers, Messrs. Coutts and Co., to sell out our last earthly investment of £1,400 Consols and send what they realize to you. Henceforth our bank is in heaven. You see we are rather afraid—notwithstanding the great earthly safety of Messrs. Coutts and Co. and the Bank of England—we are, I say, rather afraid that they may both break on the Judgment Day. And this step has been taken not without most definite reference to God's Word, and the command of the Lord Jesus, Who said, "Sell that ye have and give alms. Make for yourselves purses which wax not old." '

" 'We have felt the Spirit's drawings to this course after asking for a very long time. "To whom shall we give it?" Moreover, we have felt that in this way we shall better reach the people, as being the Lord Jesus' way of coming to preach Salvation. Hallelujah! We can also thank God by His grace that we have not done this by constraint, but cheerfully and of a ready mind and willing heart. Praise the Lord. Amen.'

" 'And we thank God too that now as regards England we are in that proud position, "Silver and gold have I none." But we don't want to be like Ananias and Sapphira, we tell you honestly we have a small amount out here. I myself at present don't know how much it is!'

" 'Now this does not come from me, for I was told that the Bible says, "He that provideth not for his own house hath denied the faith and is worse than an infidel." So I just took the whole pot and gave it to my little wife wherewith to provide for the household. And so now it is she who sends this money, regarding heaven as the safest bank, and moreover thinking it is so handy; you have no trouble about cheques or rates of exchange, but just "Ask and receive, that your joy may be full." '

" 'Now, good-bye, dear General, may the Lord keep you leading in this war for many many years, and dear Mrs. Booth too. Our united heartfelt prayer is, God bless you both and all yours in both your inner and smaller and outer and larger families. Now there only remains one other command of the Lord Jesus for us to fulfill, and that is, "When thou doest thine alms, let not thy left hand know what thy right hand doeth, that thine alms may be in secret." So, therefore, in case that voracious friend of yours, *The War Cry,* should lay hold of this document and hold it up to the public gaze, we beg to sign ourselves—your loving, we know, and getting humble, we trust, would be Soldiers of Jesus Christ. My wife and me' " (Norman Grubb, *C. T. Studd* [Fort Washington, Pa.: Christian Literature Crusade, 1972] pp. 59-62. Used by permission).

General Booth never knew who sent him the money. When they had given all their money away, C. T. Studd packed up his little wife, and they went to Africa as missionaries for the rest of their days. That is the gift of giving, and that is how God ministers. Think about what came out of that one man's gift: China Inland Mission (Hudson Taylor), George Mueller's orphanages in London, Salvation Army extensions, and Moody Bible Institute. That is how the Spirit of God operates.

Do you see yourself in any of these three gifts: leadership, service, or giving? If you do, be obedient because there will be tremendous joy.

Focusing on the Facts

1. In what ways does the New Testament urge us to behave in regard to the Spirit (see p. 120)?
2. What are the results of the Spirit's control in every believer's life (see p. 121)?
3. Why is it not important to identify your spiritual gift? What is important for you to do (see p. 121)?
4. Why is there a problem when it comes to trying to define your spiritual gift (see pp. 121-22)?
5. What is the purpose of serving gifts (see p. 123)?
6. What are the two words used to describe the gift of leadership? What does each mean (see p. 123)?
7. What abilities are encompassed in the gift of leadership? What are some abilities that may have nothing to do with the gift of leadership (see pp. 123-24)?
8. What is *cybernetics?* How does it relate to leadership (see p. 124)?
9. What is the significance of the connection that wisdom has with the Greek word *kubernēsis* in the Greek Old Testament (see pp. 124-25)?
10. What is the difference between someone who has wisdom in leadership and someone who has the gift of the word of wisdom (see p. 125)?
11. What two words define the gift of leadership? To whom can a true leader be compared (see p. 125)?
12. Who can have the gift of leadership? Why should pastors have the gift? Why are they not the only ones with the gift (see pp. 125-26)?

13. What does it mean to rule with diligence (see p. 126)?
14. Why were the Corinthians not exercising the gift of leadership (see p. 126)?
15. Why is leadership not an easy responsibility (see p. 127)?
16. What is the gift of serving? What is the literal meaning of the word *helps* (see p. 127)?
17. What are some of the positive and negative aspects of serving? Support your answer with Scripture (see pp. 127-28).
18. Why is serving the most needed gift (see p. 128)?
19. Why does Paul include "helps" right in the midst of some of the more grandiose gifts (1 Cor. 12:28; see p. 129).
20. What does *simplicity* mean in relationship to the gift of giving (see p. 129)?
21. Why is the gift of giving not a public gift (see p. 130)?
22. What are some illustrations of the gift of giving? What kind of sacrifices did these people have to make (see pp. 130-31)?

Pondering the Principles

1. List the six results of a life that is controlled by the Holy Spirit (see p. 121). On a scale from one to ten, to what degree do you experience each of these results in your own life? Look up the following verses: Matthew 20:25-28; Romans 6:22; 8:1-4; 2 Corinthians 3:17; Galatians 5:1, 22-23; Ephesians 5:18-19; 6:11-18; Philippians 3:3; Hebrews 3:14; 1 Peter 4:10-11; 1 John 4:4. Next to each result, list the verses that apply. In what ways does your life need to be more controlled by the Holy Spirit? Which results are you lacking in your life? What are some things that the Bible says that may help you to put yourself under the Spirit's control?
2. Read 1 Thessalonians 5:12-13. Do you know those people who are in leadership over you? Do you esteem them in love for their labor for your sake? Would you begin to hold up your leaders in prayer so that they might more effectively minister to the Body? In addition, memorize 1 Thessalonians 5:12-13 as a way of reminder to pray for your leaders: "And we beseech you, brethren, to know them who labor among you, and are over you in the Lord, and admonish you, and to esteem them very highly in love for their work's sake. And be at peace among yourselves."
3. Why is the gift of serving so important? List as many ways as you can in which a Christian is to serve. Who is our model? What are some things you have done to help the Body of Christ? What are some things you can do that you have not yet done? Make an effort this week to serve in some way that you have not yet tried.
4. Read again the excerpt from the biography of C. T. Studd (see pp. 131-34). What are the characteristics of giving that both he and his wife manifested? What did his giving reveal about his faith in God?

What was his view of God's Word? What was his main objective in giving away his money? Now, ask yourself these same questions. What characteristics of giving do you manifest when you give to a need? How does your giving reveal your faith in God? What is your view of God's Word? What is your main objective when you give? Compare your giving with that of C. T. Studd. What changes do you need to make in your attitude and action in giving?

8

The Permanent Edifying Gifts—Part 3

Outline

Introduction
A. The Indwelling Spirit
   1. Ephesians 2:22
   2. 1 Corinthians 3:16, 17*b*
B. The Influential Spirit
   1. The priority of His control
   2. The products of His control
      a) Unity
      b) Fellowship
      c) Worship
      d) Evangelism
      e) Love
      f) Obedience
      g) Submission to the lordship of Christ
      h) Ministry

Review
 I. The Speaking Gifts
II. The Serving Gifts
   A. Leadership
   B. Serving
   C. Giving

Lesson
   D. Mercy (Rom. 12:8)
      1. The character of God
         a) Verse 8
         b) Verse 11
         c) Verse 13
      2. The confusion with grace
         a) Illuminating the difference
         b) Illustrating the difference
            (1) Proverbs 14:20-21
            (2) Proverbs 14:31

        (3) Hosea 4:1-2*a*
        (4) Hosea 14:3
        (5) Luke 10:25-37
        (6) Matthew 9:27-29
        (7) Matthew 15:21-28
        (8) Matthew 17:14-15
        (9) Matthew 20:29-31, 34
      (10) Acts 9:36-40
  3. The compassion of the heart
    a) Sympathy in suffering
    b) Sympathy with joy
E. Faith (1 Cor. 12:9)
  1. Activating the sovereign
    a) Matthew 17:20
    b) 1 Corinthians 13:2
    c) Matthew 21:22
  2. Assurance in the storm
  3. Acting as support
F. Discernment (1 Cor. 12:10)
  1. Evaluating the spirit
  2. Exercising the gift
    a) In the early church
      (1) Rejecting the counterfeit
      (2) Rejecting the heresies
      (3) Rejecting the hypocrisy
    b) In today's church
      (1) To identify demonism
      (2) To identify carnality
      (3) To identify the true spirit
      (4) To identify truth from error

Introduction

Our basic study of spiritual gifts has been from 1 Corinthians 12:8-10 and 28, although we have been incorporating Ephesians 4:11 and Romans 12:6-8. All of these Scriptures contain the lists of the categories of spiritual gifts that the Holy Spirit has granted to the church.

The Spirit of God has given gifts (i.e., enablements, manifestations, energizings, services) to the church. They are enablements of the Holy Spirit allowing us to minister to one another within the Body of Christ. We are not spectators; we are to be involved in the actual operation of the church, carrying out the ministry as God has designed it and the Spirit of God has planned it. So, as we learn our gifts and how they operate, and as we understand how the Spirit of God works through us, we can give a greater, deeper, and broader commitment to do that which God has gifted us to do.

A. The Indwelling Spirit

1. Ephesians 2:22—"In whom ye also are built together for an habitation of God through the Spirit." In other words, the Spirit of God not only indwells individual Christians but indwells the collective assembly of believers—indwells any local assembly and any individual believer. The people at Grace Community Church are an assembly of believers who have become the habitation of the Spirit of God. He lives within us individually and collectively, as He does in the worldwide Body of Christ.

2. 1 Corinthians 3:16, 17b—"Know ye not that ye are the temple of God and that the Spirit of God dwelleth in you? . . . For the temple of God is holy, which temple ye are." The "ye" is plural, thus, collectively, we are the temple of the Spirit of God. The Spirit of God doesn't dwell in a church building, and that is why we don't call it a sanctuary; we call it an auditorium. A *sanctuary* is what the Holy of Holies in the Old Testament was, where God's Spirit dwelt and was manifest. Today, the Spirit of God dwells in the Body, both of the individual Christian and the collective, corporate assembly of believers.

B. The Influential Spirit

1. The priority of His control

Since we are an assembly of believers that is the habitation of the Spirit, it seems obvious and reasonable that the Spirit of God should be in control of the assembly. We would be denying our very identity if He were not. Since He dwells in us, He should manifest His indwelling by His power and control over us. This is a fact in the Christian life. For example, you can possess the Holy Spirit and not be controlled by Him—that is carnality. And the church can be equally carnal. There are certain assemblies in which Christians manifest carnality, selfishness, and self-will, because the Spirit of God is not in control.

That was exactly the case in the Corinthian church. They were believers, they possessed the Holy Spirit, and they were the habitation of the Spirit, but due to their sinfulness and carnality, the Spirit of God had been removed from leadership. His power was usurped, and the Corinthians were running the show. I pray that Grace Community Church would be a church where the Spirit of God rules, fills, controls, and energizes.

2. The products of His control

As I look at any church, there are certain indicators that reveal if in fact the Spirit of God is in control. There are eight that I know of:

a) Unity

The Spirit is the Spirit of unity (Eph. 4:3). Where there is a loving unity without crushing individuality, the Spirit of God is in control. He seeks unity.

b) Fellowship

The fellowship will be both deep (i.e., honest, intimate, and real) and wide (i.e., inclusive of anyone who cares, who comes, and is a part of the fellowship). It will not be separatistic and superficial fellowship.

c) Worship

An assembly that worships God truly, genuinely, and honestly will have worship that is shared by all. In other words, they will come to honor God, they will come to honor Christ, and they will speak in honor of the Holy Spirit. They will praise God: they will sing praise, they will live praise, and they will talk praise.

d) Evangelism

The Holy Spirit has come to point us to Christ. He is the one who declares Christ. And in a church where the Spirit of God controls, Christ will be declared and evangelism will be spontaneous. It will be a top priority. It will be a natural outflow of the lives of the people who make up that assembly.

e) Love

This will be an assembly of people who care about each other. It will be an assembly of people controlled by the attitude of selflessness—where real love works and where sacrifice is a byword.

f) Obedience

This will be a church that is walking in the path that the Word of God prescribes. It will be a church where spontaneous obedience is the pattern and where all that ever needs to be said is: "This is what the Bible says," and the response is immediate.

g) Submission to the lordship of Christ

Christ will rule, and the people will lovingly, joyously, and willingly submit to that rule.

h) Ministry

There will be saints interchanging spiritual gifts. There won't be just a professional pulpit, consisting of hired practitioners, pastors, teachers, and ministers, but there will be the mass of the community of believers ministering their spiritual gifts. If the Spirit of God is in control of a church, there will be ministry. And the way we minister is by those enablements—those energizings, those gifts—that God has given us. It is important for us to understand them. That is why Paul said, "I don't want you to be ignorant of these things" (1 Cor. 12:1). They are vital to ministry.

Review

Now, we have studied the gifted men. God has given to the church apostles, prophets, evangelists, teaching pastors, and teachers for the purpose of instructing the saints to build them to maturity so they can use their gifts. We are now discussing the specific gifts that belong to the individual believers, through which the Holy Spirit ministers. There are a total of eleven that are mentioned in the New Testament. These eleven gifts are like colors on an artist's palette—the Holy Spirit mixes these eleven "primary colors" into combinations, so that by the time they are given to you, they are different than they are with anyone else. That is the meaning of 1 Corinthians 12:11: "The Spirit divides to every man individually." No two Christians are alike in the area of their spiritual enablement. We have been studying these primary gifts in order to gain an understanding of all the categories of ministry.

I. THE SPEAKING GIFTS (see pp. 104-22)

II. THE SERVING GIFTS (see pp. 123-53)

A. Leadership (Rom. 12:8; 1 Cor. 12:28; see pp. 123-27)

B. Serving (Rom. 12:7; 1 Cor. 12:28; see pp. 127-29)

C. Giving (Rom. 12:8; see pp. 129-34)

Lesson

D. Mercy (Rom. 12:8)

Romans 12:8 says, "He that showeth mercy, with cheerfulness." Some people in the Body of Christ have been given the gift of showing mercy. This is one of the gifts that we can be very clear in understanding—there just isn't that much deviation between what the gift is and how it operates.

1. The character of God

The word "mercy" is the Greek word *eleon*. It means "pity" or "mercy" or "compassion." It is a term that is characteristic of the character of God. Psalm 103 contains some marvelous statements about the mercy of God. For example:

a) Verse 8—"The Lord is merciful and gracious, slow to anger, and plenteous in mercy."

b) Verse 11—"So great is his mercy toward them that fear him." How great? "For as the heavens are high above the earth."

c) Verse 13—"As a father pitieth his children, so the Lord pitieth them that fear him."

God is merciful. God is pitying. God is compassionate. And God grants mercy (Matt. 5:7).

2. The confusion with grace

Generally, the concept of mercy is often confused with the concept of grace in Scripture. When we talk about God's grace and God's mercy, we sometimes don't distinguish between them. In order to distinguish mercy from grace, I will give a definition and then show how mercy works out in practice.

a) Illuminating the difference

Grace is extended to men in relation to guilt, which is a result of their sin. Mercy is extended to men in relation to misery, which is a result of their situation. Grace is related to guilt; mercy is related to misery. Grace is God taking care of our sin; mercy is God taking care of the mess we are in.

b) Illustrating the difference

(1) Proverbs 14:20-21—"The poor is hated even by his own neighbor, but the rich hath many friends." Many people try to get into the rich man's pocketbook, while poor people don't have many friends. Verse 21 continues, "He that despiseth his neighbor sinneth; but he that hath mercy on the poor, happy is he." Mercy is not connected with being sinful but with being poor. Poor people need mercy. This introduces

142

the concept that mercy is related to misery. Mercy is related to a state of being.

(2) Proverbs 14:31—"He that oppresseth the poor reproacheth his Maker." Why? God doesn't oppress the poor: He reaches out to them. The verse continues, "But he that honoreth him hath mercy on the poor." If you want to honor God, have mercy on the poor. Here is the connection: Mercy can be extended to someone who is poor, so it is connected with misery rather than sin.

(3) Hosea 4:1-2a—"Hear the word of the Lord, ye children of Israel; for the Lord hath a controversy with the inhabitants of the land, because there is no truth, nor mercy, nor knowledge of God in the land" (v. 1). This terrible society oppressed the poor, and no one gave them relief. Relieving a poor man of his poverty is mercy. Instead of anyone's helping the poor, there was "swearing, and lying, and killing, and stealing, and committing adultery" (v. 2a).

(4) Hosea 14:3—"In thee the fatherless findeth mercy." Mercy is connected with poor people and orphans. If you were to trace mercy further through the Old Testament, you would see that God's mercy is relative to man's misery. God is merciful in that He freely, without any merit on our part, takes us out of our misery and meets every need.

You say, "That is the general concept, but how does it relate to the gift? What is the gift of mercy?" The gift of mercy is the same thing. It relates to people who are in need, such as poor people and orphans.

(5) Luke 10:25-37—Jesus is having a conversation with a rich lawyer. Their dialogue centers on the law. The lawyer desires to know who his neighbor is so that he might inherit eternal life, although he is really testing Jesus. So Jesus responds in verse 30: "A certain man went down from Jerusalem to Jericho, and fell among thieves, who stripped him of his raiment, and wounded him, and departed, leaving him half dead. And by chance there came down a certain priest that way; and when he saw him, he passed by on the other side" (vv. 30-31). This was a really strong indictment of the Jewish priesthood. In verse 32, a Levite also passed on the other side. Verse 33 says, "But a certain Sa-

143

maritan, as he journeyed, came where he was; and when he saw him, he had compassion on him."

There was nothing to motivate this man but compassion. If he helped this poor, beaten Jew, he knew he wasn't going to receive a great reward from the Samaritans. In fact, he wouldn't even tell a Samaritan because the Samaritans held animosity toward the Jews. And he also wouldn't be popular with his own people by helping this poor, beaten Jew. So, he does this knowing he will never receive any credit from his own people. He does this with absolutely no ulterior motive, knowing there will be no response, no remuneration, and nothing to be gained except the relief that comes from dispensing the compassion that was in his heart. That is the beauty of the selflessness of the operation of a spiritual gift.

Verse 34 continues, "And went to him, and bound up his wounds, pouring in oil and wine, and set him on his own beast, and brought him to an inn, and took care of him." Now, this man was probably in a hurry. We don't know what kind of business he had in Jericho, but he stopped and took the day to take care of this man. He healed his wounds the best he could, took him to an inn, and took care of him. Then verse 35 says, "And on the next day, when he departed, he took out two denarii, and gave them to the host, and said unto him, Take care of him; and whatever thou spendest more, when I come again, I will repay thee." You say, "Why did he do this? What did he have to gain? Was this a famous man lying by the road?" No, it doesn't say a thing about him. The Samaritan did it because he had compassion. In his heart was pity and mercy unmixed with any self-motive.

Then Jesus said to the lawyer, "Which, now, of these three, thinkest thou, was neighbor unto him that fell among the thieves? And he said, He that showed mercy on him. Then said Jesus unto him, Go, and do thou likewise" (vv. 36-37). That is the spirit of mercy. It is giving without any thought of return and giving to someone who is in misery. It is the poor, the orphans, the mugged, the beat-up, the maimed, the rejected, and the despised who are the recipients of mercy.

144

(6) Matthew 9:27-29—"And when Jesus departed from there, two blind men followed him, crying, and saying, Thou Son of David, have mercy on us. And when he was come into the house, the blind men came to him; and Jesus saith unto them, Believe ye that I am able to do this? They said unto him, Yea, Lord. Then touched he their eyes, saying, According to your faith be it unto you." Jesus had mercy. Mercy is eliminating human misery.

(7) Matthew 15:21-28—"Then Jesus went from there, and departed into the borders of Tyre and Sidon. And, behold, a woman of Canaan came out of the same borders, and cried unto him, saying, Have mercy on me, O Lord, thou Son of David; my daughter is grievously vexed with a demon" (vv. 21-22). Here is a lady whose misery is a demon-possessed daughter. She is also asking for mercy. To the Jewish mind, mercy is related to misery. So, misery can be expressed in poverty, in being an orphan, in being beaten up and left for dead, in being blind, and in having a demon-possessed daughter. It is human suffering. Jesus healed the people who had these miseries—these terrible sins and diseases.

In this particular case there was an interesting result: "But he answered her not a word" (v. 23a). The reason was that she was a Gentile, and Jesus was dealing first with the Jews. But then verses 24-28 say, "But he answered and said, I am not sent but unto the lost sheep of the house of Israel. Then came she and worshiped him, saying, Lord, help me. But he answered and said, It is not right to take the children's bread, and to cast it to dogs. And she said, Truth, Lord; yet the dogs eat of the crumbs which fall from their master's table. Then Jesus answered and said unto her, O woman, great is thy faith; be it unto thee even as thou wilt. And her daughter was made well from that very hour." Such a persistent Gentile He could not turn back, even though His primary ministry was to Israel.

(8) Matthew 17:14-15—"And when they were come to the multitude, there came to him a certain man, kneeling down to him, and saying, Lord, have mercy on my son; for he is epileptic, and greatly vexed; for

often he falleth into the fire, and often into the water."

(9) Matthew 20:29-31, 34—"And as they departed from Jericho, a great multitude followed him. And, behold, two blind men sitting by the wayside, when they heard that Jesus passed by, cried out, saying, Have mercy on us, O Lord, thou Son of David. And the multitude rebuked them, that they should hold their peace; but they cried the more, saying, Have mercy on us, O Lord, thou Son of David. . . . So Jesus had compassion on them, and touched their eyes; and immediately their eyes received sight." The fact that mercy is connected with human misery is found throughout the New Testament (Mark 10:46-47; Luke 17:11-19).

(10) Acts 9:36-40—Here we meet a very lovely lady who is dead, but not for long—Peter raised her from the dead. Verse 36 begins: "Now there was at Joppa a certain disciple, named Tabitha, which by interpretation is called Dorcas [meaning "gazelle"]; this woman was full of good works and almsdeeds which she did."

In the English language, the word *eleemosynary* is used to speak of a nonprofit corporation—it doesn't seek to make a profit. It is considered a charitable organization. The word *eleemosynary* comes from the Greek word for *almsdeeds; eleemosune* comes from *eleon,* which means "mercy." So this could be translated: "The woman was full of good works and mercy deeds." Here is a lady with the gift of mercy.

What do we find out about her mercy deeds? Verse 37 continues: "And it came to pass, in those days, that she was sick, and died; whom, when they had washed, they laid in an upper chamber." Then Peter heard about it, and verse 39 says, "Then Peter arose and went with them. When he was come, they brought him into the upper chamber; and all the widows stood by him weeping, and showing the coats and garments which Dorcas made, while she was with them." The gift of mercy is meeting the misery of orphans, the poor, the sick, the beaten, the abused, and the widows, even if it is making coats or blankets for them. The gift of mercy is doing whatever needs to be done in order to extend compassion and pity to someone in misery. Verse 40 concludes: "But Peter put them all forth, and kneeled down, and prayed; and turning to the body said, Tabitha, arise. And she opened her eyes; and when she saw Peter, she sat up."

3. The compassion of the heart

The gift of mercy is relative to the compassion of the heart, not the giving—that's a different gift. Often these two gifts are given in combination. But mercy emphasizes the compassion of the heart. The idea is conveyed by 1 Corinthians 12:26: "And whether one member suffer, all the members suffer with it."

a) Sympathy in suffering

The gift of mercy is the enablement to sympathize with a suffering person—to come alongside the poor, the sick, the destitute, the orphan, the widowed, and those in prison, and minister. And maybe you won't give them anything, except your heart.

W. A. Criswell tells a beautiful story of a little girl who came home from school and said, "Mommy, my best friend came to school today and said that her mother died." The mother said to her little child, "Well, what did you say to her, dear?" The child replied, "Oh, I didn't say anything, mother. I just went over to her desk, sat beside her, and cried with her." The gift of mercy includes sympathy.

b) Sympathy with joy

Romans 12:8 says to show mercy with cheerfulness. The Greek word for *cheerfulness* is *hilaros,* from which we get *hilarious.* "With cheerfulness" is to joyously offer sympathy to the sufferer.

Some of you are gifted in the area of mercy. The Spirit of God has given you areas of ministry such as hospital visitation, convalescent homes and shut-ins, the poor, and the needy. Some people have this ministry, and God bless them for it. If God has given you this enablement, use it.

E. Faith (1 Cor. 12:9)

You say, "What is the gift of faith?" Obviously, it is a supernatural capacity for believing God. Obstacles are only challenges to someone with this gift—they believe what is beyond the visible.

1. Activating the sovereign

   Now in the early years of the church, in the first century, this gift was connected with very astonishing miracles. But in our day, the gift of faith is connected with prayer, and with God's response to prayer as we see Him work. By the gift of faith I don't mean saving faith—all believers have received that. I don't mean the general faith by which we live—all believers manifest that. This is a special gift, limited to certain Christians, that involves an intensive ability to trust God—an unusual capacity to believe God in the face of a storm, in the face of enormous obstacles.

   a) Matthew 17:20—"If ye have faith as a grain of mustard seed, ye shall say unto this mountain, Remove."

   b) 1 Corinthians 13:2—"And though I have all faith, so that I could remove mountains." The gift of faith can lay hold of the promises of God.

   c) Matthew 21:22—"And all things, whatever ye shall ask in prayer, believing, ye shall receive." Faith activates God.

   You say, "But I don't always have a lot of faith." Well, you can thank God that someone else has faith on your behalf. When I have a need, I want certain people to know about it because they have the faith to activate the power of God.

2. Assurance in the storm

   Acts 27 provides an illustration of the power of this faith. Paul was in a ship traveling to Rome. There was a storm, the ship was falling apart in the midst of the wind, called Euroclydon (Acts 27:14). Since the ship was being torn to pieces, they frapped it, meaning that they undergirded the hull by tightening it with the winch. They were afraid they were going to go down toward North Africa's coast and be smashed on the Syrtis. So they lowered the gear and were driven with the wind (Acts 27:15-20). In the midst of this horrible northeaster that they thought was going to destroy them all, Paul stood up and said (v. 21), "Sirs, ye should have hearkened unto me, and not have loosed from Crete, and to have gained this harm and loss. And now I exhort you to be of good cheer; for there shall be no loss of any man's life among you, but only of the ship. For there stood by me this night an angel of God, whose I am, and whom I serve, saying, Fear not, Paul, thou must be brought before Caesar; and, lo, God hath given thee all them that sail with thee. Wherefore, sirs, be of good cheer; for I believe God, that it shall be even as it was told me" (vv. 21*b*-25). I know some Christians who would be down in the bottom of the ship panicking. But there was Paul on deck, telling everyone to cheer up because they would be all right, in the middle of the severest storm that ever hit the Mediterranean. That is special faith.

3. Acting as support

This kind of faith supports and undergirds all of us, because all of the gifts edify others. This kind of faith is the power to lay hold of God's promises for the benefit of everybody. As you go through the list of the heroes of faith in Hebrews 11— Abel, Noah, Abraham, Moses, Joshua, and David—you see their faith strengthening someone else. Throughout the history of the church, there have been thousands of saints who believed God in the face of terrible fear and death, yet who strengthened those around them. Today, there are people with this gift who don't see the obstacles; they just believe God.

Hudson Taylor believed that God could win the Chinese people of his day. Without any money, without any support, and refusing to ask for a penny, he founded the China Inland Mission and accomplished the greatest work in the history of that nation. George Muller had the same kind of faith. There have been missionaries who have gone into countries and claimed tribes, people, and nations for God. There have been evangelists who have claimed an entire city, an entire county, and an entire country for God, and it has happened in response to faith. And what is exciting is that we, who don't have that kind of faith, get caught up and swept along in all the glory of God's work.

When I first came to Grace Church, I was one with not too much faith. I figured that, if the Lord was good, by God's grace we might be able to build the church up to a thousand people. But there were some people way beyond me in their faith. Their faith is the engine, and I'm just riding along in one of the cars. I thank God for what He has done in all of our lives because some people activated His power with faith to move beyond obstacles. As a result, I believe God today more than I ever did in the past. I have been a part of seeing His response to the faith of others.

If you have the gift of faith, use it. Spent time on your knees. Spend time believing God, and encourage others by allowing them to see what God does in response.

r. Discernment (1 Cor. 12:10)

Add to the serving gifts of leadership, serving, giving, mercy, and faith, the gift of discerning spirits.

1. Evaluating the spirit

The Greek root for *discern, diakrino,* means "to judge through, to see through to the truth, to truly evaluate something." So, discerning spirits is simply to evaluate the spirit—whether it is God or a spirit other than the Holy Spirit.

2. Exercising the gift

a) In the early church

Now, in the early church, this gift was the watchdog—the patrol, the guard, the sentinel—for the church. In the early years of the church the New Testament had not been written, and people would say, "God says . . ," or, "I'm a prophet of God," or, "I speak for the Holy Spirit." It was difficult to know who did or did not speak for the Holy Spirit. So, the Spirit of God gave a supernatural ability to certain people who could determine the true from the false. They would say, "That is not the Spirit of God speaking; that is a demon spirit from Satan."

Sadly, the Corinthian church had people with the gift who were either not using it or, when they did use it, they were ignored by the rest. As a result, someone had actually stood up in the assembly and cursed Jesus, and they had agreed that it was from the Holy Spirit (1 Cor. 12:3). Someone with the gift of discernment should have stood and said, "That is not the Spirit of God speaking." And they all should have listened. In 1 Corinthians 14:29 Paul calls on the Corinthians to exercise the gift: "Let the prophets speak two or three, and let the others judge." In other words, "Let them discern; let's have someone checking on what is being said." This is a very important gift for the protection of the church.

(1) Rejecting the counterfeit

Paul illustrates the use of this gift in Acts 16:16-18. There was a young maiden following Paul and Silas. She was saying, "These men are the servants of the Most High God, who show unto us the way of salvation" (v. 17). That sounds like good PR. Verse 18 continues: "And this did she many days. But Paul, being grieved, turned and said to the spirit, I command thee, in the name of Jesus Christ, to come out of her. And he came out the same hour." Paul knew that was not the Holy Spirit but a demon spirit. How did he know? Not by what the spirit said, but because God had given him the discernment to know. The gift of discernment in those days was given to recognize the Satanic counterfeit.

Has the Gift of Discernment Ceased?

Some argue that this gift is no longer needed because you can always recognize a counterfeit by comparing that person with Scripture. But I think that is difficult to determine when there is no place in the Scripture that says the gift of discernment has ceased. It is best to allow the gift to shift and change through the flow of the history of the church, so that it can serve any period of history. Today it is just as important to protect the church from impure doctrine as it ever was. Only now the style of operation of the gift is different.

(2) Rejecting the heresies

After the New Testament was complete, a movement arose in the church known as Montanism. It was a disastrous movement in which Montanus claimed to be the only voice of the Holy Spirit. It was very unbiblical. One historian said that the whole Montanist movement was rejected by the church because some in the church discerned that one of his spokesmen, Maximilla, was not speaking from the Spirit of God. As a result, the church denied the credibility of the movement, and it was written off as a heresy. God protected the church in those early years from that heresy by some who had the gift of discernment.

The Gift on Gifts

On a certain night, a girl came into the prayer room and began to speak and to pray with one of our staff. He stopped right in the middle of the prayer and said, "I demand to know what spirit that is. That is not the Holy Spirit." That is the gift of discernment. And praise God that it protected the church from a very difficult situation. In addition it protected her because God delivered her as well. What is the gift of discernment? It is like "The Committee on Committees" in the United States House of Representatives. Discernment is the gift on gifts. A. T. Robertson says, "It was given to tell whether the gifts

151

(3) Rejecting the hypocrisy

Peter exercised it in Acts 5:3 when Ananias and Sapphira came and supposedly were worshiping God: "But Peter said, Ananias, why hath Satan filled thine heart to lie to the Holy Spirit?" How did he know? He had discernment. This kind of gifted Christian can intuitively identify truth from error; hypocrisy from genuineness.

b) In today's church

False prophets are everywhere today. I believe there are some people who are gifted by God to unmask these false prophets. Some of them write books to unmask them. I think that some of the people who have done good work on the cults and on the occult may be exercising the gift of discernment. They have the capacity to see through something to the core of its hypocrisy.

The gift can be exercised in many ways today:

(1) To identify demonism

It can be used to reveal demonism in any form. It can be used to reveal false prophets and spiritual phonies. I have a very dear friend who has this gift. One of the most convincing things to me that this gift still exists is that I see it operate in this person's life. This person can spot a spiritual phony, usually without missing: "Something's wrong in that person's life. I don't know what it is, but something is wrong." While I would blissfully go on, thinking the best, something is wrong. Sometimes, someone will say to me, "You better not put that person in that position. Something is not right." He is protecting the church.

(2) To identify carnality

I think the gift can even be used to perceive the intrusion of carnal elements into worship. In any ministry throughout the church, there are people who might be ministering in the flesh. And there are some people who can read that, while the rest of us don't know what is going on.

152

(3) To identify the true spirit

The gift can discern one in whom the Holy Spirit is genuinely working. My friend will often say to me, "There is a person really energized by the Spirit of God."

(4) To identify truth from error

Perhaps the gift of discernment can be used when two Christians are arguing. Instead of going to a pagan court, they are brought before some people who will make a judgment (1 Cor. 6:5). Someone with the gift of discernment might be able to determine who is right and who is wrong.

Those people with this gift are the watchmen of the church. I don't have any reason to believe that this gift has ceased. I do have reason to believe that the ministry is altered from what it was in the first century. But I want to warn you: This gift can easily deteriorate into critical, proud condemnation and degenerate into a judgmental spirit when operated in the flesh.

So, there are the six categories of serving gifts: leadership, supervising the saints; serving, supporting the leaders; giving, supplying the needy; mercy, sympathizing with the sick, the poor, and the destitute; faith, securing God's power; and discernment, saving the saints from the counterfeits. All of these dimensions, together with the speaking gifts, make the church mature in Christ. We have seen the eleven primary colors on the palette of the Spirit, as He paints the portrait of Christ on the canvas of the church. They are a beautiful combination designed to reveal Christ, but they only really work when you are faithful to minister in your area of giftedness.

Focusing on the Facts

1. In what two ways does the Spirit of God indwell the church, the Body of Christ (see p. 139)?
2. Why should the Holy Spirit be in control of all believers? What is the result when He is not (see p. 139)?
3. What are the eight indicators of the Holy Spirit's control of the church? Explain each one (see pp. 140-41).
4. What is the meaning of *mercy* (see p. 142)?
5. In what ways is God merciful, according to Psalm 103 (see p. 142)?
6. What is the difference between God's grace and God's mercy (see p. 142)?

7. If you want to honor God, what is one thing you can do (Prov. 14:31; see p. 143)?
8. How is God merciful to us (see p. 143)?
9. How is the gift of mercy different from the concept of mercy (see p. 143)?
10. Why did the Samaritan help the man who had been beaten up? What were his motives? What kind of reward would he receive? What kind of reward would he not receive (see p. 144)?
11. What is another way to translate *almsdeeds?* What were Tabitha's "almsdeeds" (Acts 9:39; see p. 146)?
12. What characteristic does the gift of mercy emphasize (see p. 147)?
13. What is a good word for describing the action of the gift of mercy (see p. 147)?
14. What is the gift of faith (see p. 147)?
15. What was the gift of faith connected with in the early days of the church? What is it connected with in our day (see p. 148)?
16. How did Paul manifest special faith in the midst of the storm in Acts 27:15-25 (see pp. 148-49)?
17. How is the gift of faith able to support and undergird other believers? Give some examples (see p. 149).
18. What does *discern* mean? What is the gift of discerning spirits (see p. 150)?
19. How was the gift of discernment used in the early days of the church? What happened in the Corinthian church when the gift was not exercised (see p. 150)?
20. What are some of the things that the gift of discernment is able to reject? Support your answer with some illustrations (see pp. 150-51).
21. Why can the gift of discernment be considered as the gift on gifts (see pp. 151-52)?
22. In what ways can the gift of discernment be exercised today (see pp. 152-53)?
23. What is the danger of discernment when it is operated in the flesh (see p. 153)?

Pondering the Principles

1. Look up the following verses: Exodus 34:6-7; Psalm 78:38-39; Lamentations 3:22-23; Luke 1:50; Ephesians 2:4-7; Titus 3:5; Hebrews 4:16; 8:12. In your own words, how would you describe God's mercy towards you? How much does God forgive? According to Psalm 78:39, what does God remember about man? How long does God's mercy last? According to Ephesians 2:4-7, what has God done for us? What must we do to obtain God's mercy? For how long does God remember our sins? How does your practice of mercy to others compare with God's mercy toward you? Take this moment to ask

God to help you to learn more of His mercy so that you might reflect more of Him to others.

2. Read Luke 10:25-37. What motivates you to serve Christ? Do you do everything without any regard for reward or acknowledgment, or do you hope that someone will recognize what you are doing? Perhaps you have an opportunity right now, like the Samaritan, to help someone by showing mercy to him in his need. Do not delay, but be a true neighbor to this person by showing the love of Christ. Allow the compassion of your heart to move you to act without any thought of what you might receive.

3. Read Hebrews 11. What characteristics of faith can you find that are exemplified by these heroes of faith? Which of these characteristics are true of your faith? Which ones are not? According to verse 13, what happened to the group of heroes in verses 4-12 before they could see God's promises? According to verses 36-39, what happened to this group before they could see God's promises? What does this tell you about faith? How does this relate to your own personal faith? In what ways does your faith need to grow? To help you in your striving to grow in your faith, memorize Hebrews 11:1: "Now faith is the substance of things hoped for, the evidence of things not seen."

9

The Temporary Sign Gifts—Part 1

Outline

Introduction
A. The Certainty of Miracles
  1. The operation of God
    a) His intention
    b) His intrusion
  2. The operation of Christ
    a) Commending Christ
      (1) John 2:11
      (2) John 5:36
      (3) John 20:30-31
      (4) Acts 2:22
    b) Confirming Christ
B. The Conditions of Miracles
  1. The limited period
    a) The historical pattern
      (1) Christ's revelation
      (2) God's revelation
    b) The present pattern
  2. The limited persons
    a) The demonstrators
      (1) Jesus
      (2) Apostles and prophets
    b) The demonstration
      (1) Acts 14:2-3
      (2) 2 Corinthians 12:12
      (3) Hebrews 2:3-4
  3. The limited purpose
    a) Revelation is complete
    b) Revelation is convincing

Lesson
I. Miracles
A. The Power of Miracles

B. The Practice of Miracles
   1. By Christ
      a) Luke 4:13-14
      b) Luke 4:36
      c) Luke 6:17-19
      d) Mark 1:34
      e) Luke 9:42-43
      f) Matthew 8:16
   2. By the apostles
      a) Luke 9:1
      b) Luke 10:17-19
      c) Romans 15:19

Introduction

There are four temporary sign gifts listed in 1 Corinthians 12:10: miracles, healings, languages, and the interpretation of languages. First, we want to examine the gift of miracles.

A. The Certainty of Miracles

   1. The operation of God

   a) His intention

   I am not going to say that God can't do miracles. God can do, and does, whatever He wants to do. If He wants to do something that is against the normal natural law, He will do it. We are not attempting to put any limitations on God; we are only attempting to categorize His operation and deal fairly with Scripture. Please don't say that I don't believe God does miracles—I believe He does. In fact, He does them hour by hour. And the greatest miracle of all is the miracle of the new birth—people created as new creatures in Christ. We are not denying God the power, the desire, or the will to do miracles.

   b) His intrusion

   It is also important that we carefully define what we mean by a miracle. People will say, "Oh, the other day I found a parking place at the store. It was a miracle!" That is not a miracle in terms of the biblical definition. Or people will say, "My son passed a course. It was a miracle!" Or they might say, "I needed this, and it came in the mail. It was a miracle!" We throw that word around very easily.

So, what is a miracle? A miracle is a supernatural intrusion into the natural law that can have no explanation other than that God is acting. There are some things that have other possible explanations: circumstances could allow you to find a parking place at the store, and circumstances could allow your son to pass a course—he studied hard. Circumstances can accommodate many things. But when a miracle occurs, it is a supernatural intrusion into the natural law, and only God could be responsible.

For example, suppose a man builds a model city. In this huge model city, the cars, trains, and lights actually work. And he runs everything from a remote control electronic board. But every once in a while he will pick something up and move it to another place. Now, if you were alive in that model city, you would say, "What's going on! That building used to be over here. Now it's over there." God created the universe, and He usually lets it run on its own. But every once in a while He picks something up and moves it. In other words, He will raise somebody from the dead, or make an axhead float on water, or part the Red Sea, or do something astonishing just so people don't forget that He is the one running the show. A miracle is something that has no other explanation.

2. The operation of Christ

Now, we have to understand the general category of miraculous operation before we can study the miracle gifts. Jesus Christ, who is the greatest miracle worker, will give us what we need in order to understand more about miracles.

In his excellent book entitled *Counterfeit Miracles,* B. B. Warfield begins with these words: "When our Lord came down to earth He drew heaven with Him. The signs which accompanied His ministry were but the trailing clouds of glory which He brought from heaven, which is His home. The number of miracles which He wrought may easily be underrated. It has been said that in effect He banished disease and death from Palestine for the three years of His ministry. If this is exaggeration it is pardonable exaggeration. . . .

"We ordinarily greatly underestimate His beneficent activity as He went about, as Luke says, doing good.

"His own divine power by which He began to found His church He continued in the Apostles whom He had chosen to complete this great work."

a) Commending Christ

Jesus was a miracle worker. Why?

(1) John 2:11—"This beginning of miracles did Jesus in Cana, of Galilee, and manifested forth his glory." Why did Jesus do miracles? To manifest His glory. What is His glory? The composite of His attributes as deity. Why did He do miracles? To reveal Himself as God. Miracles are confirming signs of the revelation of God. That is, always has been, and always will be their intent.

(2) John 5:36—"But I have greater witness than that of John; for the works which the Father hath given me to finish, the same works that I do, bear witness of me, that the Father hath sent me." In other words, "My heavenly origin and My divine commission are proved by My miracles."

(3) John 20:30-31—"And many other signs truly did Jesus in the presence of his disciples, which are not written in this book; but these are written, that ye might believe that Jesus is the Christ, the Son of God; and that believing ye might have life through his name." Jesus did miracles to prove that God was being revealed in His living Word.

(4) Acts 2:22—"Ye men of Israel, hear these words: Jesus of Nazareth, a man approved of God among you by miracles and wonders and signs." God wants you to know who Jesus is, so He approved of Him, established Him, and commended Him by miracles, wonders, and signs.

b) Confirming Christ

Why does God do miracles? In order to corroborate His self-disclosure and in order to confirm His own revelation. Miracles are in Scripture for one purpose: to prove that God is speaking, whether it is in the Old Testament written Word, the New Testament living Word, or the New Testament written Word. Miracles corroborate God's revelation. When God wanted people to know He was speaking, He did miracles. God normally operates the universe according to His created natural law, but when it comes time for God to make a self-revelation, He will, contrary to natural law, make things occur that have no explanation other than that God is revealing Himself. So, the purpose of Jesus' miracles was to reveal His deity.

B. The Conditions of Miracles

1. The limited period

It is important to understand that there are only certain times when God does miracles.

a) The historical pattern

(1) Christ's revelation

Jesus lived thirty-three years, yet for thirty of those years He did not do one single miracle. Now, there are some apocryphal writings that say, when He was little, He became angry with an evil child and killed him with a word. It has also been said in apocryphal writings that when He was little He made clay pigeons, then blew on them, and they flew away. Others have said that He made things instantly for His father to help him in his business. That isn't so. Jesus never did a single miracle for the first thirty years of His life.

You say, "How do you know that?" When Jesus turned water into wine, John 2:11 says, "This beginning of miracles did Jesus in Cana, of Galilee." You say, "What does that prove?" It proves that not all ages, times, and periods are intended by God for miracles, only those times when God wants to reveal Himself. And Jesus never revealed Himself until He began His ministry after His baptism. These miracles lasted for the duration of His three-year ministry. Jesus never did a single miracle before the hour of His revelation as God.

(2) God's revelation

Not all ages are miracle ages. If you study the Old Testament, there really are only two periods of miracles: one, the revealing of the law to Moses; and two, the lives of Elijah and Elisha when God was laying down the platform of prophetic revelation through His prophets. The rest of the Old Testament contains very few references to the use of miracles and none at the end of the Old Testament. Miracles have not been occurring all the time since the first one. And the reason is that God had a specific word to reveal, with limits and boundaries. When God was revealing either His written Word or Christ, His living Word, it was then and only then that He used miracles as a corroborating and confirming sign.

b) The present pattern

We must still allow for God to do a miracle, never confining Him, but that is not the norm or pattern. Some Christians today think miracles are the norm. There is no end to their appearance on some of the television programs. In fact, there are so many efforts at healing that none of them mean anything. There just is no evidence that those healings are legitimate.

God has designed miracles for a single purpose—to confirm His revelation. Once God has revealed Himself, then the miracles have no continuing purpose. For example, when God finished revealing Himself in the Old Testament, that period was closed. In the four-hundred-year period of history between the Old and New Testaments, God gave no revelation and certainly nothing miraculous. Then, in the New Testament, miracles occurred again. Now the New Testament is finished, the Book is closed, and there are no more miracles.

2. The limited persons

a) The demonstrators

(1) Jesus

Jesus did miracles to convince people that He was of God and that He was God. Matthew 13:54 says that He did mighty works. Verse 58 says, "And he did not many mighty works there because of their unbelief." Jesus did miracles to convince people that He was God, but only those people who already were open to believing—people in whom the Father had already generated faith. And He didn't convince many people, only those who were ready and prepared (cf. John 20:30). So, the miracles were confirming signs. God has never used miracles to save people; He has always saved people with the preaching of the gospel. Once the evidence was complete that Jesus was God, Christ finished His work, the apostles wrote it down, and then you find the gift fading away.

(2) Apostles and prophets

Jesus not only had the ability to do miracles, but so did the apostles and prophets—the New Testament writers, the ones who were the heartbeat of the early church.

Since there was no written word to corroborate their preaching, God gave them miraculous abilities. And God gave them these abilities because there was no other way for God to prove to people that these men were the only ones speaking the truth among the myriad of people speaking in that part of the world. Today, if someone says that he is a prophet of God, we don't need him to do a miracle; we just compare him with the Bible—the confirming Word. But in those days there was no standard and no revealed written Word, so miracles were the attestation.

Miracles, then, were given to authenticate the living Word and the written Word. They belonged to just two categories: Christ, and the apostles and those that worked with the apostles in the foundations of the church. Those are the only two groups that ever did miracles in the life of the church.

b) The demonstration

(1) Acts 14:2-3—"But the unbelieving Jews stirred up the Gentiles, and made their minds evil affected against the brethren. A long time, therefore, abode they speaking boldly in the Lord, who gave testimony unto the word of his grace." How did God give testimony to the Word? Here were these people preaching the Word—people who had touched the lives of the apostles, who were foundational in the early church, and who were on the cutting edge of laying out the foundations. "And [they] granted signs and wonders to be done by their hands." God confirmed His Word in the early church by miracles, signs, and wonders.

After the Spirit had come in the New Testament church age, the only people that we ever know of who were able to do miracles were either the apostles or those whom the apostles personally commissioned. Miracles never extended any further.

(2) 2 Corinthians 12:12—"Truly the signs of an apostle were wrought among you in all patience, in signs, and wonders, and mighty deeds." What were the signs of an apostle? The ability to do signs, and wonders, and mighty deeds. You say, "What were those miracle powers?" They were the signs of an especially sent one—the twelve and a few of the other New Testament apostles.

(3) Hebrews 2:3-4—"How shall we escape, if we neglect so great salvation, which at the first began to be spoken by the Lord, and was confirmed unto us by them that heard him" (v. 3). Who was it that heard the Lord? The apostles. Verse 4 is the key: "God also bearing them witness, both with signs and wonders, and with diverse miracles and gifts of the Holy Spirit, according to his own will?" They had special gifts of the Spirit—special miracle powers to confirm the Word.

If someone said, "I speak the gospel of God," and another said, "Well, how do I know it's true?" and then wonders and signs appeared that have no other explanation, then I agree that God was behind him. Today the same thing is accomplished when someone's preaching is compared to the Word of God, which has proved itself to be just what it claims. That is verification enough. B. B. Warfield says, "These miraculous gifts were part of the credentials of the Apostles as the authoritative agents of God in founding the church. Their function thus confined them to distinctively the Apostolic Church and they necessarily passed away with it." So these marvelous abilities to confirm the Word occurred only when God was revealing the Word.

3. The limited purpose

 a) Revelation is complete

If we say that miracles continue to occur today, and that their only purpose is to confirm God's revelation, then God is still revealing His Word. If He is still revealing His Word, your Bible is incomplete, and Revelation 22:18 is a lie: "If any man shall add unto these things, God shall add unto him the plagues that are written in this book." So, when people, particularly charismatic people, say that miracles are still occurring, they will also say that God is still revealing Himself today. And supposedly many of them receive visions, revelations, and words from God. Even they recognize that miracles are a corroboration of God's revelation. But if we believe that the Word of God is complete and closed and that revelation has ceased, then there is no reason for a continuing, normal flow of miracles. It is clear from the gospels through Acts that there is a progressive lessening of miracles. By the time of Paul's epistles, miracles are gone. People become sick in Paul's epistles, and they stay sick—including Paul. Once the revelation and the Bible were finished, the purpose for miracles was finished.

b) Revelation is convincing

You say, "But what if people won't believe the Bible?" Then they won't believe in miracles, because the Bible is full of miracles that can be historically verified. Jesus said, "Woe unto thee, Chorazin! ... And thou Capernaum ... for if the mighty works, which have been done in thee, had been done in Sodom, it would have remained until this day. But I say unto you, That it shall be more tolerable for the land of Sodom in the day of judgment, than for thee" (Matt. 11:21*a*, 23-24). He is saying, "You don't need any more miracles. There have been enough in the past to be convincing. It is not a question of miracles, it is a question of your own unbelief." I say the same thing. People don't need miracles today; they just need to understand the Word of God. If they won't believe the Word of God, they won't believe miracles either. In the story of the rich man and Lazarus, the rich man says, "Nay, father Abraham; but if one went unto them [his brothers] from the dead, they will repent. And he said unto him, If they hear not Moses and the prophets, neither will they be persuaded, though one rose from the dead" (Luke 16:30-31). And Jesus did, and still many didn't believe.

So miracles had a limited time, only for the early era; limited persons, only the apostles and prophets and early New Testament preachers; and a limited purpose, only for the confirmation of revelation. They were signposts pointing to God's revelation, first in the living Word and then in the written Word. Now that the reality is here, we don't need the sign anymore. It is the same as the difference between a picture and a person. For example, maybe you sent your son to college, or he moved away. You have his picture as a reminder of him. But when your son comes home, you don't stand around looking at his picture; you enjoy your son. We don't need to look at the signs anymore; we have the Bible right here.

To allow for miracles causes all kinds of problems, because that allows for continuing revelation. If there is continuing revelation, then all sorts of people today are claiming miracles, and how do we separate the claims? It was easy in the New Testament: It was either Christ, or His apostles, or those working with the apostles. Richard Baxter says, "Since the primary purpose for which miracles were performed in biblical times is no longer operative, it is reasonable to believe that miracles performed through the agency of man, as in Bible times, no longer are to be seen on earth today." And I agree.

Now remember, we are not trying to say God can't do miracles. We are only saying that God did some miracles at certain periods of time strictly to confirm His Word—strictly as sign gifts for a period of confirmation. They have no place in the ongoing life of the church.

Now, four of these gifts are mentioned in the New Testament: miracles, healings, languages, and the interpretation of languages. They appear only in the list in 1 Corinthians 12. In the other lists, Romans 12, Ephesians 4, and 1 Peter 4, there is never a discussion of these miracle gifts. They only had a purpose in the infancy of the church. We have discussed the overall category of supernatural ability given to those early men as well as Christ; now, what about the specific gift of miracles?

Lesson

I. MIRACLES (1 Cor. 12:10)

A. The Power of Miracles

Verse 10 calls the gift "the working of miracles." The word "miracles" is the Greek word *dunamis,* which means "power." That is the way I would translate it. This is the gift of power—supernatural, special power. It is translated in the New Testament as "power, mighty deeds, strength, and miracles." According to Kittel *(Theological Dictionary of the New Testament),* the root in the Greek means "being able" to do something. It is referring to an ability, a power, an energy.

B. The Practice of Miracles

This word is used 120 times in the New Testament. The verb is used over 100 times. It is a very common word. Remember this: the word that is translated *miracle* in 1 Corinthians 12 is the exact same word translated *power* throughout the gospels. For example:

1. By Christ

    a) Luke 4:13-14—This is the point at which Jesus began His ministry: "And when the devil had ended all the testing, he departed from him for a season" (v. 13). Jesus has just been in conflict with Satan, and Christ has come out the victor. When the devil had ended all the testing, he departed from Him only for a little while. The entire life of Jesus was a day-by-day fight with Satan, because He was invading the kingdom of darkness and rescuing people.

165

Verse 14 continues: "And Jesus returned in the power of the Spirit into Galilee." When the devil had ended all the testing, he departed from Him for a season. What was it that allowed Jesus to be victorious over Satan? The power of the Spirit. Notice that the concept of power is connected with a struggle against Satan. Power, as it is often used in the gospels, is seen in reference to Christ's conflict with Satan's kingdom.

b) Luke 4:36—In verse 35, Jesus rebukes a demon who has taken over a man, and casts him out. Then verse 36 says, "And they were all amazed, and spoke among themselves saying, What a word is this! For with authority [Gk., *exousia*] and power [Gk., *dunamis*] he commandeth the unclean spirits, and they come out." Power is the controlling sock that Christ has on the kingdom of Satan.

c) Luke 6:17-19—"And he came down with them, and stood in the plain, and the company of his disciples, and a great multitude of people out of all Judea and Jerusalem, and from the seacoast of Tyre and Sidon, who came to hear him, and to be healed of their diseases, and they that were vexed with unclean spirits; and they were healed. And the whole multitude sought to touch him; for there went power out of him, and healed them all." Power is connected with dealing with the kingdom of darkness.

d) Mark 1:34—"And he healed many that were sick of diverse diseases, and cast out many demons; and permitted not the demons to speak, because they knew him." The demons couldn't even speak. Verse 39 says that He preached and cast out demons. Notice that His amazing ability to cast out demons is connected with His preaching, because the gift of miracles is connected to the revelation of God.

In Mark 5 the same thing is found: Jesus exercising great power casting demons out of a demoniac (a demon-possessed man who became a maniac). In Mark 7:24-30 there is another casting out of demons (cf. Matt. 9:31-33; 12:22-23).

e) Luke 9:42-43—"And as he was coming [a father is bringing his child to Jesus], the demon threw him down, and tore him. And Jesus rebuked the unclean spirit, and healed the child, and delivered him again to his father. And they were all astonished at the mighty power of God." Power is again connected with conflict and victory over Satan's kingdom.

166

You say, "What are you getting at?" I believe the gift of powers (or miracles) was primarily the supernatural and instantaneous ability to cast out demons. It may have had broader application, and I would not limit it as I would not limit any of the gifts and their varieties as indicated in 1 Corinthians 12, but the primary use of the gift of powers by Christ was in showing that the kingdom of God ruled the kingdom of darkness. That instantaneous ability to cast out Satan was saying to the world: "Why would you be a part of that kingdom, which I control, when I offer you My kingdom?"

f) Matthew 8:16—"When the evening was come, they brought unto him many that were possessed with demons; and he cast out the spirits with his word, and healed all that were sick." I don't know anyone who can do that today. Would-be Christian exorcists go through long sweaty hours of trying to get rid of demons, but that is not the apostolic gift of powers or miracles. With a single word Jesus cast out the demons and healed all that were sick. There are the two gifts: powers and healing. Jesus could handle demon-induced, physically-induced, and congenitally-induced illnesses. I believe that the gift of miracles dealt with demonic influence and the gift of healing with physical problems. These seem to be the intentions of these two gifts, although there is some overlap. The gift of miracles could extend beyond demon-induced problems, but this seems to be its primary function.

2. By the apostles

You say, "Well, that's fine for Jesus, but what about the apostles? Is that the same gift they had?"

a) Luke 9:1—"Then he called his twelve disciples together, and gave them power and authority over all demons, and to cure diseases." Miracles are related to the demons, healing is related to diseases. Verse 2 says, "And he sent them to preach the kingdom of God." Why? These miracles were to confirm their preaching. It does no good to heal people if that healing is not corroborating the message from God.

b) Luke 10:17-19—The personal commission of Jesus extended beyond the twelve to the seventy. "And the seventy returned again with joy, saying, Lord, even the demons are subject unto us through thy name." They had never seen this before. This was not a normal thing, and it is not one now. Verse 18 continues: "And he said unto them, I beheld Satan as lightning fall from heaven. Behold, I give unto you power of the enemy; and nothing shall by any means hurt you." In other words, "Satan may want to use poison, he may want to use serpents, but I give you power over the kingdom of darkness." The gift of powers is the ability to deal with Satan.

c) Romans 15:19—"Through mighty signs and wonders, by the power of the Spirit of God [Gk., *en duna-mei pneuma-tos,* 'in the dynamite of the Spirit'] . . . I have fully preached the gospel of Christ." Paul had the gift of powers, or miracles—the ability to deal with Satan and cast out demons.

Now, this ability belonged to Christ, the apostles, and the few that were touched by their lives. The book of Acts is full of examples of the apostles having the ability to do this. The demons had to respond; they didn't have any choice. For example, in Acts 6:8: "And Stephen, full of faith and power, did great wonders and miracles among the people." What does this mean? It means that he showed himself more powerful in the kingdom of God than the kingdom of Satan was. In Acts 8:7 unclean spirits leave Philip's ministry. The apostles had the ability to deal with the kingdom of Satan, and it confirmed that they were of God (Acts 13:6-13; 19:11-12).

How do you eliminate demons?

You say, "If that gift doesn't exist anymore, how do you get rid of demons? How does an unsaved person get rid of demons?" The Bible says to receive Jesus Christ (John 1:12). How does a Christian eliminate the external influence of demons on his life? The Bible says we ought to minister to each other, reprove one another, rebuke one another, love one another, teach one another, edify one another, and pray for one another (Gal. 5:13; 2 Tim. 4:2; Rom. 13:8; Col. 3:16; 1 Thess. 5:11; James 5:16). It doesn't say to cast out demons from one another. All of the instruction in the New Testament is very clear. You have to deal with that problem alone but with the power of the Holy Spirit. The Bible is very explicit on how to deal with the devil. For example:

1. James 4:7—"Resist the devil, and he will flee from you."

2. Ephesians 6:11—Here we read, "Put on the whole armor of God."

3. 2 Corinthians 2:11—We are not to be ignorant of Satan's devices that will give him an advantage.

4. 1 Peter 5:8-9—"The devil, like a roaring lion walketh about, seeking whom he may devour; whom resist steadfast."

5. 2 Timothy 2:22, 26—Live a pure life so he doesn't have any way to invade you.

This is all personal instruction. Jesus and those early apostles had the power to cast out demons, instantly and completely, and perform other wonders to confirm the revelation. We don't find any reference to that for today because it is not needed by Christians. There is no reference in the entire New Testament epistles to having a Christian cast demons from another Christian. According to Romans 16:20, the believer has Satan under his feet. All you have to do in order to deal with the devil is put on the armor of God (Eph. 6:11).

America's supposed number one demon exorcist says that even he has problems, and some of them won't leave. Then he doesn't have the gift. Do you think that if Jesus cast them out they wouldn't leave? Of course they would.

How will people believe without miracles?

People say, "Well, if you don't allow for miracles, how will people believe?" Miracles have never been the issue in people's believing.

Jesus fed thousands of people on a hillside and did miracles all day long. They followed Him to the other side of the Sea of Galilee. Then He said to them, "You didn't come here because of who I am or what I did, you came here because you want more food" (John 6:26).

Jesus raised Lazarus from the dead, but the Jews got angry and killed Jesus over it.

In Acts 14:8-11, Paul healed a crippled and impotent man. But in verse 19 a little group got together and persuaded the people to stone him. They did and threw him out of the city, presuming he was dead. That is how great of an effect he had.

Miracles never were the reason people were saved. People are saved because God gives them faith in their hearts. The apostles never evangelized through miracles; they evangelized

169

through the preaching of the Word. The miracles only confirmed the Word. Once the Word was finished, the miracles had no reason for existing.

Incidentally, miracles will appear once more in the future when all the Christians are gone and the world is void of any witness. Then the two witnesses will appear with miraculous ability (Rev. 11:3-6). In the meantime, miracles have not occurred since around A.D. 100 as the norm in the life of the church. God is not revealing His Word anymore. All Scripture is inspired by God, and it is complete, that the man of God may be thoroughly furnished (2 Tim. 3:16*a*, 17*a*).

The Amazing Miraculous Claims

You say, "But what about all of these miracles that people claim?" I don't have to answer that question because I can show from the Word of God that this is not a miracle age. But you say that there have been miracles throughout history. Interestingly enough, for years after the New Testament church was established no miracles appeared until the beginning of Roman Catholicism. All of a sudden miracles started occurring.

You say, "What were the miracles?" They were really amazing miracles. For example:

In 415 the bones of Stephen were found. The bones were moved to Africa, and everywhere they went, miracles happened.

A merchant in one town stole the arm of John the Baptist, which had been preserved in a shrine. As long as he kept it in his closet, he became rich; but when somebody found it and took it away, he became a beggar.

In the early years of the forming of the Roman church, Christians preserved feather droppings that supposedly came from the wings of Gabriel when he came to announce the birth of Jesus to Mary.

Pilgrim monks boasted that they had been to Jerusalem and seen the real finger of the Holy Spirit.

The churches of the saints Cosmas and Damien at Rome exhibited a miracle-working vial of the breast milk of the virgin Mary. This became such a popular miracle worker that many churches in France had bottles of Mary's breast milk to do miracles. They even said that this wasn't necessarily the milk that the virgin used to nourish the infant, but that she, through all the ages, had continued to nourish her children in times of deadly need. Even her statues and paintings would give milk at certain times to certain saints.

Bernard of Clairvaux said that he was rewarded for his holy life by Mary's visiting him in his cell and letting his lips be moistened by the food of the heavenly child.

Many people claim to have stigmatizations—the signs of the cross showing up in their hands and feet with bleeding, much as St. Francis claimed.

One saint, Pantaleon, had supposedly drunk so much of Mary's milk in his life that when he died they cut him open and out of his veins came blood and milk. They caught it in a vial, and the blood and milk would switch places each year. When the blood was on top, the country had a bad year; and when the milk was on top, it had a good year.

Supposed apparitions of Mary have occurred all over the world at places like Guadeloupe and Lourdes.

Was God confirming Roman Catholicism by all of these things? What about today, when they tell us that in Indonesia God made porridge for many people at a party?

The evangelical church from the post-New Testament era on has to operate this way: We are to walk by faith and not by sight (2 Cor. 5:7). People who want more and more miracles give evidence of the most infantile faith. Sure, the counterfeit miracles continue. There are so many counterfeits that if God did do something miraculous, it would be hard to separate it from all the mess.

The gift of miracles had a unique purpose: to confirm the revelation of God. Beloved, the revelation is finished. And just as there was no reason for miracles during the first thirty years of Jesus' life, there is no reason to assume that miracles have to continue on and on. People who say, "Oh, we have faith in miracles," don't have faith; they have doubt looking for proof.

Focusing on the Facts

1. What is the greatest miracle that God accomplishes every day (see p. 157)?
2. What is a miracle (see p. 158)?
3. Why did Jesus do miracles? What is the intention of miracles? Support your answer with Scripture (see p. 159).

4. What is the one purpose for the appearance of miracles in Scripture (see p. 159)?

5. When did Jesus accomplish His first miracle? Why is this significant (see p. 160)?

6. Why are not all ages miracle ages? What was God's purpose in the miracle ages (see p. 160)?

7. Why do miracles have no continuing purpose (see p. 161)?

8. Who did Jesus accomplish His miracles for (see p. 161)?

9. How does God save people? What part do miracles play in salvation (see. p. 161)?

10. Why did the apostles and prophets have the ability to do miracles, in addition to Jesus? Give some examples of their miraculous ability (see pp. 162-63).

11. Why is it wrong to say that a continuing, normal flow of miracles occurs today, given that their purpose is to confirm God's revelation (see p. 163)?

12. As far as belief in God is concerned, people don't need miracles. What do they need (see p. 164)?

13. What are the three limitations that are imposed on miracles (see p. 164)?

14. What is the best way to translate *miracle?* What does the root word mean in Greek (see p. 165)?

15. What is the concept of power connected with in many verses of the gospels? Support your answer with Scripture (see pp. 165-67).

16. What was the primary purpose of the gift of powers as used by Christ (see p. 166)?

17. What is the basic difference between the gift of miracles and the gift of healing (see p. 167)?

18. Did the apostles have the same gift as Jesus? Use Scripture to support your answer (see p. 167-68).

19. How should Christians deal with the devil? Support your answer (see pp. 168-69).

20. What was the typical response that people had to miracles in the New Testament? What kind of effect do miracles have on salvation? How are people saved (see pp. 169-70)?

21. How does the evangelical church need to operate (see p. 171)?

Pondering the Principles

1. According to Acts 2:22, Jesus was "a man approved of God . . . by miracles and wonders and signs, which God did by him." Look up the following verses: Matthew 14:14-21; 15:31; John 2:1-11; 3:2; 5:5-9; 9:1-7. What were the things that Jesus either created or recreated? What was Nicodemus's response to what Jesus did? Is your response the same? What are the differences that you see in the miracles of Christ, as opposed to the miraculous claims that people make today?

As a result, what should be your response to the miraculous claims made today?

2. Is God able to do miracles today? If so, how does He accomplish them? Does He still use human instruments to accomplish them? In other words, do some still possess the gift of miracles? How would you respond to someone who says that God still uses human instruments to produce miracles? What are some of the verses you would use to prove your point? In order to be ready and able to give a defense of the hope that is in you (1 Pet. 3:15), take this time to prepare your defense of this issue. Ask God to give you the wisdom and discernment to set forth the proper defense.

3. How would you answer those who believe that miracles are important because they will help people to believe in God? Look up the following verses: Matthew 5:18; John 17:17; 1 Corinthians 2:7-14; 1 Thessalonians 2:13; 2 Timothy 3:16-17; Hebrews 4:12; 2 Peter 1:20-21. What do these verses teach about the Word of God? Make a list. Now read Romans 10:17. Based on these verses, how is a person able to come to saving faith in Jesus Christ? What do you think would be the result if a specially appointed man of God were to arrive in the world today and do many signs and wonders that point to God? Would the reaction of the people be any different than it was in John 6:26 or Acts 14:8-11, 19? What is it that truly will help to bring a person to have faith in God?

10

The Temporary Sign Gifts—Part 2

Outline

Introduction
A. Healing: The Controversy of Opinions
B. Healing: The Criteria for Analysis
C. Healing: The Choice of God

Review
I. Miracles

Lesson
II. Healing (1 Cor. 12:9, 28, 30)
A. The Problem of Disease
1. Searching for cures
2. Seeking to heal
3. Saving the soul
B. The Pretense of Healers
1. The counterfeit claims
a) The historic claims
b) The present claims
(1) Satanic influence
(2) Sincere illusions
(3) Strategic intention
2. A clarifying commentary
3. The critical causes
a) There is evidence
b) The people are Spirit filled
c) The healing is biblical
d) The healing is based on sound teaching
e) People are desperate
C. The Pattern of Christ's Healing
1. Jesus healed with a word or touch
a) A word
b) A touch
2. Jesus healed instantaneously
a) Mark 5:29

b) Mark 7:31-35
3. Jesus healed totally
4. Jesus healed everybody
5. Jesus healed organic disease
6. Jesus raised the dead

Introduction

There are three verses in 1 Corinthians 12 that mention the gift of healing. First Corinthians 12:9 says: "To another, faith by the same Spirit; to another, the gifts of healing by the same Spirit." Then verse 28 says, "And God hath set some in the church: first apostles, second prophets, third teachers; after that miracles [powers], then gifts of healings, helps, governments, diversities of tongues [languages]." Then verse 30 says "Have all the gifts of healing? Do all speak with tongues [languages]? Do all interpret?" The gift of healing is one of the spiritual gifts cataloged in this chapter and therefore is an important one to study.

Now, I want to begin our study of the truths relative to this gift with a few preliminary remarks:

A. Healing: The Controversy of Opinions

First, I realize that the gift of healing is a very controversial subject. There is much concern, because the number one human problem in the world is illness. I am well aware of the variety of opinions, and I have done my very best to read as much and as widely as I could in order to understand the varying viewpoints. I am going to attempt to give you what I believe is God's clear Word relative to this area of ministry. Despite my frailties and humanness, I am trusting that God can use me to speak for Him. I am going to do the best I can to open my mouth and share with you what I see is in the Word of God. This is not a question of my opinion; this is what I believe the Bible says, and we ought to understand it.

B. Healing: The Criteria for Analysis

Second, what I say is not directed as an attack; it is simply directed at dealing with the truth and exposing what appears to be error. I am not trying to attack or judge someone; and I am certainly not trying to wound, grieve, injure, or cause bitterness within the Body of Christ. I have to make that statement, because there will be some who think that this is my approach. It is not. Whenever you deal truthfully with the Word of God, there will be some people who are outside that area of influence. As a result, they need to be recognized as being in error. But at the same time, what I say I want to be understood as being said in a spirit of gentleness, in a spirit of love, and in a spirit of concern for people who have not understood the truth about the area of healing.

C. Healing: The Choice of God

Third, please do not assume by what I say that I do not believe God heals. I do believe God heals. God heals in answer to prayer. God heals miraculously in answer to prayer. God heals miraculously in answer to prayer in order to reveal His glory. I do not question God's miraculous healing in response to the prayers of saints. What I want you to understand is the difference between the healing by God and the gift of healing. There is a great difference between God's healing someone immediately and God's healing someone through a human instrument. That is the distinction that needs to be made.

Review

We have studied the spiritual gifts and ministries in three categories. The first one was the gifted men (1 Cor. 12:28; Eph. 4:11). God has given to the church apostles, prophets, evangelists, teaching pastors, and teachers. Second, among the members of the church, God has given a second category of ministry which we have called the permanent edifying gifts. These are the divine enablements that equip the saints to minister to each other and to build the Body. These gifts will function for the duration of the church. There were two kinds: speaking gifts and serving gifts.

Now we come to the third category: temporary sign gifts—certain enablements and energizings given to certain believers for the purpose of authenticating and confirming the Word when it was still being proclaimed in the early church, before the Scriptures were completed. These were temporary gifts. Their primary purpose was not to edify, though they accomplished that in a secondary sense. Their primary purpose was to authenticate the message of the apostolic community. The first one we considered was the gift of:

I. MIRACLES (1 Cor. 12:10; see pp. 165-76)

The primary function of the gift of miracles (or powers) is the ability to cast out demons. For example, no apostle ever performed what would be called a miracle of nature. No apostle ever fed five thousand men by multiplying bread and fish. No apostle ever did any miracles connected with nature. The gift of miracles was primarily connected with the casting out of demons—God's power over the kingdom of darkness.

Lesson

II. HEALING (1 Cor. 12:9, 28, 30)

A. The Problem of Disease

Now, I think we are aware that disease is the most tragic human reality. Disease is the number one human problem. It is that which hits hardest and hurts the most, especially when it culminates in death.

1. Searching for cures

Since the Fall of man in the Garden of Eden, disease and death have been a reality. Since that time, the search for cures to alleviate the reality of illness and suffering continues. In the darkest part of an aboriginal society, witch doctors have potions and approaches to curing disease. Even the most sophisticated, complex hospital in the world today is doing the very same thing. The primitive beginning of medicine occurred centuries ago in Egypt. Throughout the history of Western civilization, man has continually searched for cures for the terrible reality of disease and illness.

2. Seeking to heal

I know that many people seek certain gifts of the Spirit. There are people who tarry for the gift of languages, or tongues. If I could have any gift of the Spirit, beyond the gift the Holy Spirit has already given me, I would seek, beg, plead, and tarry for the gift of healing. I wish I had the gift of healing. I have stood by a mother and father in a hospital and watched their child die of leukemia and wished I had the gift of healing. I have prayed with a dear friend while cancer was eating up his insides and watched him die and wished I had the gift of healing. I have been in intensive care units again and again, seeing people crushed from accidents. I have seen people torn by surgery. I have watched people eaten by disease and wished that I could heal them with a word and a touch. But I can't.

Think of how thrilling it would be to have the gift of healing. Think of what it would be like to go to a hospital, to all the sick and dying, and just touch them and heal them. Fantastic! Think of all the efforts and years that doctors go through in medicine. Think of the millions of dollars spent on technology when all we need is the gift of healing. Sickness and disease is heartbreaking. It's all over the world.

Imagine that all of the people who had the gift of healing got together, got on an airplane, flew to the great pockets of disease in the world, and went through the crowds healing everyone. Fantastic! How humanity and sympathy would speak for Christianity! Just imagine what would happen if we went through the world with the gift of healing and banished illness from the world. It has been said that in three years Jesus banished disease from Palestine.

Why don't we do it? Why is it that the people who claim to have the gift don't leave their tents? Why do they perform their gift in a controlled environment? Why aren't they in the hospitals? Why aren't they out in the areas of the world where people are really hurting? Why aren't they in India or the other places where masses of humanity are racked with disease? It just doesn't happen. Why? I submit that they don't have the gift of healing because it was a temporary sign gift for the authenticating of the Scriptures as the Word of God. Once the Word of God was authenticated, the gift ceased.

3. Saving the soul

Jesus doesn't say to us, "Go into all the world and banish disease." He says, "Go into all the world and preach the gospel" (Matt. 28:19). Jesus is more concerned about the soul of a man than He is about the body of a man (Matt. 10:28). He didn't say to go and banish disease; He said to go and banish damnation. Many people are naive in their assumption that if we healed everyone in the manner Jesus did, all would believe the gospel. Do you believe that? If you do, then you totally misunderstand the life of Christ. For three years Jesus Christ banished disease from Palestine, and when He was at the end of His ministry, the population agreed that they ought to kill Him. After healing all of the multitudes, when His true followers gathered in the Upper Room to wait for the birth of the church, there were only 120 of them.

Saving faith is a gift from God according to His sovereign will. It is given to whom He wills, and it comes through hearing the gospel and mixing it with the divine gift of faith. It doesn't come through being healed. In Romans 10:17, Paul says, "So, then, [saving] faith cometh by hearing, and hearing by the word of God [a speech about Jesus Christ]." Saving faith comes by hearing a speech about Jesus Christ. Don't think that if we could heal that everyone would be saved. They weren't in Jesus' day, and they weren't in the apostles' day. The apostles did miracle after miracle of healing and were thrown into jail (Acts 3-5). Then in Acts 8 a wholesale persecution broke out against them.

B. The Pretense of Healers

1. The counterfeit claims

What are the claims that are being made about healing today?

a) The historic claims

Historically, the oldest of all the claims comes out of the Roman Catholic church. They have claimed to be able to heal people with the bones of John the Baptist, the bones of Peter, and the relics of the cross. They have claimed to be able to heal at the shrines where Mary has appeared. They have claimed to be able to heal with vials of Mary's breast milk. They have claimed many healings at the shrine at Lourdes.

b) The present claims

(1) Satanic influence

There are Oriental psychic healers—those who do "bloodless surgery," using only their hands as scalpels, and even claiming to raise the dead. There are witch doctors who are using their fading fetishes on the diseases of the aboriginal few left in our world. There are occultists who use black magic, operating in the power of Satan to do lying wonders such as will appear in the Great Tribulation (2 Thess. 2:9). Raphael Gasson, the former spiritualist medium converted to Christ, says in his book *The Challenging Counterfeit,* "There are many spiritualists today who are endowed with this remarkable gift by the power of Satan; and I myself, having been used in this way, can testify to having witnessed miraculous healing taking place at healing meetings in spiritualism."

There are actually demonic counterfeit healings done by Satan using God's words. Kurt Trampler, a Munich author and lawyer, uses the names of God and Christ in his healings but denies the clear teaching of the Word.

(2) Sincere illusions

I have talked with one woman who said that her pastor had the gift of healing. His wife had cancer, but he healed her. I said, "Well, that's interesting. How's she doing now?" She said, "Oh, she's dead." I said, "She's dead? How long after the healing?" "One year." What kind of healing is that? She had the mentality to believe that everything of that nature was a healing.

This same pastor said that his gift of healing works in this way: "In the morning services the Lord tells me what healings are available. The Lord will say, 'I've got three cancers available, one bad back, and two headaches.' I announce this to the congregation and tell them that whoever comes in the evening with enough faith can claim the available healings."

Mary Baker Eddy claimed to heal through telepathy. Today there are men who claim all kinds of healing. You can turn on your television, and they will heal you from a distance, even on a delayed tape.

(3) Strategic intention

Well-known healers make tremendous claims and employ startling procedures. Behind them are many lesser-known healers plying their trade. Each has his own technique. Each operates in a controlled environment. Each operates with a set strategy. But I have never yet seen any of them walk down the hall of a hospital and heal everyone. Yet they all claim that God heals through them.

Operate in the Spirit

All the gifts of the Spirit operate truly only in a Spirit-filled life. If your life isn't controlled by the Holy Spirit, will your gifts function in the Holy Spirit's energy? No, they will function in the energy of the flesh. If you are walking in the flesh, you will function in the flesh. If you walk in the Spirit, your gift will be ministered in the Spirit. Now, if you say, "I have the spiritual gift of healing," then several things should be true of you: You will have a pure life. You will have pure doctrine. You will be characterized by humility. You will have a life of total submission and obedience to Scripture. You will have a life set on completely exalting Jesus Christ. And you will manifest all the fruit of the Spirit. The gifts of the Spirit must operate in the energy of the Spirit, and that only happens when the Spirit is in control. Study the people who claim to have this gift.

2. A clarifying commentary

There is an interesting book entitled *Healing: A Doctor in Search of a Miracle,* by William Nolen, M.D. (New York: Random House, 1974). He is not a Christian, but he writes from a very objective viewpoint. He has a section in his book on charismatic healers. I believe this will provide some really solid answers.

Functional vs. Organic Disease

In your mind you must make a distinction between a functional disease and an organic disease. A functional disease is diagnosed when a perfectly good organ does not function properly. An organic disease is diagnosed when the organ is organically destroyed, maimed, or crippled. The functional disease has only a symptom without a reality. An organic disease has a reality and a symptom. And you will find that in all the cases of so-called healers, the only types of healings they ever accomplish are functional, never organic. They are dealing only with the symptom.

Nolen says: "A healer—can sometimes influence a patient and cure symptoms or a functional disease by suggestion, with or without a laying on of hands. Physicians can do the same thing. These cures are not miraculous; they result from the corrections made by the patient in the function of his autonomic system. We don't know yet how to control this system, but we're learning. . . .

"Doctors use hypnosis, or suggestion, frequently. When I give a patient a pill or a shot, I make a point of saying, 'This medicine should make you better in twenty-four or forty-eight hours. . . . This medicine always works very well.' I know that in some cases I'm going to get better results if I suggest to the patient that the medicine will work than I would if I said, 'Well, I don't know about this medicine . . . sometimes it works pretty well, sometimes it's not so hot. We'll give it a try and hope for the best.' There's a lot to the power of positive thinking, particularly where functional disorders are concerned. . . .

"Now, finally, in our attempt to understand 'healing,' we must deal with organic diseases—diseases that are caused not simply by dysfunction of an organ but by derangement of the structure of an organ or organs. Infections, heart attacks, gallstones, hernias, slipped discs, cancers of all kinds, broken bones, congenital deformities, lacerations, and multitudes of other diseases and subdivisions of those I've mentioned are included in the organic-disease classification. Some organic diseases are self-limited, i.e., healed by the body itself; the common cold and minor sprains are examples of such ailments. But to cure many oganic diseases, the body needs help.

"These are the diseases that healers, even the most charismatic, cannot cure. When they attempt to do so—and they all fall into this trap, since they know and care nothing of the differences between functional and organic diseases—they tread on very dangerous ground. When healers treat serious organic diseases they are responsible for untold anguish and unhappiness; this happens because they keep patients away from possibly effective and lifesaving help. The healers become killers.

"Search the literature as I have, and you will find no documented cures by healers of gallstones, heart disease, cancer or any other serious organic disease. Certainly, you'll find patients temporarily relieved of their upset stomachs, their chest pains, their breathing problems; and you will find healers, and believers, who will interpret this interruption of symptoms as evidence that the disease is cured. But when you track the patient down and find out what happened later, you always find the 'cure' to have been purely symptomatic and transient. The underlying disease remains" (pp. 250-60).

3. The critical causes

   a) There is evidence

   I want you to understand that there is another way to view the claims of healing. So, when someone says, "You have to believe; look at all the evidence," where is the evidence? Where are the organic, spontaneous healings? Where are the healings of broken bones?

   b) The people are Spirit filled

   You say, "Well, I believe in healings because the healers are so obviously Spirit filled." I am not sure, given the kind of production and the kind of things that go on in the lives of the people in those positions, that they really manifest the fruit of the Spirit. As I have examined the lives of the people who are involved in this, I have been very distressed at what I have found.

c) The healing is biblical

Someone else says, "The reason I believe is that they do it biblically." The fact is: They don't do it biblically, as we will see.

d) The healing is based on sound teaching

Someone else says, "I believe it because it is based on the sound teaching of the Bible that by His stripes we are healed. Healing is in the atonement." That is a gross misinterpretation of Isaiah 53:5. It is not talking about physical healing; it is talking about spiritual healing—salvation.

e) People are desperate

You say, "If people don't go for any of these reasons, why do they go?" They go because people who are sick are desperate. There is a certain amount of desperation in disease. Sickness drives people to do things that they normally wouldn't do. Ordinarily clear-minded, intelligent, balanced people become irrational. Job 2:4 says, "Skin for skin, yea, all that a man hath will he give for his life." People will do anything to live. All you need to have happen is for your doctor to say, "You've got a terminal illness," and the panic sets in as well as the desire to be healed. People will do anything to be healed. So one reason the healers do so well is that there is a fantastic market of people who are really sick and desperate. But the really organically ill are not healed by healers. Then there are those who aren't really sick at all; they just have psychosomatic disorders. And then there are those who are ill because they just can't believe God—they are so doubtful that they attempt to have their doubts reinforced by "miracles."

C. The Pattern of Christ's Healing

In order to make a comparison between what goes on today and what the Bible teaches, we just look at Jesus. How did He heal? He set the pattern for all the spiritual gifts. There are six points that are absolutely critical:

1. Jesus healed with a word or touch

a) A word

Matthew 8:5-8 says, "And when Jesus was entered into Capernaum, there came unto him a centurion, beseeching him, and saying, Lord, my servant lieth at home sick of the palsy, grievously tormented. And Jesus saith unto him, I will come and heal him. The centurion answered and said, Lord, I am not worthy that thou shouldest come under my roof; but speak the word only, and my servant shall be healed." You say, "How did the centurion know that?" That was the common way in which Jesus healed.

b) A Touch

Jesus also healed with a touch. Mark 5:25-34 tells the story of a woman, with an issue of blood, who crawled through the crowd to reach Jesus. Verse 27 says, "When she had heard of Jesus, came in the crowd behind, and touched his garment. For she said, If I may touch but his clothes, I shall be whole. And straightway the fountain of her blood was dried up; and she felt in her body that she was healed of that plague" (vv. 27-29). Jesus didn't push her over; she simply reached up and grabbed one of the rabbinical tassels hanging on His robe (rabbis had four tassels on their robes), and she was healed instantly. With a word or a touch He healed all. There were no dramatics and no theatrics.

2. Jesus healed instantaneously

a) Mark 5:29—"And straightway the fountain of her blood was dried up; and she felt in her body that she was healed of that plague." When? Immediately. I have heard people say, "The Lord healed me. Since He did I have been getting better progressively." Jesus never did a progressive healing. When He sent away the lepers, they were healed instantaneously as they traveled on the road (Luke 17:14). When the blind man washed his eyes in the pool, he saw instantly (John 9:7). What about the man who first saw men like trees, walking (Mark 8:24)? He was just focusing what God had just created. Instant healing—the Scripture knows no other kind; otherwise, if Jesus healed progressively, that kind of miracle would be worthless to demonstrate His deity. Someone would say it was just a natural process. His healing had to be instant.

b) Mark 7:31-35—"And again, departing from the borders of Tyre and Sidon, he came unto the Sea of Galilee, through the midst of the borders of Decapolis. And they bring unto him one that was deaf, and had an impediment in his speech" (vv. 31-32*a*). Now, very frequently when someone has always been deaf, it is difficult for him to articulate clearly. So he speaks with a certain impediment because he cannot hear himself talk. This is an organic problem.

Verse 32 continues: "And they beseech him to put his hand upon him. And he took him aside from the multitude, and put his fingers into his ears, and he spat, and touched his tongue; and looking up to heaven, he sighed, and saith unto him, Ephphatha, that is, Be opened. And straightway his ears were opened, and the string of his tongue was loosed, and he spoke plainly" (vv. 32b-35). No healer today has ever done that. All of a sudden, a person who was stone deaf from birth, and who talked in the manner characteristic of one who had never heard himself speak, was given the freedom to speak clearly and to hear everything instantaneously. That is what Jesus did to prove that God was intervening. There was no other possible explanation; otherwise the miracle ceases to have significance.

3. Jesus healed totally

Luke 4:38 says, "And he arose and left the synagogue, and entered into Simon's house. And Simon's wife's mother was taken with a great fever." Peter's mother-in-law was very ill. In fact, the implication here is that she was dying. Verse 39 says, "And he stood over her, and rebuked the fever, and it left her; and immediately she arose and ministered unto them." She got up and made dinner. Here was a woman lying on her deathbed, and when Jesus healed her, He healed her totally. He didn't say, "Now that you've been healed, I want you to just take a little honey and hot tea, and then I want you to make sure that you stay around the house and just lie down." She was healed of a deathly disease, then got up and made dinner. That is instant, total healing.

4. Jesus healed everybody

Jesus didn't allow all the people with organic diseases to leave the same way they came. Luke 4:40 says, "Now when the sun was setting, all they that had any who were sick with various diseases, brought them unto him; and he laid his hands on every one of them, and healed them." He healed with a word and a touch, instantaneously, totally, and everybody. That is why He didn't have to heal in His own environment; He could go where they were.

5. Jesus healed organic disease

People who were crippled from birth could walk. People who were blind could see. People who were deaf and dumb could speak and hear. These were all organic problems. Jesus didn't go around healing low back pain, palpitation of the heart, and breathing problems.

6. Jesus raised the dead

Mark 5:35 says, "While he yet spoke, there came from the ruler of the synagogue's house certain who said, Thy daughter is dead. Why troublest thou the Master any further?" The ruler of the synagogue had asked Jesus to help his sick daughter (v. 23). Verse 41 picks up the narrative: "And he took the child by the hand, and said unto her, Talitha cumi; which is, being interpreted, Little girl, I say unto thee, arise. And straightway the child arose, and walked; for she was the age of twelve years. And they were astonished with a great astonishment" (vv. 41-42). The miracle was in the resurrection. He raised the dead.

I wish the people who claim to have the gift of healing would spend a little time in funeral parlors. They could sure make some exciting things happen. Wouldn't it be super if the next time you went to a funeral someone with the gift of healing came in and said, "I feel bad about this situation. Would you please get up?"

Why did Jesus heal with a word or a touch, instantaneously, totally, everybody, those with organic diseases, and raise the dead? Did He do it to infatuate or play games with the people? John 20:30-31 gives the reason: "And many other signs truly did Jesus . . . but these are written, that ye might believe that Jesus is the Christ, the Son of God; and that believing ye might have life through his name." This gift was an authenticating gift to confirm the statement of Jesus that He is God. You say, "But what about when the apostles healed?" It was to confirm their proclamation.

I'm not saying that God doesn't do miracles. I'm not saying that God doesn't heal. He does heal, and He can do anything He wants to do. Miracles are neither impossible nor necessary—that is up to God. But there is no evidence biblically or practically that anyone today is operating the gift of healing. If God wants to heal, that is His business and privilege. He may heal through the prayers of an individual. He promises that "the prayer of faith shall save the sick" (James 5:15a). But let's not confuse God's healing in response to prayer with the ability to heal everyone at will, as in the case of Jesus and the apostles.

Focusing on the Facts

1. Does God heal? What motivates God to heal (see p. 176)?
2. What is the number one human problem (see p. 177)?
3. What benefit would be derived if some people actually had the gift

of healing? Why don't those who claim to have the gift function in this manner (see pp. 177-78)?
4. What was the purpose of the gift of healing? Why was it only a temporary gift (see p. 178)?
5. What is Jesus most concerned about in relation to man (see p. 178)?
6. After Christ spent three years banishing disease from Palestine, what did the people decide to do with Him? How many true followers met in the Upper Room? What happened to the apostles as a result of their healing people (see pp. 178-79)?
7. Why do people believe in the gospel? What effect does healing have on bringing someone to Christ (see pp. 178-79)?
8. Where do the oldest claims of healing originate? Give some examples (see p. 179).
9. What are some of the claims of healing that is influenced by Satan (see p. 179)?
10. What is characteristic of someone who is operating under the control of the Holy Spirit (see p. 180)?
11. What is the difference between a functional disease and an organic disease (see p. 181)?
12. Why do doctors use suggestion to help patients in their recovery? What type of disease will this technique help (see p. 181)?
13. How is it possible for "healers to become killers" (see p. 182)?
14. Why do so many people go to healers if they are not truly healers (see p. 183)?
15. What are the six ways in which Jesus healed? Explain each one and give an example (see pp. 183-86).
16. Why did Jesus heal, according to John 20:31 (see p. 186)?

Pondering the Principles

1. Matthew 16:26 says, "For what is a man profited, if he shall gain the whole world, and lose his own soul? Or what shall a man give in exchange for his soul?" How would you answer those two questions? Look up the following verses: Matthew 4:4; 10:28; 16:24-26; 26:41; John 3:3-8; 1 Corinthians 2:11; 2 Corinthians 4:16-5:9. In what ways do these verses reveal that Jesus is more concerned about the soul of man that He is the body of man? What is the most important disease that man needs to be healed of? If you know someone who is afflicted by an organic disease, memorize 2 Corinthians 4:17 so that you might have an encouraging word to share: "For our light affliction, which is but for a moment, worketh for us a far more exceeding and eternal weight of glory."
2. Is your gift being operated in the energy of the Spirit? Do you manifest the following: a pure life, pure doctrine, humility, total submission and obedience to Scripture, a life that exalts Jesus Christ, the fruit of the Spirit (Gal. 5:22-23)? These characteristics will be

manifest in a life that is under the control of the Holy Spirit. Which of these characteristics are not being manifest as they should? Take this moment for some self-examination. Ask God to reveal to you how you might more effectively use your gift to God's glory.

3. What new insights have you gained from the excerpts from William Nolen's book? What changes has it produced in your view of modern healing? In what ways has it reaffirmed your present view? If you were confronted by someone who believes that some people today have the gift of healing, what things could you share with them? Make a list of those things, then add to it when you find any new information that will help. Remember, be ready to make a defense of your faith to anyone who asks (1 Pet. 3:15).

11

The Temporary Sign Gifts—Part 3

Outline

Introduction

Review
I. Miracles
II. Healing
    A. The Problem of Disease
    B. The Pretense of Healers
    C. The Pattern of Christ's Healing

Lesson
    D. The Power of the Apostles
       1. The progression
          a) To the twelve
            (1) Miracles
            (2) Healing
          b) The seventy
          c) The associates
       2. The purpose
          a) The confirmation of the message
            (1) Acts 3:1-15
            (2) Acts 19:10-12
          b) The controversy of the message
            (1) Acceptance
            (2) Rejection
       3. The pattern
          a) They healed with a word or touch
            (1) A word
            (2) A touch
          b) They healed instantaneously
          c) They healed totally
          d) They healed everybody
            (1) Acts 5:12, 14-16
            (2) Acts 28:9

Introduction

It is important for Christians to be discerning, especially in the area of spiritual gifts. Today, we hear that all of the miracles and all of the apostolic gifts are still occurring. Some promise that if you invest in their ministry, they will give you the promise of God for a miracle a day. There is a book entitled *A Miracle a Day Keeps the Devil Away.* I received in the mail a special miracle prayer cloth, with these instructions: "Take this special miracle prayer cloth and put it under your pillow and sleep on it tonight. Or you may want to place it on your body or on a loved one. Use it as a release point wherever you hurt. First thing in the morning send it back to me in the green envelope. Do not keep this prayer cloth; return it to me. I'll take it, pray over it all night. Miracle power will flow like a river. God has something better for you, a special miracle to meet your needs." This is just one in a long line of claims that are being made.

Television is being inundated by Christian programming that is, in many ways, a misrepresentation of biblical Christianity. That is a sad thing. People are claiming miracles and healings all the time. It makes you wonder just how much people perceive. In every city and every Christian group I address, people ask me questions regarding this whole subject of healing: "Is God restoring this marvelous gift? What do you think?" The result is that the people across America who aren't saved are confused, to say nothing of the poor Christians who are untaught in Scripture. In our studies we have been endeavoring to clear up many of the misconceptions surrounding spiritual gifts.

Review

In our study of the temporary sign gifts, we mentioned that there are four: miracles, healings, languages, and the interpretation of languages. They are the four miraculous sign gifts given by the Spirit to authenticate the new revelation that constituted the New Testament. Once the New Testament was finished, these sign gifts ceased to have a function. They do not belong to the continuing life of the church.

The people today who claim to have these abilities to conduct and experience healing after healing need to be carefully brought to the test of Scripture. The question is not, "Well, I had this experience; what's your experience?" The question is: "What does the Bible say?" I have nothing against these people. I simply want to deal with what the Word of God has to say about their claims and leave the results to God.

The temporary sign gifts do not exist today. We have seen that this is true from Scripture in our past studies.

I. MIRACLES (1 Cor. 12:10; see pp. 165-76)

II. HEALING (1 Cor. 12:9, 28, 30; see pp. 177-86)

    A. The Problem of Disease (see pp. 177-79)

B. The Pretense of Healers (see pp. 179-83)

C. The Pattern of Christ's Healing (see pp. 183-86)

Lesson

D. The Power of the Apostles

  1. The progression

    a) To the twelve

      In Luke 9:1 our Lord passes on to His apostles this power:

      (1) Miracles

        "Then he called his twelve disciples together, and gave them power and authority over all demons." That is the gift of miracles (or powers). This gift was never the ability given to the apostles and their associates to work natural miracles (i.e., making food, walking on water, feeding a multitude, making a tree fall over dead, building an instant house, or similar miracles). The miracle gift was simply the gift of *dunamis*—power over Satan, the ability to cast out demons.

      (2) Healing

        The end of verse 1 says, "And to cure diseases." He gave them the power over disease, with an unqualified ability to cure diseases. The twelve had that power.

    b) The seventy

      In Luke 10:1 Jesus extends these abilities to another group: "After these things the Lord appointed other seventy also, and sent them two by two." In verse 9 He says to them, "And heal the sick that are there, and say unto them, The kingdom of God is come near unto you." He gave to the seventy the ability to heal the sick. You say, "Does anyone else in the New Testament have the ability to heal?"

    c) The associates

      A few of the associates of the apostles, used of God, were given the gift.

So, the gift belonged to Christ, His apostles, the seventy, and some of the associates of the apostles. We never see the gift used at random in the churches. It was always associated with Christ, the twelve, the seventy, and the associates of the twelve (such as Philip). It was never extended beyond those men. It was a very limited gift in terms of the people who possessed it, as was the gift of miracles (or powers).

2. The purpose

   a) The confirmation of the message

   As this early band went out preaching, proclaiming the gospel of the kingdom (this phenomenal, unbelievable new message), God gave them the ability to heal diseases instantaneously and totally in order to convince people that they were from God and that their message was indeed believable. These gifts were given in order to authenticate and confirm the proclamation of these particular individuals. This is seen throughout the book of Acts. For example:

   (1) Acts 3:1-15—In verse 1 Peter and John are going into the temple. Then verse 2 says, "And a certain man, lame from his birth." We know from Acts 4:22 that he was over forty years old. He was congenitally deformed. Verse 2 continues: "Whom they laid daily at the gate of the temple which is called Beautiful, to ask alms of them that entered into the temple; who, seeing Peter and John about to go into the temple, asked an alms. And Peter, fastening his eyes upon him, with John, said, Look on us. And he gave heed unto them, expecting to receive something from them. Then Peter said, Silver and gold have I none, but, such as I have, give I thee. In the name of Jesus Christ of Nazareth, rise up and walk. And he took him by the right hand, and lifted him up; and immediately his feet and ankle bones received strength. And he, leaping up, stood and walked, and entered with them into the temple, walking, and leaping, and praising God. And all the people saw him walking and praising God; and they knew that it was he who sat for alms at the Beautiful Gate of the temple; and they were filled with wonder and amazement at that which had happened unto him. And as the lame man who was healed held Peter and John, all the people ran together unto them in the porch that is called Solomon's, greatly wondering" (vv. 2*b*-11). The healing drew the crowd. Here was a man they knew had been crippled for forty years, and now he was instantaneously walking and leaping. Incredible!

   The key to this healing starts at verse 12: "And when Peter saw it, he answered the people." The point is, the healing simply generated the amazement that could make the message believable. Then Peter launched into a great sermon: "The God of Abraham, and of Isaac, and of Jacob, the God of our fathers, hath glorified his Son, Jesus, whom ye delivered up and denied in the presence of Pilate, when he was determined to let him go. But ye denied the Holy One and the Just, and desired a murderer to be granted unto you; and killed the Prince of life, whom God hath raised from the dead, of which we are witnesses" (vv. 13-15). The point is, these miracles were signs and wonders pointing to the message they were preaching.

This pattern occurs throughout the book of Acts. Paul would go into a city, perform a miracle, and then preach a sermon. Peter would go into a city, perform a miracle (raise somebody from the dead), and people would believe the Word. The gift was given to those who were the proclaimers of the message in order for them to attend the message with divine confirmation, so people would know that it wasn't just their own opinion.

(2) Acts 19:10-12—"And this continued for the space of two years; so that all they who dwelt in Asia heard the word of the Lord Jesus, both Jews and Greeks. And God wrought special miracles by the hands of Paul, so that from his body were brought unto the sick handkerchiefs or aprons, and the diseases departed from them, and the evil spirits went out of them." The word for "handkerchiefs" in the Greek means "sweat bands." And the word for "aprons" had reference to the type of apron Paul wore when he was making tents. In other words, Paul didn't do this. They actually came to where Paul was working, took his sweatbands and aprons, and put them on sick people. So tremendous were the miracles that they knew this man had power. In Acts 5:15 Peter would walk along the street, and people would try to get under his shadow in order to be healed because so much power attended his preaching.

b) The controversy of the message

The new message delivered by the apostles was confirmed by these signs. Once the message was written down, the signs ceased to be the confirming agent, and the Bible confirms itself. To the Jews, the new message was shocking. Here came these men saying, "You have executed your Messiah. You have been set aside by God, and He is calling out the church from among the Gentiles." You cannot imagine the drama of that message. This was so shocking, so dramatic, and so transforming, that their responses were absolutely amazing.

(1) Acceptance

In Acts 2:37 is one response: "Now when they heard this, they were pricked in their heart, and said . . . what shall we do?" In other words, "This is incredible! We've killed our Messiah! What do we do now?" They heard Peter's sermon with spiritual ears.

(2) Rejection

The others were furious. They threw the apostles in jail and said, "Ye have filled Jerusalem with your doctrine" (Acts 5:28b).

The jolt that was involved in this message was so tremendous that God had to attest to the truth of it by miracles and healings, or men never would have believed. But as it was accompanied with these mighty signs and wonders, they believed it, and three thousand were saved the first day (Acts 2:41). In Acts 4:4 five thousand more men believed. Just for them to hear that they had killed their Messiah was enough to shock them. A new age had come, and God gave His men miraculous ability so the people would understand the truth of the message.

3. The pattern

Now, in giving these men this power of healing, God allowed them to heal in the exact manner in which Jesus healed.

a) They healed with a word or touch

(1) A word

Acts 9:32-35 says, "And it came to pass, as Peter passed throughout all quarters, he came down also to the saints who dwelt at Lydda. And there he found a certain man, named Aeneas, who had kept his bed eight years, and was sick of the palsy. And Peter said unto him, Aeneas, Jesus Christ maketh thee well; arise, and make thy bed. And he arose immediately. And all that dwelt at Lydda and Sharon saw him, and turned to the Lord." Why? The healing was attended by the preaching of the gospel of the kingdom.

(2) A touch

The apostles could also heal with a touch. In Acts 28, Paul is on the island of Melita after the shipwreck. Verse 8 says, "And it came to pass that the father of Publius lay sick of a fever and a bloody flux; to whom Paul entered in, and prayed, and laid his hands on him, and healed him." Here the apostle Paul healed with his hands. Jesus also healed with a word or a touch. They had the same power for healing.

b) They healed instantaneously

Acts 3:4 says, "And Peter, fastening his eyes upon him, with John, said, Look on us. . . . Then Peter said, Silver and gold have I none, but, such as I have, give I thee. In the name of Jesus Christ of Nazareth, rise up and walk. And he took him by the right hand, and lifted him up; and immediately his feet and ankle bones received strength. And he, leaping up, stood and walked, and entered with them into the temple, walking, and leaping, and praising God" (vv. 4, 6-8). There was no rehabilitation. The man had never walked in his entire life. There was no therapy, just instantaneous wholeness.

c) They healed totally

The apostles, like Jesus, healed totally. For example, in Acts 9:34 Peter said, "Aeneas, Jesus Christ maketh thee whole." There is no progression in any apostolic healing. There is nothing like, "I've been healed and I am steadily getting better." No. There is instantaneous, total healing.

d) They healed everybody

(1) Acts 5:12, 14-16—"And by the hands of the apostles were many signs and wonders wrought among the people (. . . . And believers were the more added to the Lord, multitudes both of men and women), insomuch that they brought forth the sick into the streets, and laid them on beds and couches, that at the least the shadow of Peter passing by might overshadow some of them. There came also a multitude out of the cities round about unto Jerusalem, bringing sick folks, and them who were vexed with unclean spirits; and they were healed every one." The apostle Peter healed every single one.

This is not the same as when a person goes to a healing meeting and goes away sick. The healer says,

"Well, I don't do it; only God can do it." But anyone in the Bible who had been given the gift operated it strictly on the basis of volition. The leper came to Jesus in Matthew 8:2 and said, "Lord, if thou wilt, thou canst make me clean." And Jesus said, "I will" (v. 3b). It is the will of the one with the gift that makes it operational. That is why Romans 12:6-8 says that if you have the gift of giving, give; if you have the gift of prophecy, prophesy; if you have the gift of showing mercy, do it, and so on. Any time there is a command to use your gift, there is the assumption that you have the will to control it. This is true of the gift of healing, like every other gift. The people of today say that they are not the ones who heal because they don't heal. They have to say this because, if they claim the gift, then they are forced to answer this question: "Well, why don't you heal this person?" Their copout is: "It's not me; it's the Lord." That proves they don't have the gift, because it was exercised at the will of the one who possessed it—like any spiritual gift.

(2) Acts 28:9—"So when this was done, others also in the island, who had diseases, came and were healed." Who was healed? Everybody who came with a disease.

Jesus and His apostles healed the same way—with a word or a touch, instantaneously, totally, everybody, and:

e) They healed organic disease

They did not deal with functional, symptomatic, psychosomatic things but with actual organic diseases. The man spoken of in Acts 3 had been crippled for forty years. They didn't heal low back pain, migraine headaches, palpitations of the heart, or anything else that was not visible and not organic.

f) They raised the dead

This was part of the gift of healing. Acts 9:36 says, "Now there was at Joppa a certain disciple, named Tabitha, which by interpretation is called Dorcas." When she died, Peter came to see her (vv. 37-39). Verse 40 says, "But Peter put them all forth, and kneeled down, and prayed; and turning to the body said, Tabitha, arise. And she opened her eyes; and when she saw Peter, she sat up. And he gave her his hand, and lifted her up; and when he had called the saints and widows, presented her alive. And it was known throughout all Joppa; and many believed in the Lord" (vv.

40-42). Here, again, is another connection of healing with proclamation and salvation. Next time someone claims to have the gift of healing, take him out to the cemetery and have him raise someone from the dead.

Jesus and the apostles healed with a word or a touch, instantaneously, totally, everybody, organic diseases, and raised the dead. I have yet to see anyone today who can do any of those things. That is the continuity of the apostolic gift of healing. They were confirming signs connected with the preaching of the gospel.

4. The period

Once the Word was complete, the signs ceased.

a) The reality of the Word

Joshua 5:11-12 says, "And they did eat of the old grain of the land on the next day after the passover, unleavened cakes, and parched grain in the very same day. And the manna ceased on the next day after they had eaten of the old grain of the land; neither had the children of Israel manna any more, but they did eat of the fruit of the land of Canaan that year." The miracle of the manna was no longer needed when they entered the Promised Land, so the miracle stopped. In the same manner, once we have the Bible (the land of Canaan in this little allegory), the miraculous sign gift (the manna) is no longer needed. We have the living Word. The gift was never intended to be used to keep Christians healthy; it was to be used as a sign to unbelievers to motivate them to hear the gospel.

b) The restraint of Paul

We know that Paul had the gift of healing. Paul shows us the purpose of this gift because he never used it outside of its purpose. For example:

(1) Toward Epaphroditus

Philippians 2:25-27 says, "Yet I thought it necessary to send to you Epaphroditus, my brother and companion in labor, and fellow soldier. . . . For he longed after you all, and was full of heaviness, because ye had heard that he had been sick. For, indeed, he was sick near unto death, but God had mercy on him; and not on him only, but on me also, lest I should have sorrow upon sorrow." Now here was Paul's friend sick to the point of death. But the Lord didn't let him die.

You say, "Well, what's the big deal, Paul? Why don't you heal him? The gift of healing is something you can use at will." Paul didn't heal him because he would not pervert the purpose of the gift to his own personal ends. The purpose of the gift was not to keep Christians healthy; it was given as a sign to unbelievers. The gift was used only at the point when God revealed that the purpose was clear, the time was right, and it was necessary for proclamation.

(2) Toward Trophimus

In 2 Timothy 4:20 Paul says, "Trophimus have I left at Miletus sick." You say, "You have the gift of healing. Why did you leave him sick?" The purpose of the gift was not to keep the Christians healthy; it was a sign to unbelievers to hear the gospel of the kingdom.

(3) Toward Timothy

According to 1 Timothy 5:23, Timothy was sick, and Paul didn't say, "Find someone with the gift of healing." He said, "Use a little wine for thy stomach's sake."

(4) Toward himself

Paul himself was racked with a thorn in the flesh (2 Cor. 12:7-9), yet he never healed himself, and he never went to someone for healing. Why? That was never the purpose.

E. The Perspective on Illness

1. The heart of salvation

a) Is not physical wholeness

I am tired of hearing people say that God wants every Christian to be well. There is a book titled *God Wants You Well.* I would like to write a sequel, *God Wants You Sick.* God even wants some people dead. God's healing purposes should not be perverted and twisted as they are today. The gift of healing is rampantly being claimed all over as the panacea for everyone's ills. The charismatic movement grows because there are so many sick people looking to get well.

A certain book says, "God has made it perfectly clear in His Word that it is His will to heal the sick—period!" Then why are people sick? It seems much simpler if they just didn't get sick. Then people say, "Well, Isaiah 53:5 says that by His stripes we are healed." Please don't associate that verse with physical healing. That is a corruption of the message of Isaiah 53. Jesus didn't die on a cross so you won't get a cold; Jesus died on the cross to heal your soul of its diseases. Many of the cults promise healing because there is a tremendous market for it.

b) Is spiritual wholeness

In a world where sin is not excluded from the permissive will of God, why should we assume that suffering is? Paul had no such exemption. He prayed three different times for God to remove the thorn in his flesh, and He never removed it because He wanted him to have it. Paul had so many revelations that he could have easily become proud, so God kept him humble by his illness (2 Cor. 12:7-9).

If every Christian were well, and health were a part of the atonement, then all people would be running to get saved for the wrong reason. God's picture of salvation would become cloudy. God wants people to come to Him in repentance of sin and because of His glory, not so they can be healthy physically. What nonsense would be made of such virtues as long-suffering, patience, and endurance— so highly prized in the New Testament—if we were always well. How dumb it would be for salvation to provide physical wholeness on earth but spiritual wholeness only in heaven. How foolish for God to decree that all of us must die but none of us can ever get sick. Paul was sick, and he left a lot of other people sick, but that is the way it is because God wants some people sick.

(1) Hebrews 12:6—"For whom the Lord loveth he chasteneth, and scourgeth every son whom he receiveth." Part of that scourging is illness.

(2) Exodus 4:11—"And the Lord said unto him, Who hath made man's mouth? Or who maketh the dumb, or deaf, or the seeing, or the blind? Have not I, the Lord?" God makes people deaf and dumb and blind because it fits His purpose.

(3) John 9:2*b*-3—"Who did sin, this man, or his parents, that he was born blind? Jesus answered, Neither hath this man sinned, nor his parents, but that the works of God should be made manifest in him." God has His own purposes.

Jesus, Peter, Paul, and all the rest could heal by saying, "I will." They could use that gift anytime, and it was true of any of the sign gifts. First Corinthians 14 was written to regulate the control of the gift of tongues. If the gift were of the type that required waiting on God, regulations would not be needed. God wouldn't use a gift out of its purpose. These gifts were used at the volition of the one who possessed them. Peter possessed it: "Such as I have, give I thee" (Acts 3:6). So, when people say, "I don't heal; it's God," that is strictly a cop-out when a healing doesn't occur. It is true, they don't heal.

2. The hypocrisy of modern healers

The question I hear all the time is: "Well, how do you explain what goes on?" All right, let me ask you a question. Since none of the healers can heal with a word or a touch, instantaneously, totally, everybody, organic diseases, and raise the dead; since none of them have received the gift of healing from Jesus or the apostles; since the Bible is complete, the revelation has ceased, and more signs are no longer necessary; since the Word needs no confirmation—it is sufficient that the man of God might be perfect; since their healings are based on faulty theology of the atonement and salvation; since they disallow God His own purposes in having some people remain sick; since their personal lives are not known to manifest the fruit of the Spirit; since so many tricks, gimmicks, and special effects are often used; since the evidence is weak, unsupported, and so-called testimonies exaggerated; since they do not go to where the sick are, as Jesus did; since they cannot heal all who come to them; and since their healings can have other possible explanations rather than that God has acted supernaturally, let me ask you this question: "How do you explain it?" You can't explain it biblically—it is fraud; they are deceived. Maybe they don't know they are deceived; maybe they are honestly deceived, but they are deceived.

3. The healing of God

You say, "Are you saying God doesn't heal?" No. God answers prayer. Second, God heals in answer to prayer. God heals miraculously in answer to prayer. God heals miraculously in answer to prayer where there is faith. God heals miraculously in answer to prayer where there is faith to manifest His own glory. Don't say I don't believe God heals. I've seen Him heal. I've seen Him heal miraculously. I've seen Him heal miraculously to manifest His glory in response to faithful prayer. God heals. But God does not heal everybody, and God no longer heals through the apostolic gift of healing. That gift has ceased.

4. The health of the soul

In looking at this from another angle, why are Christians sick? There are several possibilities:

a) God makes you sick

God has made the deaf and the dumb and the blind. God allowed the man in John 9 to be born blind. God wanted Lazarus dead. Jesus wanted him dead—He stayed away (John 11:1-11). Some people are sick because God wants them sick. You may have a little baby who is sick. That is God's plan, and the baby is a gift of God's love, so He will reveal His purpose to you as you seek Him. Some of you may have a congenital deformity. There is a great book titled *Grace Grows Best in Winter* that gives beautiful insights into why God allows these things to happen. The author, Margaret Clarkson, has lived all of her life with a congenital problem.

b) Satan makes you sick

Luke 13:11 says, "And, behold, there was a woman who had a spirit of infirmity eighteen years, and was bowed together, and could in no way lift herself up. And when Jesus saw her, he called her to him, and said unto her, Woman, thou art loosed from thine infirmity. And he laid his hands on her; and immediately she was made straight, and glorified God" (vv. 11-13). She had a spirit from Satan. God may choose to cast out those demons and heal people of infirmities.

c) God allows Satan to make you sick for special reasons

God had a purpose for Job. God said to Satan, "I want you to see that I have a man who can handle you. He can handle any test you give him" (Job 1:8). God may allow Satan to buffet you. In 2 Corinthians 12:7 Paul says that his thorn in the flesh is a messenger of Satan sent to buffet him. So it could be God, it could be a demon, or it could be God letting it happen—letting Satan do it to perfect you.

d) God makes you sick to perfect you

God might allow you to catch a certain disease because He has a purpose. David pours out his heart in Psalm 119:67:

"Before I was afflicted I went astray, but now have I kept thy word." Then verse 71 says, "It is good for me that I have been afflicted, that I might learn thy statutes." Sometimes illness, affliction, infirmity, and trouble drive us to His side. That is His intention. It is better for you to be sick and godly than well and ungodly.

e) God chastens you for sin

(1) The sin

God could be allowing you to be sick because of your sin.

(a) Numbers 12:9-10—"And the anger of the Lord was kindled against them; and he departed. And the cloud departed from off the tabernacle; and, behold, Miriam became leprous, white as snow." God got angry with Miriam and gave her leprosy. Then they prayed, and the Lord healed her. If illness comes as a result of chastening, and you will just eliminate the cause for the chastening, the chances are you will eliminate the illness.

(b) Deuteronomy 28:21-22—"The Lord shall make the pestilence cling unto thee, until he have consumed thee from off the land, to which thou goest to possess it. The Lord shall smite thee with a consumption, and with a fever, and with an inflammation, and with an extreme burning, and with the sword, and with blight, and with mildew." God uses illness as a chastening.

(c) 2 Kings 5:15-27—Gehazi sinned and got leprosy.

(d) 2 Chronicles 26:5, 21—"And he sought God in the days of Zechariah, who had understanding in the visions of God; and as long as he sought the Lord, God made him prosper. . . . And Uzziah, the king, was a leper unto the day of his death, and dwelt in a separate house, being a leper; for he was cut off from the house of the Lord." As long as he sought God, he was healthy; as soon as he didn't, he got leprosy.

(e) Exodus 15:26—"If thou wilt . . . keep all his statutes, I will put none of these diseases upon thee."

(f) 1 Corinthians 11:30—When God chastened the Corinthians because of their desecration of the

203

Lord's Table, Paul said, "For this cause many are weak and sickly among you, and many sleep."

(2) The confession

Now, if God makes you sick for His own intents and purposes, that is His choice. If it is Satan, then when you become a Christian I believe God will deliver you from the demon. I believe salvation cleans you. If it is God letting Satan do it, or God allowing it to be done to perfect you, then it will have to run its course until you are perfected in the way He wants. Peter said, "After you have suffered awhile, God will make you perfect" (1 Pet. 5:10b). If it is chastening for sin, then as soon as you deal with the sin, I believe that God begins to withdraw the chastening. James 5:14-16 says, "Is any sick among you? Let him call for the elders of the church; and let them pray over him, anointing him with oil in the name of the Lord; and the prayer of faith shall save the sick, and the Lord shall raise him up; and if he have committed sins, they shall be forgiven him. Confess your faults one to another, and pray one for another, that ye may be healed. The effectual, fervent prayer of a righteous man availeth much."

Here is sickness related to chastening. There are two things to do when you are sick: First, call for the elders and pray; and second, confess your sins. That is the reason the elders are brought in. Every time you are sick, it isn't necessarily an issue for the elders, because "the effectual, fervent prayer of a righteous man availeth much." But when it is a sickness that is a result of sinfulness, then it is a matter of purity for the church. The elders are the overseers of church purity, and they need to be involved in hearing that confession and joining with the person in seeking God for the removal of that illness.

So, there is the promise that when confession is made believing in God's power and will to heal in regard to chastening, God will respond. God heals when you pray believing and confessing your sin, if the disease is the result of chastening. The first thing I tell people when they are sick is: "Have you checked out every area of your life for sin? Have you confessed it openly? If there's a sin in your life and you know it, meet with the elders; we will pray about it and believe God." If your life is pure and the sickness is still there, then it is God's choice for your perfection.

5. The heaven of healing

It is ridiculous to say God always wants everyone well. The Bible doesn't teach that, yet you have the right to look to heaven in every illness because God may want to remove the illness for His glory. There are three reasons that you have the right to look to heaven:

a) God's person

In Exodus 15:26 God says: "For I am the Lord that healeth thee [Jehovah Ropheca]." He is a healer. You have a right to look to Him in every illness.

b) God's promise

God says, "Call unto me, and I will answer thee, and show thee great and mighty things, which thou knowest not" (Jer. 33:3). He promised to hear every prayer (1 John 5:14). He promised that whatever we asked in His name He would do (Matt. 21:22). The promise of God is that if it is His will, He will heal.

c) God's pattern

God's pattern was established in Jesus. If you want to know how God feels about disease, look at Jesus. How did He feel about disease? He went everywhere healing. I believe He gave us a pattern of God's attitude: "When the evening was come, they brought unto him many that were possessed with demons; and he cast out the spirits with his word, and healed all that were sick, that it might be fulfilled which was spoken by Isaiah, the prophet, saying, he himself took our infirmities, and bore our sicknesses" (Matt. 8:16-17).

Here is the promise that God heals because of His person, His promise, and His pattern.

6. The honor due medicine

Did you know that Christians believe in doctors?

a) Isaiah 38:1-5, 21—"In those days was Hezekiah sick unto death. And Isaiah, the prophet, the son of Amoz, came unto him, and said unto him, Thus saith the Lord, Set thine house in order; for thou shalt die, and not live. Then Hezekiah turned his face toward the wall, and prayed unto the Lord, and said, Remember now, O Lord, I beseech thee, how I have walked before thee in truth and with a perfect heart, and have done that which is good in thy sight. And Hezekiah wept bitterly. Then came the word of the Lord to Isaiah, saying, Go, and say to Hezekiah, Thus saith the Lord, the God of David, thy father, I have heard thy prayer, I have seen thy tears; behold, I will add unto thy days fifteen years." Now that is answered prayer! Then verse 21 says, "For Isaiah had said, Let them take a lump of figs, and lay it for a plaster upon the boil, and he shall recover." If you are healed of God, why do you need the remedy? I think God is laying down a principle. Do two things when you get sick: Pray, and go to the doctor.

b) Matthew 9:12—"They that are whole need not a physician, but they that are sick." Jesus assumed that sick people needed a doctor.

c) Acts 28:8-10—On the island of Melita, verse 8 says that Paul "laid his hands on him [the father of Publius], and healed him." The Greek word *iaomai* means "healing." It is also used as a spiritual term for healing. Then verse 9 says that many were healed. Here it is implied that Luke practiced medicine (Gk., *therapeuō*) on them. So, if you get sick, find a Paul to pray for you and a Luke to help you get better. Just let God do His will.

Remember, sometimes it is in God's will for people to die. May everyone face death like Peter. Jesus said to him that by his death he would glorify God. I hope that in your illnesses and everything else you keep your biblical perspective and glorify God in His purpose. Remember, you do have the promise to seek heaven because *Jehovah Ropheca* is there—the Lord that heals.

Focusing on the Facts

1. To whom did the Lord pass on the power of healing (see p. 192)?
2. Why were the gifts of miracles and healings given to the apostles and their associates (see p. 193)?
3. What was the key aspect in the healing of the lame man in Acts 3 (see p. 194)?
4. According to Acts 19:10-12, what did the people do that showed their belief in Paul's power (see p. 194)?
5. Why was the message that the apostles gave so shocking to the Jews? What were the responses to the message? How did God confirm the truth of this shocking message (see p. 195)?
6. In what ways did the apostles heal? In what ways were they similar to the ways Jesus healed (see pp. 195-97)?

7. On what basis is a spiritual gift operated? What then is wrong when someone who claims to have the gift of healing says that he doesn't control who is healed and who isn't, but the Holy Spirit does (see p. 197)?

8. What happened to the miraculous signs after the Word was complete? Why (see pp. 198-99)?

9. How does Paul reveal the true purpose of the gift of healing? Give examples (see pp. 198-99).

10. What disease did Jesus die on the cross for? Does God heal all who are sick (see p. 200)?

11. Why didn't God remove Paul's thorn in the flesh (see p. 200)?

12. Why would it be dangerous if health were part of the atonement? For what reason does God want people to come to Him (see p. 200)?

13. Why does God want some people sick, or deaf, or dumb, or blind (see p. 200)?

14. Why was 1 Corinthians 14 written? Why were regulations needed? What does this prove regarding the gift of healing (see p. 201)?

15. Can healings today through those who claim to have the gift of healing be explained? Why not (see p. 201)?

16. Does God heal today? How does He heal (see p. 201)?

17. Why are Christians sick? Give the five reasons and explain each one (see pp. 202-3).

18. How can the sickness be eliminated in each of these cases? When sickness is a result of chastening for sin, what two things are necessary to do in order to eliminate the sickness (see pp. 204-5)?

19. When do the elders of the church need to be involved in hearing the confession of sin from someone who is sick (see p. 204)?

20. Why does every Christian have the right to look to God for healing in every illness (see p. 205)?

21. What biblical proof shows that Christians believe in doctors? Explain (see p. 206).

Pondering the Principles

1. Review the pattern of healing that was revealed by both Jesus and the apostles (see pp. 195-97). What kinds of diseases did they heal? In what ways were their methods of healing different from the healings you hear of today? In what ways were their results different? In view of this pattern, how would you define the biblical gift of healing? If someone were to ask you to explain why the gift of healing is not active today, what would you tell him? What verses would you use to support your position?

2. Suppose you had a choice to live the rest of your life on earth in only one of these two situations: one, to be healthy physically but dead spiritually; or two, to be sick physically but alive spiritually. Which

one would you choose? Why? Take a moment to do some self-examination. Do you live thinking more about your physical circumstances or more about your spiritual circumstances? Read Philippians 4:8 and begin to dwell on those things.

3. Do you think that you have ever been sick as a result of chastening for sin? If so, what did you do? What should you have done based on James 5:14-16? Do you know someone who is sick, perhaps even as a result of chastening for sin? What encouraging words could you share with them? Based on James 5:16, would you begin to pray faithfully for that individual? In addition, memorize James 5:16: "Confess your faults one to another, and pray one for another, that ye may be healed. The effectual, fervent prayer of a righteous man availeth much."

4. In your own mind, how do you harmonize the idea that God wants you to look to Him for healing, but that He also wants you to go to doctors? What danger is inherent if you only depend on God for healing and do not go to a doctor for treatment of some illness? What danger is inherent if you only depend on doctors for treatment of illness but not on the power of God to heal? What is the most important perspective for you to have?

12

Spiritual Baptism

Outline

Introduction

Review

Lesson
I. The Illustrations
  A. The Unity in the Body
    1. The common designation
    2. The creative design
    3. The contrasting duplication
    4. The culminating diversity
  B. The Universality of Members
  C. The Unity with Christ
    1. One life in Christ
      a) Biological life
      b) Abundantly alive
      c) Eternally alive
    2. One body in Christ
    3. One life source
II. The Reality
  A. The formation of the Body
    1. The beginning
      a) A significant translation
      b) A significant transformation
        (1) The examples of the baptizer
          (*a*) Matthew 3:11-12
          (*b*) Mark 1:7-8
          (*c*) Luke 3:16
          (*d*) John 1:33, 34*b*
          (*e*) Acts 2:32-33
        (2) The element of the baptism
      c) A single Spirit
    2. The baptism
      a) The recipients

Introduction

Lessons from Scripture vary a great deal because the Scripture varies in its style. Some lessons are by nature very practical, and some are very theological. Some are more exciting to listen to than others, simply by virtue of what you know or don't know. The context of this lesson is centered on a very theological statement made by the apostle Paul. He does not interpolate it into practical areas; he simply makes a very straightforward theological statement in 1 Corinthians 12:12-13. It is an important statement and one we must understand.

The subject of Paul's statement is the baptizing by the Holy Spirit. Today, this is a very misunderstood and controversial subject. In any controversy, you need to take a side and have an opinion. And it had better be that your opinion is defensible biblically. So our approach to this passage of Scripture is to read it and determine what it means by what it says, theologically. What I say is not an attack on any individuals, but simply an attempt to honestly, and with as much integrity as possible, understand what the Spirit of God is saying. From this we can then apply it.

Review

Paul's theme throughout 1 Corinthians 12-14 is to help the Corinthians deal with carnality as it manifested itself in the area of spiritual gifts. First Corinthians 12:12-13 becomes the very core of Paul's argument. In verses 1-3 he says that he doesn't want them to be ignorant about spiritual gifts. There were two basic things he wanted them to understand: one, the diversity of gifts. The Spirit of God does not want everyone to do the same thing in the same way. There is a tremendous and beautiful diversity. That is Paul's message in verses 4-11. We have learned that every believer is unique and possesses a unique combination of divine enablements that make him a spiritual snowflake. In that uniqueness and individuality of giftedness that God has given to every believer, there is a marvelous ability to minister to the Body. This ability is so unique that no one else can minister to the Body in the same way if you don't. That is why it is critical for you to minister in the energy of the Holy Spirit, because you are irreplaceable.

Now, two: as he comes to verses 12-13, he talks about the other side of this dichotomy—the unity of the church. The church is not only diverse, but it is one. There is a basic unity that we must be committed to. It is fine to have diverse gifts, but we must always remember that there is a oneness that has to be maintained in practice because it exists in position.

In order to help us understand this statement of unity, Paul gives an illustration. The illustration is in verse 12, and the statement of reality is in verse 13.

Lesson

I. THE ILLUSTRATION (v. 12)

"For as the body [the physical body] is one [a unit], and hath many members, and all the members of that one body, being many, are one body, so also is Christ."

A. The Unity in the Body

Here is Paul's simple statement: The Body is one, but it has many parts. The many parts function diversely, and yet they are one. Now, every organism—every organic whole—possesses diversity and unity. In the body there is diversity—diversity of the members and diversity of the functions. But there exists one whole body and one life energy that makes the body an organic unit.

1. The common designation

This is a common designation on the part of the apostle Paul. In 1 Corinthians 10:17 he refers to us as one body. In Romans 12:4-5, where he also discusses the theme of spiritual gifts, he says, "For as we have many members in one body, and all members have not the same office, so we, being many, are one body in Christ, and every one members one of another" (cf.

Eph. 1:23; 2:16; 4:4, 12, 16; Col. 1:18, 22). So for Paul, the single, most clear illustration of the unity of the believer with Christ is to see the believers as a body and Christ as the head—the source of the body's life.

2. The creative design

The human body is amazing—surely the most amazing organic creation of God. It is the highest of His creation. It is the pinnacle of His creation. It is sublime, beautiful, and valuable beyond understanding. The life principle that makes up a man has tremendous value beyond what could be measured. The body is much more than the sum of its parts; it is a fantastic creation of God that manifests diversity and unity.

3. The contrasting duplication

Even your duplicated parts are unique and function differently. You have two feet, but when you try on shoes you may find that your feet are not the same size. You may also find that you can do certain things better with your right foot than with your left foot. You have two arms and two hands, but you are either right-handed or left-handed. I wear glasses because my eyes are different; one has one problem, and the other has another problem. They can't even agree. So there is a diversity in my eyes. Even those members that are duplicated are diverse and have unique functions.

4. The culminating diversity

There is one organic whole that makes up the body. The body is the most perfect illustration of diversity and unity in perfect combination and function. You can see that this is true in anyone who does something with dexterity (e.g., an athlete or an artist who has a beautiful touch with a brush or chisel). There is a common life principle that ties all this diversity together so that it becomes a unit. And the church is no different. Basically, it is one organic whole—a plurality of members with a common life principle.

B. The Universality of Members

There are not now, there never has been, and there never will be two different kinds of Christians—there is only one. Verse 13 says that we were all baptized into one Body no matter who we are—Jew, Greek, bond, or free. There are no Christians who are out of the Body. We are all in the Body of Christ; we are all members of His Body; we are all a part of the organic whole through which pulses the very lifeblood of Christ Himself; and we all have the

212

common energy of the living Christ, who dwells in us. The Body, then, is one organic whole. And it is the illustration that Paul used to refer to the church.

C. The Unity with Christ

The illustration becomes clearer at the end of verse 12 in the little statement: "So also is Christ." I would have expected Paul to say, "So also is the church." But when you think of the church, what do you think of? You normally think of many disconnected people. So Paul, in keeping with his metaphor, says, "So also is Christ." To say that we are Christ is the same as saying that we are the church.

1. One life in Christ

What does "so also is Christ" mean? Why doesn't he say, "So the church is one body"? The church is Christ, and he wants to emphasize the fact that you and I, as believers, are one with the living Christ. We are one living organism through which pulses the eternal life of God by the Spirit of Christ living in us.

a) Biological life

You are not just someone with *bios*—the Greek word for biological life. Biological life simply means being alive as opposed to being dead. You are still working; you are still functioning.

b) Abundantly alive

We are not just *bios,* we are also *zōē*—not just alive as opposed to being dead, but we are really alive! For example, if I say, "This person is alive," that could mean one of two things: one, he is almost dead and is barely pulling through; or two, he is really turned on. The Greeks had the same concept, only they used two different words.

c) Eternally alive

But there is another step for the Christian. We are not just biologically alive, we are not just turned on, we are eternally alive. Why? The life of God is in us. The one common denominator that all believers possess is the life of God in the soul of man. That is what Jesus meant when He said, "Because I live, ye shall live also" (John 14:19b). That is what John meant when he said, "He that hath the Son hath life; and he that hath not the Son of God hath not life" (1 John 5:12). The one without Christ is stuck with either *bios* or *zōē*—he might be biologically alive, and he may be turned on, but he doesn't know what it is to have real life.

2. One Body in Christ

We are Christ. The only Christ the world is going to see is us. Christ became incarnate once in a single body. He has become incarnate once again in all of our bodies, making us the one Body that is Christ in the world. Paul is emphasizing the fact of the incarnation of Jesus in His church—in His Body. It is a living incarnation. Christ is alive in me; He is alive in you. He is alive in every believer. That is what salvation means. All of us are one in Christ Jesus.

3. One life source

First Corinthians 6:17 says, "But he that is joined unto the Lord is one spirit." Thus he is one with every other person joined to the Lord. Paul is saying to the Corinthians, "I know there is to be diversity, but that doesn't mean you should continue fracturing the fellowship; there is also to be unity." I have one personality. I have one life source. The church, the one Body made up of all of us, is pervaded by one life source, one personality, and that is Christ. We are literally flesh and bones manifesting the living Christ.

As a result, it is so ridiculous and incongruous when we exalt self. It would be no different than if Christ, in His incarnate body, had to fight someone else. He should be freely manifested through us. When we operate and minister our spiritual gifts, it is Christ ministering and manifesting His life.

We possess the common life of Christ. He lives in us. Paul says, "I am crucified with Christ; nevertheless I live; yet not I, but Christ liveth in me" (Gal. 2:20a). Paul also says, "For to me to live is Christ" (Phil. 1:21a). The same is true for you. The life of Christ is in you—God's eternal life. That is why when you die, you don't die—you already have eternal life. You are not going to get it; you have it! What you are now, you are going to be forever. When you die, it is less of a change for you than your salvation was. You already have eternal life. Dying is simply leaving the physical body so you can enjoy life in its fullness. So, we have eternal life. Christ is alive in us.

Now, do all Christians have this life? Yes. Do all Christians possess the life of Christ? Yes, that is salvation—to receive Jesus Christ, to have Him enter my life. That is Paul's illustration. Now, he goes on to explain the significance of this theologically in verse 13.

II. THE REALITY (v. 13)

"For by one Spirit were we all baptized into one body, whether we be Jews or Greeks, whether we be bond or free; and have been all made to drink . . . one Spirit."

This is a tremendous verse that is, unfortunately, greatly misunderstood today. What does it mean to be baptized into one Body by the Holy Spirit? Paul gives us two thoughts in this verse: first, the formation of the body ("were we all baptized into one body"); and second, the inner life of the believer ("have been all made to drink [into] one Spirit"). The word "into" was added because it is not in the original manuscript. Unity is Paul's point. There are two unifying concepts: We have all been put into the Body in the same way, and we all possess the same inner life. Therein lies our unity.

A. The formation of the Body (v. 13a)

1. The beginning

"For by one Spirit."

a) A significant translation

Many people are confused at this point. The Greek *en heni pneumati* could be translated "for, by, or with one Spirit." Some would translate it *in*. I don't feel that is a proper translation, because those Greek prepositions are translated differently depending upon the case ending of the word following. The safest and most consistent translation in the context of the New Testament is to use the word *by* or *with*. We are baptized by or with the Holy Spirit.

One word that never could be used here is *of*. The phrase that you hear so often, the baptism *of* the Holy Spirit, appears nowhere in Scripture. That is not a scriptural term. In fact, I would go a step further and say that there is no place in the Bible where you can find that the Spirit does the baptizing.

b) A significant transformation

(1) The examples of the baptizer

(a) Matthew 3:11-12—"I, indeed, baptize you with water unto repentance, but he who cometh after me is mightier than I, whose shoes I am not worthy to bear; he shall baptize you with the Holy Spirit, and with fire" (v. 11). Who was the baptizer? Christ. The One who was coming who was mightier than John the Baptist, the One whom he came to announce was Christ. Later, Jesus would baptize with fire. Now, that is not the fire of Pentecost. You say, "What fire is it?" Verse 12 says, "Whose fan is in his hand, and he will thoroughly purge his floor, and gather his wheat into the granary, but he will burn up the chaff with unquenchable fire." It is the fire of hell.

If you are not baptized with the Holy Spirit, what is going to happen? You will be baptized with fire. I would add, then, that there are only two kinds of people in the world: the people baptized with the Holy Spirit and the people who go to hell. So, you can't be a Christian and not be baptized with the Holy Spirit.

(*b*) Mark 1:7-8—"There cometh one mightier than I after me, the latchet of whose shoes I am not worthy to stoop down and loose. I, indeed, have baptized you with water, but He shall baptize you with the Holy Spirit." Again, Christ is seen as the baptizer.

(*c*) Luke 3:16—"John answered, saying unto them all, I indeed baptize you with water; but one mightier than I cometh, the latchet of whose shoes I am not worthy to loose; he shall baptize you with the Holy Spirit and with fire." And in verse 17 he details what the fire means.

(*d*) John 1:33, 34*b*—"And I knew him not; but he that sent me to baptize with water, the same said unto me, Upon whom thou shalt see the Spirit descending, and remaining on him, the same is he who baptizeth with the Holy Spirit. . . . this is the Son of God." Who is the baptizer? Christ is the baptizer.

(*e*) Acts 2:32-33—"This Jesus hath God raised up, whereof we all are witnesses. Therefore, being by the right hand of God exalted, and having received from the Father the promise of the Holy Spirit, he hath shed forth this, which ye now see and hear." Who is it that shed forth the Holy Spirit on the day of Pentecost? It was Christ, in fulfillment of the prophecy that John the Baptist gave.

(2) The element of the baptism

The baptizer is Christ, not the Holy Spirit. People who say, "We have had the baptism of the Holy Spirit," think that the Holy Spirit does something to them. They even go so far as to say, "We have been baptized by Christ in conversion, but the baptism of the Spirit comes later." That is a misunderstanding of the Word of God. The element of baptism is the Spirit. The baptizer is Christ. Just as John was the baptizer baptizing people into water, so Christ is the baptizer baptizing us into the Spirit of God, the act which places us in the Body. That is a very mystical concept, but we have to understand what the Bible is saying. Christ is the baptizer. He is the One who sends the Spirit. He is the One who had to go back to the Father in order to send the Spirit. And He is the One who baptizes us with the agency of the Spirit.

Could you say that we are saved by the Lord Jesus Christ? I think so; I was. Weren't you saved by the Lord Jesus Christ? But who was the agent of your salvation? You were born of the Spirit (John 3:5). Christ and the Spirit are involved, and so is the Father. Somehow, when you are saved, the Lord Jesus Christ, by the agency of the Spirit of God, places you into His Body. He is the baptizer!

c) A single Spirit

Verse 13 says, "For by one Spirit." How many Spirits are there? One Spirit.

2. The baptism

"Were we all baptized into one body."

a) The recipients

How many Christians have had the baptism by the Holy Spirit? All Christians. When someone says, "Have you had the baptism of the Holy Spirit?" my first answer is, "There is no such thing as the baptism of the Holy Spirit. If you mean the baptism by the Holy Spirit, yes." Paul's point is that all Christians have had the baptism by the Holy Spirit. This is the basis for which we are all one Body, possessing the one life source, and indwelt by the one Christ. If you take away the baptizing by Christ by the agency of the Holy Spirit, you destroy the doctrine of the unity of the

217

Body, because we then have some people who aren't yet a part of the Body. Then where are they? How can you be saved but not be a part of the Body of Christ? How can you be a Christian but not in Christ? That makes no sense. It is clear—we were all baptized.

b) The role

What does Paul mean by "baptized"? First, verse 13 is not referring to water baptism. There are some verses in the New Testament that do, but this isn't one of them. Some of Paul's theological passages cannot be simplistically interpreted in terms of water. But there are some people who say that when you are baptized in water, that is the baptism that imparts to you the Holy Spirit. No, that can't be. There are many people who have been baptized in water and haven't any idea of what has happened. Perhaps they were baptized as babies or at some later point in their lives, but they don't believe in Christ, they don't practice the Christian life, and they know nothing of the changing power of Christ and the indwelling presence of the Spirit of God. Paul is not talking about water baptism.

(1) A spiritual immersion

The Greek word *baptizō* is used in the New Testament to refer to a "spiritual immersing." Paul is saying that the same Spirit has immersed every believer in the same unity with Christ that constitutes His Body. The baptism Paul is referring to is a spiritual reality that brings the believer into a vital union with Christ. The word means "to immerse." And as somebody could be immersed in water, so somebody could be immersed in the Body of Christ. In other words, you are in a new environment, a new atmosphere, a new union, a new identification, a new oneness with Christ. That is the New Testament usage of the word. For example:

(*a*) Baptism into repentance

Matthew 3:11 mentions that there is the baptism unto repentance. What does that mean? It means you are immersed into a repentant heart and a repentant attitude.

(*b*) Baptism into Moses

In 1 Corinthians 10:2 the nation of Israel left Pharaoh and the old land of Egypt to become immersed and identified with a new leader (Moses) and a new land (Canaan).

Baptism by the Holy Spirit is Christ placing you, by means of the Spirit's operation, into the unity of the Body and giving you a common life principle. When you became a Christian you were joined to Christ; and when you were joined to Christ, you were connected up with everyone who is joined to Him (Gal. 3:27). We are all one.

(2) A superabundant inheritance

I will never understand why people want to say that you have to wait for a second experience for the baptism of the Holy Spirit. It just isn't so! They are tampering with the doctrine of salvation, and that is why it is so serious. They are saying that salvation doesn't really give you everything you think it gives you. I don't like to hear that about salvation. Spirit baptism unites you to Jesus Christ, and that means that all that He is and all that is His are yours. You say, "You mean it all becomes ours?" Yes.

(a) John 7:37-39—Some people use this passage to refer to the baptism of the Holy Spirit. They say, "Well, you may be saved, and you may possess the Holy Spirit, but you don't have the rivers of living water flowing out of you." They claim that there is another step needed to receive the rivers of living water. Verse 37 says, "In the last day, that great day of the feast." This is the Feast of Tabernacles. In this ritual, a priest would pour a pitcher of water. This was one reminder of God's giving water to the children of Israel at Meribah (Ex. 17:6-7). They would quote Isaiah 12:3, "Therefore, with joy shall ye draw water out of the wells of salvation." It was a great ceremony. It was probably at this point that Jesus said, "If any man thirst, let him come unto me, and drink" (v. 37b). In other words, "If you are really thirsty, it isn't that water that will satisfy you; it is the water I give." Who is a thirsty man? Someone who sees his need. Let him come to Christ and drink—that is salvation. You know you have a need, you go to the source, and you take what He has. This is just an invitation for salvation.

219

Now you say, "Then what happens?" Verses 38-39 say, "He that believeth on me, as the scripture hath said, out of his heart shall flow rivers of living water. (But this spoke he of the Spirit, whom they that believe on him should receive.)" Who receives the Holy Spirit? Someone who believes. And how much of the Holy Spirit does he receive? So much that out of his being flow rivers of living water. There is nothing lacking.

Now whether or not the river is flowing out of me is dependent upon my obedience and submission. But Jesus says, "Come and drink, and you will have the rivers of living water." There isn't any other condition given. Throughout Scripture there is only one single condition for the fullness of the Spirit of God in your life, one single condition for the rivers of living water, one single condition for the baptizing with the Holy Spirit, and that is to believe. That is saving faith.

(b) Acts 11:15-17—Peter is reporting about the Gentile conversion, which was a great shock to him: "And as I began to speak, the Holy Spirit fell on them, as on us at the beginning. Then remembered I the word of the Lord, how he said, John indeed baptized with water; but ye shall be baptized with the Holy Spirit. Forasmuch, then, as God gave them the same gift as he did unto us, who believed on the Lord Jesus Christ." Who receives the baptism by the Holy Spirit? Anyone who believes in the Lord Jesus Christ.

(3) A synonymous identification

The baptism by the Holy Spirit is not an experience. It is a fact that occurs at your salvation. It is the fact that when you believe God, He places you into the Son by His Spirit. That is the baptizing by the Holy Spirit. In Galatians 3:26-27 Paul says, "For ye are all the sons of God by faith in Christ Jesus. For as many of you as have been baptized into Christ have put on Christ." There are four parallel statements in those verses. Let me give you four definitions of a Christian: A Christian is a son of God. A Christian is somebody who has put his faith in Christ Jesus. A Christian is somebody baptized into Christ. And a Christian is somebody who has put on Christ. All of those are synonyms. "As

220

many of you as have been baptized into Christ have put on Christ" and are the sons of God.

That is why there is no command in Scripture to be baptized with the Spirit. There is no exhortation to receive the Holy Spirit. Why? You already have the Spirit. That is the whole point of our unity in Christ. If this truth is removed, then a part of the doctrine of salvation is destroyed, because that would mean Christians are saved but don't have all there is in salvation. But our salvation is complete, according to Colossians 2:10: "And ye are complete in him."

(4) A scheduled increase

In 1 Corinthians 12:13 Paul says that by one Spirit we all have been baptized—past tense. It happened when we were saved. You don't experience it—it's a fact. It is a union and an identification with the Body—the life principle of Christ coming to live in you.

(a) For Pentecost

People say, "What about the book of Acts? People in Acts 1 believed, but they had to wait." Yes, they had to wait because the Holy Spirit hadn't come yet. They had to wait until the Spirit came the first time at Pentecost (Acts 2:1-4). Anna (the prophetess who stayed in the Temple) had waited for the Messiah. People who believed had to wait for the Spirit. But that doesn't mean Pentecosts are going on all the time any more than Jesus is born in Bethlehem every two weeks. He came once, and that was it. The Spirit came once, and that was it.

(b) For Samaritans and Gentiles

You say, "But why was there a gap in Acts 8 with Samaritans getting saved but not receiving the Spirit?" God's design was to have them wait to receive the Spirit until the Jews and the apostles could see it, in order that the Jews and the apostles would know the Samaritans (Acts 8:16) and the Gentiles (Acts 10:44-45) had received the same Holy Spirit they had. God wanted them all to know that the church was one. But they never sought after the Spirit. The only people who ever waited for the Spirit were those in transition in the book of Acts.

221

(c) For disciples of John the Baptist

Some people say, "Well, what about Acts 19? Those people were asked, 'Have you received the Holy Spirit since you believed?' And they said, 'We don't even know about the Holy Spirit.' " And from that these people say, "There you have Christians without the Holy Spirit." No. They were not Christians; they were disciples of John the Baptist. When they found out about Christ, they received Christ and the Spirit at the same time (Acts 19:1-6).

But from then on the statement of doctrine is clear: "For by one Spirit were we all baptized into one body" (1 Cor. 12:13a). We have all been placed into the Body. So don't let anyone tell you that there are some Christians who have never been baptized with the Holy Spirit. We all have.

3. The benefactors

"Whether we be Jews or Greeks, whether we be bond or free."

It doesn't matter who we are. Religious background doesn't matter; social status doesn't matter. We are one church, and God has made clear that everyone is a part. Now you may not like the fact that we are all one, but we are. I am sure there are some young people who look at some of the older folks and say, "You mean we are in the same Body with them?" Then there are some older folks who look at those kids and say, "It can't be, it can't be!" There may be some people who rub you the wrong way, but you might as well get used to them, because you are going to spend eternity with them. We are all in the same Body. This is the universal gift to all Christians.

Baptism or Filling

People who say that my salvation does not give me everything that God wants for me the moment I have it are tampering around with the doctrine of salvation. That is serious business. There is no second Pentecost. These people have confused the baptizing (placing you into the Body) with the filling of the Spirit of God (where the Spirit of God is released in your life to empower you for service). When you are filled with the Spirit, you are simply yielding to the Spirit within you. You are simply being obedient. Do you know how to be filled with the Spirit of God and see the energy of the Spirit in your life? You say, "Tarry." No, don't tarry. You say, "Get with a group of people who can teach you how to speak in tongues." No. In order to release the Spirit of God in your life, simply obey. When you walk in obedience to the Word of God, the Spirit of God is energized in your life. That is the basic principle of the New Testament.

So, we have seen the formation of the Body by one Spirit placing everyone into one Body.

B. The Inner Life of the Believer (v. 13b)

"And have been all made to drink . . . one Spirit."

Not only have we been placed into something, but we have had something placed into us—the Holy Spirit. I suppose there are some people who think we didn't receive all of the Spirit either. But He doesn't come in doses.

1. John 3:34—"For God giveth not the Spirit by measure unto him." You have the Holy Spirit.

2. 1 Corinthians 6:19—"What? Know ye not that your body is the temple of the Holy Spirit who is in you, whom ye have of God?"

3. 2 Corinthians 6:16—"As God hath said, I will dwell in them." God is in me and alive in me.

4. Romans 8:9—"If any man have not the Spirit of Christ, he is none of his."

I not only have been put into something, but something has been put into me. I am not only immersed into an environment of the life of God, but the life of God is in me. All of the resource is there, all that I need is there. I have received the promise of the Holy Spirit fully and totally. The Holy Spirit is yours the minute you believe. That is what 1 Corinthians 12:13 says: We have all been made to drink one Spirit. This is the common life principle. If you haven't received the Holy Spirit, you don't have eternal life, because that life is in the Spirit who lives in you.

The Most Misunderstood Doctrine

The fact of the baptism by the Holy Spirit has to be the most confused, misrepresented, misunderstood doctrine among Christians today. It is a cause for continual controversy. People continually intimidate Christians by saying, "You haven't had something that God wants you to have. You have to seek for it, and here is how you can."

I read ten different writers who gave ten different ways to obtain the baptism of the Spirit. That's incredible! I read my

Bible, and I have read evangelical writers, and I have never read a true evangelical writer who ever gave more than one way to get saved. If this baptism of the Spirit is so important, how come we can't figure out what the key to it is? It's difficult because the Bible doesn't say. And the reason the Bible doesn't say how to be baptized with the Spirit of God is that Christians have already been baptized with the Spirit. It is very important for us to make these distinctions. It doesn't do any justice to the Holy Spirit to misconstrue His work; it only dishonors Him. It bothers me because it undermines the doctrine of salvation. It bothers me when someone tells me that I don't have some aspect of the Spirit, because that tells me that the Spirit isn't what I thought He was. And He doesn't like that either. Now, I believe that these people are Christians; I just think that we all have to get back to the study of the Word of God.

You say, "Where did the idea of the baptism of the Spirit come from?" Some Catholic theologians have taught that when an infant is baptized, he receives salvation. Years later, when he is confirmed, he receives the Holy Spirit. So this dichotomy has its roots in Roman Catholicism.

It also has roots in John Wesley, Charles Finney, R. A. Torrey, and others. In fact, Torrey has been one of the greatest contributors to the modern Pentecostal movement because he wasn't a Pentecostal. When he taught that the baptism of the Spirit was a later work, they quoted him because he was such a well-known evangelical, mainline theologian.

John Wesley taught that you were saved first and then later on there was a second work of grace subsequent to salvation. I think this might have been a holdover from the environment that he was in. John Wesley's biographers say that he died never having attained that second work.

Finney, Andrew Murray, and Watchman Nee were all proponents of this. The Holiness and Keswick movements had the same thinking. In 1901 in Topeka, Kansas, the modern Pentecostal movement was born, and they fostered this teaching. The Pentecostal movement came out of the Holiness movement. Later, in 1906 in Los Angeles, it began on Azusa Street. This movement developed into the International Church of the Foursquare Gospel, the Churches of God, the Assemblies of God, the United Pentecostal Church International, the Pentecostal Fire-Baptized Holiness churches, and many other denominations. They hold to this old, traditional viewpoint that you get something at conversion and something later. However, that position does injustice to the doctrine of salvation, and it violates 1 Corinthians 12:13, which says you were placed into the Body when you were saved. That was the baptism by the Spirit, and you received the fullness of the Spirit at the same time. All Christians have received that fullness. I just want you to understand that you are not missing anything.

Focusing on the Facts

1. What is Paul's theme in 1 Corinthians 12-14? What are the two basic things he wanted the Corinthians to understand (see pp. 210-11)?
2. What two things make up an organism (see p. 211)?
3. What is the most common designation used by Paul to describe the unity of the believer with Christ (see p. 211)?
4. What could be considered the most amazing creation of God (see p. 212)?
5. How many different kinds of Christians exist? Why (see p. 212)?
6. Why does Paul close 1 Corinthians 12:12 with "so also is Christ" and not with "so also is the church" (see p. 213)?
7. In what three ways are Christians alive? Which one is the most important? What is the one common denominator that all believers possess (see p. 213)?
8. How is Jesus Christ incarnate today (see p. 214)?
9. Why is it ridiculous for Christians to exalt themselves (see p. 214)?
10. What happens to a Christian when he dies? What kind of change takes place (see p. 214)?
11. What two thoughts does Paul present from 1 Corinthians 12:13 (see p. 215)?
12. Explain why the baptism *of* the Holy Spirit is not the proper translation of the preposition in 1 Corinthians 12:13 (see p. 215).
13. Who is it that performs the baptizing of every believer? Support your answer with Scripture (see pp. 215-17).
14. In what two ways does Christ baptize? How does He baptize a believer? How does He baptize an unbeliever (see p. 216)?
15. What part does the Holy Spirit play in baptism? What is His function (see p. 217)?
16. What would be destroyed if the Holy Spirit came to believers at some time other than salvation (see pp. 217-18)?
17. What kind of baptism is Paul referring to in 1 Corinthians 12:13? Explain (see p. 218).
18. What does *immerse* mean? How are Christians immersed into the Body of Christ? Give some other examples (see pp. 218-19).
19. What is the one condition necessary to have the fullness of the Holy

Spirit in an individual's life (see p. 219)?

20. Is the baptism with the Holy Spirit a fact or an experience? Explain (see p. 220).

21. What are four definitions of a Christian, based on Galatians 3:26-27 (see p. 220)?

22. Why is there no command in Scripture to be baptized with the Holy Spirit (see p. 221)?

23. Explain the three instances in the book of Acts where it seems that certain people did not receive the Holy Spirit right away (see pp. 221-22; Acts 1:5; 2:1-4; 8:16; 19:1-6).

24. What part do religious background and social status play in who gets to be a part of the Body (see p. 222)?

25. What is the difference between being baptized by the Holy Spirit and being filled with the Spirit? What must a Christian do in order to release the energy of the Holy Spirit in his life (see pp. 222-23)?

26. Where is the life of God in relation to the believer (see p. 223)?

27. Why is the baptism by the Spirit one of the most misunderstood doctrines (see pp. 223-25)?

Pondering the Principles

1. What are the three kinds of life that a Christian has (see p. 213)? What does eternal life mean? Look up the following verses: John 3:36; 4:14; 5:24; 10:27-29; 12:25; 17:3; Romans 6:22-23; Galatians 6:8; 1 Timothy 1:16; 6:17-19; 1 John 5:11-13. Based on these verses, make a list of all the things that are true about your eternal life in Christ. What happens to the people who die having only *bios* or *zōē?* What happens to the Christian when he dies? According to 1 John 5:12, if you have Jesus Christ then you already have eternal life. Based on this, how should you live right now? Why will your physical death be less of a change for you than your salvation? In order to have the proper perspective of your present life and your future physical death, memorize Philippians 1:21: "For to me to live is Christ, and to die is gain."

2. Why is it wrong for you to exalt yourself? Who are you fighting when you do? If Jesus Christ were to stand before you now, how much of an inclination would you have to exalt yourself? Where is Christ right now in relation to you (see Gal. 2:20)? Which is more significant: Jesus Christ standing in front of you or Christ living inside of you? The next time you have the desire to exalt yourself, what will you do?

3. What do you think it means to "put on Christ" (Gal. 3:27)? Look up the following verses: Romans 13:12-14; 1 Corinthians 15:51-57; Ephesians 4:22-24; 6:10-11; Colossians 3:8-14. When you put on Christ, what other things do you put on? What do you take off? What are some of the things that you have left on that you should

have removed? If you are a Christian, you have put on Jesus Christ, according to Galatians 3:27. That is your position. But in your practice you may not have removed some of the things from your past and put on the new man you are. Spend time in prayer with God, asking Him to reveal to you those things that you need to remove. Then, make the commitment to God to begin this week to put on Christ in practice.

4. In view of what you have learned from this lesson, how would you respond to those who believe that there is a second work of salvation, that being the baptism of the Holy Spirit? Write out your thoughts and organize them in a logical manner. Support your points with Scripture. What new things have you learned in regard to this doctrine? In what ways has your own understanding of the fact of your baptism into the Body of Christ been enlightened?

13

One Body, Many Gifts—Part 1

Outline

Introduction
A. The Church Is Not an Organization
   1. It is not a promotional agency
      a) Gospel birds
      b) Gospel bottles
   2. It is not a profit-making business
   3. It is not run by paid professionals
   4. It is not a community social center
B. The Church Is an Organism
   1. An organism is alive
   2. The church is alive
      a) A bride
      b) A Vine and branches
      c) A flock
      d) A family

Review

Lesson
I. The Analogy
   A. Unity
      1. Spiritual unity
         a) Ephesians 4:3
         b) Ephesians 2:15-16
         c) Ephesians 4:4-6
         d) Galatians 3:28
         e) John 17:20-23
      2. Spiritual necessity
   B. Diversity
      1. Unity demands diversity
         a) The illustrations
            (1) An auto plant
            (2) A football team

Introduction

In 1 Corinthians 12:12-31 Paul has a very important and practical word for us on the subject of one Body and many gifts. It is my prayer that the Spirit of God will use this subject not just as encouragement or instruction but as a catalyst to alter your behavior as a believer in relation to Him and to His church during all the years to come.

A. The Church Is Not an Organization

Unfortunately, Christianity has become very organized. As one writer put it: "When Christians get organized, they get very un-Christian." It is clear from any study of church history that this is the time when the church has become most like the world's organization. Today, organization is more sophisticated than it has ever been. There is no question about the fact that the church, for the most part, has been turned into an organization.

1. It is not a promotional agency

The church was never designed to be ordered along the lines of the world's organizational principles. It was never designed to be a management outfit. It was never designed to follow business philosophy. It was never designed to be a selling agency in which people are motivated by Madison Avenue promotion, gimmicks, and moneymaking schemes. Unfortunately, it has become just that.

Two church ads illustrated this to me. The church uses amazing gimmicks to fulfill what Christians assume is their responsibility.

a) Gospel birds

One ad said to attend a certain church because that coming Sunday they were featuring the Hanson Gospel Birds. The ad said, "These birds eat with a fork, fly backwards, open padlocks, ride airplanes, and swallow small swords." Those were the Hanson Gospel Birds.

b) Gospel bottles

Another ad advertised a service on a Sunday night in which a converted alcoholic was going to play gospel music on converted booze bottles to illustrate the transformation in his life. Instead of drinking out of the bottles, he was going to blow gospel music back into them.

You say, "That is ridiculous!" Of course it is, but it does illustrate the fact that the church has lost the concept of what it is supposed to be. The church is not a place to go to watch gospel birds. It is not a place to go to hear a man play converted booze bottles. The church was never designed to be a gimmick to attract people.

2. It is not a profit-making business

The church was never intended to be a business for profit-making. There are churches today that own money, property, businesses, and corporations, and they are turning a profit. At one of our elders' meetings, one very kind and well-meaning organization wanted to give us a lot of stainless steel. This was tremendous, because stainless steel is very valuable. However, it was all built to fit a certain kitchen, and we would have to take it as it was. The question immediately came up: "Will it fit our kitchen?" "No." "Can we use it in our kitchen?" "No." "But it's very valuable. What are we going to do with it?" One idea that surfaced was to sell it for a profit. Well, it was a kind gesture, but our thinking was that we were not in the stainless steel business; we were a church. The church is not a profit-making brokerage for people who want to unload certain items as a charity write-off. That is not our business.

3. It is not run by paid professionals

The church was never designed to be run by paid professionals who do all the work while everybody else watches. We live in a society like this. We are all watchers. We sit at home and watch the world happen on the tube. If we leave home, it is to go and watch something, such as people playing games, or people singing and making music. We have no involvement, no responsibility, and no commitment—but we watch. The church has also fallen into this category. If you look at the church page on Saturday night, you will have difficulty distinguishing it from the movie page. "Who is playing where? Where will we go this week? Over here they are showing a movie." "Yes, but in this church it's a double feature." "Over here they have Hanson's Gospel Birds." "But over here there is a converted man blowing into booze bottles." Where do we go? In other words, the church has been turned into a spectator place—the local religious production.

4. It is not a community social center

I am also convinced that the church was never intended by God to be a community social center where everybody goes because it's a nice place to go. It is not like a country club— you don't have to pay.

B. The Church Is an Organism

What is the church? The church is an organism, not an organization. This is the perspective at Grace Community Church.

1. An organism is alive

Paul, in 1 Corinthians 12, is attempting to show that the church is an organism. And an organism is living. It is different from an organization. A corpse is organized, but it isn't alive. A corpse has all the limbs in the right place, the bone structure is flawless, all the organs are in the right spot and connected to the right things—everything is there—but it is not living. It is an organization at that point, but it has ceased to be an organism.

The difference between an organism and an organization can also be illustrated as the difference between you and your car. The dictionary says that an organization is a structured system.

But an organism is a living system. Your car is structured. It has a frame, it has steel, it has everything it needs, and it works to perform a certain function when you carry out the things that are commensurate with its structure. But it isn't a living organism. You don't call your car and say, "Come and get me; I'm stuck down here!" Your car cannot respond as a living thing.

2. The church is alive

The church is also not like a car. The church is not a highly structured organization with all the right parts, with nice, comfortable seats, with many supertrained, tremendous technicians and mechanics, and driven by a hotshot preacher. No. The church is an organism. It is a living, breathing, vital life. I think that Paul wanted to get this truth across with great fervency. Every individual in the church is alive. Pulsing through all of us is the life of God—eternal life (Gk., *aiōnios zōē*), God's life, and God's Spirit. We are living. Just as every cell and every member in your body is alive, so everyone in the church is alive. We are a Body.

Now, when the New Testamant wants to speak of the church in terms of analogies, it frequently uses analogies of living organisms.

a) A bride

b) A Vine and branches—Christ is the Vine, and we are the branches.

c) A flock—We are sheep, and Christ is the Shepherd. Sheep are living, breathing, and vital.

d) A family—This analogy comes from Ephesians 2:19 and Romans 8:14-17. The church is a family, and we are sons who cry out, "Abba, Father." A family is living and organic.

So when God the Holy Spirit wants to show us the church, He shows it to us in organic terms—in terms that will say to us, "Everybody is a living part; nobody is a spectator." The church isn't a structured organization run by professionals; it is a living, breathing, vital organism.

But the best metaphor that has ever been used to define the church—the one never appearing in the Old Testament but unique to the church—is that the church is a body. First Corinthians 12:12 says, "For as the body is one . . . so also is Christ." Christ's church is like a human body. We are an organism. We are not a structured system; we are a living system. We are not just organized; we are alive. The church is a plurality of living cells beating with eternal life (Gk., *aiōnios zōē*).

Review

Paul's message to the Corinthians was directed to the fact that they were not functioning as a body. They were totally chaotic. Their particular manifestation of the Body of Christ was definitely crippled, spastic, and out of control. They were not portraying the proper image of Christ in the world. They were carnal. They were immature. They were immoral. They were selfish. They were proud. They were heretical. They were divisive. They fostered parties of opposition. They were enamored with human philosophy. They identified in little cliques under certain spiritual teachers. They tolerated sin. They were suing each other. They had a Women's Lib movement. They were gluttonous. They were drunkards. They were sexually evil. They allowed pagan worship ritual to be brought into their own worship. They committed orgiastic sins at the love feast. They desecrated the Lord's Table. And they perverted and twisted the area of spiritual ministries. As a result of all of this, the Body of Christ was distorted, and the image of Christ in the world was lost.

As Paul reaches chapter 12, the indication he gives is that in no other area was there more discord or disunity evident than in the area of spiritual gifts. In an area where the Body ought to have been functioning, there was chaos. Why? For one thing, the Corinthians had counterfeited the true gifts. For another thing, Satan had moved in and was counterfeiting the gifts in the name of the Holy Spirit. In addition to that, everybody was seeking the showy gifts—the public gifts, the speaking gifts. Terrible chaos was the result. People who didn't have the showy gifts felt inferior. People who did have them felt superior. There were people grumbling and griping because they couldn't get certain gifts, while others were lording it over the ones who couldn't get those gifts. So instead of the Body's functioning in beautiful harmony, there was chaos. The Corinthians, in their self-seeking, selfish, attention-getting, ego-pandering efforts, were seeking the showy gifts.

Paul is saying to them, "You are a body. In a body the hand doesn't say, 'If I can't be the eye, I'm leaving,' or, 'I'm frustrated,' or, 'I've been cheated.' " His point is that you must be content with the design of God. You must allow God to put the Body together the way He planned, accept the sense of divine dignity that God has placed in every member, and minister in the area God has gifted you in.

When the Corinthians began to seek for other gifts, they wouldn't minister the gifts they did have, and chaos resulted. In verse 11 Paul says, "All of the gifts are given by the same Spirit, who divides them out to every man as He wills." These are divine and sovereign gifts. There isn't anything to seek for or to chase after. To seek certain gifts shows discontent with one's own gifts and a selfish desire for the showy gifts. There are some people who do not have the gift of teaching. Other people have confirmed that they do not have the gift of teaching and yet they continue to seek the places of teaching. There are people today who believe that you haven't received a certain dimension of the spiritual life until you have received the gift of tongues. So they continually seek for it, but that is not what God intends. It is precisely this problem that Paul is confronting in 1 Corinthians 12.

Beloved, there is nothing to seek. You will find no such injunction or exhortation to seek spiritual gifts, but only to accept what God has given in humility and faithfulness, and then minister. But the Corinthians wanted the showy, self-seeking, glorifying gifts. I fear that many in the modern charismatic movement have been caught in the same trap. God never intended all of us to have all the same gifts. That is the beauty of the Body.

In this chapter, Paul wants to make the Corinthians face the truth that they are not to seek other gifts. They are not to feel inadequate because they don't have some showy gift, and they are not to feel proud if they do. Paul presents an analogy of a human body and then draws out of it an application. He says that the body and the church are similar. Each is an organism with many parts, each is complete only when all those parts function, and each part is unique and yet dependent. When the parts don't cooperate, there is chaos. So, the church is like a human body. Paul's analogy begins in verse 12 and runs through verse 26. Then in verse 27 he shifts gears and makes the application.

Lesson

I. THE ANALOGY (vv. 12-26; 28a)

Paul develops his analogy along four lines: Unity, Diversity, Sovereignty, and Harmony.

A. Unity (vv. 12-13)

"For as the body is one, and hath many members, and all the members of that one body, being many, are one body, so also is Christ. For by one Spirit were we all baptized into one body, whether we be Jews or Greeks, whether we be bond or free; and have been all made to drink . . . one Spirit."

1. Spiritual unity

The point is very simple: A body is one, and yet has many members. The church is one, and yet has many members. Our

234

unity is emphasized because we have all been placed into one Body by one Spirit and made to drink one Spirit—we are born of one Spirit. We are placed into one Body by the baptism with one Spirit. We are indwelt by one Spirit.

a) Ephesians 4:3—"Keep the unity of the Spirit." We are all one. We have the common life of God in our souls. The Spirit of God lives in us. We have eternal life (Gk., aiōnios zōē). We have that eternal life pulsing through all of us.

b) Ephesians 2:15-16—"To make in himself [Christ] of two [Jew and Gentile] one new man" (v. 15). He took Jew and Gentile and made them into one new man. The word "new" is not new in time (Gk., neos), but new in quality (Gk., kainos). He has made a new kind of man in a new kind of existence. Verse 16 says, "And that he might reconcile both unto God in one body."

c) Ephesians 4:4-6—"There is one body, and one Spirit, even as ye are called in one hope of your calling; one Lord, one faith, one baptism, one God and Father of all, who is above all, and through all, and in you all."

d) Galatians 3:28—"There is neither Jew nor Greek, there is neither bond nor free, there is neither male nor female; for ye are all one in Christ Jesus" (cf. Rom. 10:12). Paul calls us fellow citizens, fellow partakers, fellow members, and fellow heirs (Eph. 2:19; 3:6; 4:25).

e) John 17:20-23—"Neither pray I for these alone, but for them also who shall believe on me through their word; that they all may be one, as thou, Father, art in me, and I in thee, that they also may be one in us; that the world may believe that thou hast sent me. And the glory which thou gavest me I have given them, that they may be one, even as we are one: I in them, and thou in me, that they may be made perfect in one." Jesus wants us to be one. The Holy Spirit comes on Pentecost, makes us one, and Jesus' prayer is answered—positionally. Jesus wanted this unity, and the Spirit of God brought about that unity—we are one Body.

2. Spiritual necessity

There are no spiritual loners. There are no people on the outside. There are no drifters. There are no spectators. We are one. The life of God is pulsing through you and me. You are as vital to the organism as any limb of a human body is vital to that body. There are no degrees of importance or responsibility in terms of significance. Everyone is an equal, spiritual necessity. We are an organism, and an organism's entire life is dependent on every single part, no matter how minute it is.

So the church is not an organization, a business, or a group of people who come to watch what happens while the paid professionals run the show. We are a living cell—a community of people who live and breathe the same air. We are citizens of the same kingdom, members of the same family, a bride for the same Bridegroom, sheep of the same flock, branches on the same Vine, and best of all, members of the same Body. You are just as important as I am, and I am just as important as you. There is no reason for you to say, "I don't matter. I can hang loose on the fringe. I'm not really a part." Oh yes, you are! If the life of God lives in your soul by the presence of the Spirit of God, you are vital. And if you are not an active and practical part of what is happening in the Body, then the Body is crippled. You say, "You mean I'm that important?" This is what God is trying to make you understand. Maybe you don't understand how important you are because you have never tried to fulfill your importance and have never seen what could be done.

B. Diversity (v. 14)

"For the body is not one member, but many."

1. Unity demands diversity

a) The illustrations

(1) An auto plant

What would happen if the following situation occurred in an auto assembly plant? Suppose that all the workers got together and had a big labor meeting and announced to the management, "We are united. We have solved our problems. We are of one mind, and there is such great unity in this plant that we have all decided, without any dissent, that we are all going to screw on rear taillights." There would not be anything to screw the rear taillights onto! In order for one unit to come off that assembly line, there has to be diversity. The same thing is true of the Body of Christ. God does not want a bunch of spiritual rubber ducks dropping out of some divine mold. There have to be distinctions. Paul gives us this concept in verse 14: "For the body is not one member, but many." There have to be different functions. Every Christian is a spiritual snowflake—unique

236

and essential to the Body of Christ and to a local community of believers who are the representation of that greater Body. You are absolutely essential. Unity and diversity form Paul's basic theme.

(2) A football team

If all the members of a football team said to the coach, "We had a meeting, and are we united! We have all decided to play quarterback," they would not have a team.

But as I look at movements in Christianity today, I see forty-four quarterbacks. I see seven thousand people screwing on rear taillights. Many say, "If you don't have that gift, you haven't arrived." So everyone chases after the same gift. As a result, Christians don't do what they should do to make the Body what God wants it to be. The Body gets a case of spiritual hydrocephalus—everyone is flowing to the head.

I remember in one "Flash Gordon" episode that there was a race of people that was all head and no body. And I see that in the church today. Everybody is running to be the head, or to get on the face, be an ear, an eye to be seen, or a mouth that can speak. Unity demands diversity. We all have to do different things.

b) The implications

In the church at Corinth, everyone wanted the same showy gifts. In 1 Corinthians 12:29 Paul asks, "Is everyone supposed to be an apostle? Is everyone supposed to be a prophet? Is everyone supposed to be a teacher? Is everyone supposed to work miracles? Is everyone supposed to heal? Is everyone supposed to interpret?" What is the implied answer? Of course not! But you will notice that he is talking about either showy offices or gifts: apostles, prophets, teachers, miracles, healing, and speaking in languages. And today I see the church doing the same thing all over again.

Paul's point is clear: A body is one because it has all the necessary, functioning parts. We had all better be operating, or the Body is not going to properly present the picture of Jesus Christ. I don't know what your gifts are, but you ought to know how the Spirit of God uses you, and you ought to be able to define your ministries and be useful to God.

237

c) The improvement

When many of the living, breathing members of an organism are not ministering, they jam up the functioning of the body. Can you imagine a body in rebellion? It happens in the church. So we have to train a foot to do what the hand does because there aren't enough hands to do the job. We compensate. One of the reasons that the church becomes organized is to do what the organism won't do. Unfortunately, organization takes place in order to bypass the carnal people. What really ought to be done is to deal with the carnality instead of organizing around it.

2. God demands diversity

Diversity is not accidental. God doesn't say, "Let's see—I will throw a few gifts down there and see where they land." No, gifts are the very essence of the Body. The church works when every member begins to minister his gift.

a) Inspiring the flock

The first time that I had ever said anything regarding this subject, it really revolutionized our church. One day I said, "If you're waiting for this organization to give you a ministry—forget it. We are not going to give you one until you show us that you're a faithful minister of your gift. So you better take your gift and minister." One lady came up to me and said, "I have the gift of teaching, but I've checked and there are no openings in the primary department." And I said, "Are there any kids in your neighborhood that age?" "Oh, yes!" "Teach them." "You mean, just go right out and teach them?" "Go right out and teach them." Some people say to me, "I feel that I have the gift of teaching, but I don't have a class." I say, "Do you know somebody that knows less than you?" "Yes." "Then teach him." I will never forget what happened. Little by little people began to minister, and then the body was functioning. Then you are saying to people, "Be faithful at this level and God will be faithful to put you in the place of a strategic service." Begin to minister—you are a living part of this Body.

b) Instructing the flock

You say, "Well, why do you talk at us?" All I am doing is giving you the input so you can minister. I do the feeding. I am trying to pour in some fuel that you can thrive on. We provide a kind of spiritual smorgasbord. We don't expect everyone to come and do everything. We don't say, "If you don't have a Bible study, you're against the Bible." I have actually heard preachers say that. All we say is, "If you want to take advantage of what is here, we will try to feed you and give you what you need to develop a ministry within the Body of Christ." A believer who doesn't have a ministry is a contradiction—denying God the right to use him in the way He has gifted and prepared him to be used. So diversity is no accident. There is unity, diversity, and third:

C. Sovereignty (vv. 18, 24b, 28a)

1. Harmonious design (v. 18)

"But now hath God set the members, every one of them, in the body, as it hath pleased him."

Here Paul turns to the One who created the body. By implication in this analogy you can prove that Paul was not an evolutionist. He believed God created the body as well as the church by virtue of the statement in reference to the analogy of sovereignty: "But now hath God set the members." God designed every member. God did not put out a monotonous line of uniform Christians; He put out a group of people who were one and yet individually unique.

a) God's placement

The word "set" in verse 18 refers to the act of divine appointment. Just as God planned the physical body with all of its parts, so He planned the church. You have the gifts you have because you are exactly what God wanted you to be, minus your sin. Does that give you a sense of divine dignity? Instead of saying, "Well, why didn't I get this gift?" or, "Why don't I have this gift?" or, "I'm going to seek this gift," why not just be content with what God has given you and get into your mind the sense of divine dignity that God has granted you? Unparalleled dignity is given to every part of the Body.

b) God's people

How many of the members has God set in the Body as it pleased Him? Every one of them. When you are not content with your gift, you are rebelling and acting selfishly against the sovereign and supreme will of God. You are like the imaginary antagonist in Romans 9:20 saying to the potter, "Why hast thou made me thus?" instead of saying, "God, I just want to thank You for making me like this so I can minister in a way that is necessary for the Body."

The dignity in the Body of Christ does not belong to the people with the showy gifts. The dignity in the Body does not belong to the people who are up front. The dignity in the Body belongs to every member, because every member is what he or she is by the sovereign will of God. You are that spiritual snowflake; you are the marvelous one that God has made out of all the world of men to be what you are, and to be in His Body for His glory and the blessing of all the other saints.

Sometimes we think that the only people who are important are the people up front. If the people up front really think about it, they know that the people who are important are the people behind the scenes creating the opportunity for the people up front to be there. With your gift, you are God's masterpiece as it has pleased Him.

c) God's pleasure

Notice that verse 18 also says, "As it hath pleased him." Please remember this: A Christian does not select his own gift. You don't have any part in it—God does. Do you realize the chaos that would be created if everyone was selecting his own gift? Do you think that you can organize the entire Body of Christ? God had to do that! For me to question God, feel inferior, or feel superior is ridiculous. There should be a sense of dignity in every individual believer. You have not only been created in Christ Jesus, but placed within you is a marvelous capacity to minister to the Body of Christ and to God Himself. And you ought to understand that lofty dignity. I think that it is terrible when some Christians are not content with what God has given them as a ministry and, instead, are proudly pursuing something showy.

(1) No command to seek a gift

There is not a single command in the Bible to seek a spiritual gift. You say, "What about 1 Corinthians 14:39: 'Wherefore, brethren, covet to prophesy'?" Is "brethren" singular or plural? Plural—brethren, many of you, all of you. What is Paul saying? He is saying, "When you come together as a church, seek to have the gift of prophesy used. Don't forbid languages—God may want to use that gift if there are some unbelieving Jews present—but seek to prophesy." He is not saying to go seek the gift of prophecy. He is saying, "Brothers, when you come together collectively, seek that prophecy be exalted. Let's get some teaching started." That verse is not an individual command to a Christian to seek the gift of prophecy. You cannot seek a gift.

(2) No place for discontent

There is no place for discontent. There is no place for selfishness. There is no place for conceit.

(a) Hebrews 2:4—"God also bearing them witness, both with signs and wonders, and with diverse miracles and gifts of the Holy Spirit, according to his own will?" The gifts are always given according to His own will.

(b) 1 Corinthians 12:11—"Dividing to every man severally as he will."

(c) 1 Corinthians 12:18—"But now hath God set the members . . . as it hath pleased him." The bestowing of gifts is all up to the sovereign will of God.

(d) Romans 12:3—"According as God hath dealt to every man the measure of faith."

God saved us. God placed us in the Body with certain gifts. So Paul says to the Corinthians, "Quit chasing the showy gifts." If you chase a gift that you don't have, will you get it? No. What will you get? A counterfeit. Unfortunately, we see a lot of that today.

2. Harmonious blending (v. 24b)

"But God hath tempered the body together."

The word "tempered" in the Greek means "mixed together." It is a term used for mixing colors—artistic terminology. It is harmonious blending. God not only chooses the gifts for you, but He mixes you in with the right people, so that the right combination will work in the right location.

a) Painting the portrait

(1) Blending the gifts

You say, "Why am I at my church?" God mixed you in there for ministry. Imagine it this way: In a previous illustration we had an artist's palette that contained the primary colors. Those primary colors represented the gifts of the Spirit: the permanent edifying gifts such as giving, mercy, teaching, prophesying, and so on. We said that when the Spirit of God gives you your gift, He takes a certain amount from each of these different combinations and mixes up a color that is yours and yours alone. You are a unique individual. You are a combination of many gifts (or areas of giftedness).

(2) Blending the members

But this analogy goes a step further. Once the Spirit has made you the color He wants you to be, then He transfers you to the canvas of the church exactly in the spot He wants you to be right next to the other colors. So when the Body is put together, everybody is in the right spot. When the picture is finished, it is a picture of Christ. You are not only the right color, but you are the right color in the right place. Isn't that a beautiful concept? God not only gifts you, but He mixes you into the Body in just the right place.

b) Preventing the portrayal

Can you imagine some color's saying, "I'm going to fade. I'm going to run. I'm going to drip all over the color next to me," or, "I refuse to be a color?" When that happens and the portrait is held up before the world, what do people see? It is hard to tell. I'm not sure they really know. You need to think of the Body with that perspective. You are a combination of the primary colors designed to be a gifted individual like no other. You are strategic because if you are gone, part of the portrait is gone. If parts of the portrait are missing from different places, the world looks at the canvas of the church and cannot really see what it is supposed to be. It is sad, selfish, and inconsistent when we rebel and the portrait of Christ is lost.

3. Harmonious leadership (v. 28a)

"And God hath set some in the church: first apostles, second prophets, third teachers."

In this verse, Paul uses a similar phrase as in verse 18: "God hath set." This is divine appointment. In addition to the gifts, and in addition to the blending of the gifts, He gives gifted men who lead and direct the church.

a) The Spirit's helpers

Many of the famous artists, such as da Vinci and Michelangelo, had other artists that worked for them. The artist would paint his basic work, and then the other artists would fill in and touch up any gaps under the direction of the artist. The Holy Spirit is the artist, and He puts us on the canvas in the right place, but He also has some helpers—the gifted men.

b) The Spirit's perfecters

Ephesians 4:11 says, "And he gave some, apostles; and some, prophets; and some, evangelists; and some, pastors and teachers." Their job is to perfect the saints—to make those colors as vivid, as bright, and as beautiful as they can so that the portrait of Christ is clear. That is God's calling. God chooses the men and women to have the responsibility in different areas of leadership.

(1) The twelve

One of the first things the Lord Jesus did when He began His ministry was to choose out twelve men. When one of them defected, through the selection process in Acts 1:24-26 He chose Matthias.

(2) Paul

After His resurrection, Jesus chose Paul. And Paul even says he had nothing to do with it: "I was going to Damascus. The next thing I knew, I was in the ministry" (Acts 26:12-18).

(3) The first missionaries

When God wanted two missionaries to go to the Gentile world, the Holy Spirit stopped off in Antioch and said, "Separate me Barnabas and Saul for the work unto which I have called them" (Acts 13:2*b*).

So it is that God's sovereignty chooses the leadership. His sovereignty selects those who shall be the gifted men to assist the Holy Spirit in making the portrait of Christ all that it should be.

We have to recognize that we are in a Body and that the Body is one. We are a part of that oneness. We must sense that. We have the life of the Spirit in us just like everyone else. "He that is joined unto the Lord is one spirit" (1 Cor. 6:17), so we are all in it together. Yet there is diversity, and every one of us is unique and exactly as God made us. There is a tremendous dignity in that. You are not an accident. You were planned before the foundation of the world to be you (Eph. 1:4). And you are to use what you have been given. Realize that this is God's plan, and don't chase something you don't have, don't be something you can't be, but say, "God, if this is what I am, then I sense that You wanted it so. I sense the dignity in that, and I will minister for You."

You Ain't Nothin' till He Calls It!

We should never have movements. They always seem to be about the showy gifts. Have you ever heard of a giving movement, where everyone is seeking the gift of giving? Have you ever heard of a helps movement? In the history of the church there has never been a helps movement. Has there ever been a showing mercy movement? No. But there have been movements involving tongues and healing. All the movements do is create chaos. God has put the Body together in the way He wants. And when God says it, that's the way it ought to be.

There was a baseball umpire in the major leagues by the name of Bill Clem. One day he was umpiring an important game. There was a runner on third base. The batter hit a deep fly to left field. The left fielder went way back, caught the ball, and rifled the ball home with his shotgun arm as the runner on third broke for the plate. It was a perfect throw on one hop to the catcher. The ball, the catcher, and the runner all hit the plate at the same time as dust flew everywhere. The umpire hesitated in his decision until the dust cleared. One bench screamed, "He's out! He's out!" The other bench screamed, "Safe! He's safe!" Bill Clem turned around and looked at both benches and said, "He ain't nothin' till I call it!" God looks at us and says, "You ain't nothin' till I call it." But when He has called it, then you are something. And the something that you are is the something He wanted you to be, and it is desperately needed by the rest of us.

Focusing on the Facts

1. What things was the church never designed to be? Explain each one (see pp. 230-31).
2. If the church is not an organization, what is it (see p. 231)?
3. How is the church different from an organization? Give some examples (see pp. 231-32).
4. What is it that pulses through the life of every believer (see p. 232)?
5. What are the different analogies that the New Testament uses to describe the church? Why does the Holy Spirit use these particular analogies (see p. 232)?
6. In what ways were the Corinthians not functioning as a body? What was the result of their behavior (see pp. 233-34)?

7. Why was there chaos in the Corinthian church in the particular area of spiritual gifts (see p. 233)?
8. How are the human body and the church similar (see p. 234)?
9. Along what four lines does Paul develop his analogy (see p. 234)?
10. Why does Paul emphasize the unity of the Body of Christ (see p. 235)?
11. Why are there no spiritual loners in the Body of Christ (see pp. 235-36)?
12. What does unity demand? Explain (see p. 236).
13. What were the kinds of gifts the Corinthians were seeking (see p. 237)?
14. What is one reason for the church's becoming organized? What should the church do instead of organizing (see p. 238)?
15. Why is a believer without a ministry a contradiction (see p. 239)?
16. What does the word "set" refer to in 1 Corinthians 12:18? Explain (see p. 239).
17. Why should every Christian possess a sense of divine dignity? What is the result when a Christian is not content with his gift (see pp. 239-40)?
18. Why does dignity belong to every member of the Body of Christ (see p. 240)?
19. Why can't 1 Corinthians 14:39 be used as a proof text that Christians should seek for spiritual gifts (see pp. 240-41)?
20. Why should a Christian have no discontent over his spiritual gift (see p. 241)?
21. What does the word "tempered" mean in 1 Corinthians 12:24? What significance does this word have for believers in the Body of Christ (see p. 241)?
22. Explain the concept of the believer as a color that the Holy Spirit uses to paint the portrait of Christ for the world. What is the result when some of the colors are missing (see pp. 241-42)?
23. Who are the people who help the Spirit as He paints the portrait of Christ? What is their job (see p. 243)?

Pondering the Principles

1. Does your church operate primarily as an organization or as an organism? What are some of the characteristics that are revealed in your church that make you view it as an organization? What are some of the characteristics that are revealed that make you view it as an organism? What do you think a church should do in order to stop being run as an organization? Read Ephesians 4:11-16. What responsibility should the leaders have? What responsibility should the congregation have? According to verses 13-15, what are the results when the Body is built up? Please be in prayer for your church and its leaders. Take this moment to pray.

2. Do you realize that you are essential to the Body of Christ? Do you experience the fact of your necessity to your brothers and sisters in Christ, or do you feel unnecessary? Read John 17:20-23. Who do you suppose Jesus is praying for? If two thousand years ago Jesus prayed for all the future believers, don't you think He prayed for you as well? If on the night before His crucifixion Jesus prayed that you might be one with all the other believers, how important do you think Jesus Christ feels you are to His Body? How does that change your perspective on your importance?

3. Are you presently ministering your spiritual gift? If not, why? Are you waiting for your church to give you a ministry? Read Matthew 25:14-30. God has entrusted some of His possessions to you. What are you doing with them? Are you helping the Body to grow by the use of what God has given you, or have you hidden what God has given you? If you want to experience a greater ministry, be faithful right now. Memorize Matthew 25:21: "Well done, good and faithful slave; you were faithful with a few things, I will put you in charge of many things, enter into the joy of your master" (NASB). Pray that this might be true of you.

4. Take this moment to reflect on your position within the Body of Christ. Based on your practical unity with other believers, what kind of portrait of Christ does the world see? How is your attitude affecting that portrait? Do you have a sense of divine dignity with your position in the body of Christ, or are you discontented with your position? Why? Take time to allow God to search your heart and reveal to you what may be causing any discontent (Ps. 139:23-24). Remember that God, by His sovereign will, has placed you in the perfect spot within the Body of Christ. Confess any of those thoughts and attitudes that are questioning God's sovereignty in your life. Turn from those attitudes and seek to develop a trusting heart in God.

14

One Body, Many Gifts—Part 2

Outline

Introduction
A. The Appeal of Rugged Individualism to the World
  1. God's desire for dependence
  2. Satan's desire for independence
B. The Attitude of Rugged Individualism in the Church
  1. The proponents of interdependence
    a) Jesus
    b) Paul
  2. The problem with individualism
    a) The individualism of isolation
    b) The individualism of pride

Review
 I. The Analogy
  A. Unity
  B. Diversity
  C. Sovereignty

Lesson
  D. Harmony
    1. The disharmony of inferiority
      a) The requirement in the physical body
        (1) The principle: removal is impossible
          (*a*) The perspective of the foot
          (*b*) The perspective of the ear
        (2) The problem: reorganization is irrational
      b) The reality in the spiritual body
        (1) The plan of God
        (2) The peril of no body
        (3) The point of Paul
    2. The disharmony of superiority
      a) Examining the members
        (1) The external superiority
        (2) The internal support

   (*a*) Recognizing the necessity of the feeble members
   (*b*) Recognizing the needs of the lesser members
    i) Less honorable
    ii) Uncomely
  b) Equalizing the members
  c) Encouraging the members
II. The Application
 A. Remember Your Unity
 B. Remember Your Diversity
 C. Remember God's Sovereignty
III. The Appeal
 A. Start a New Practice
 B. Stop the Old Practice

Introduction

A. The Appeal of Rugged Individualism to the World

I am sure that you have seen the television commercial with the rugged, bearded, strong he-man type who runs around the woods with a big bear, advertising beer. There is a method in a commercial like that. It has a tremendous appeal to people because most people really admire rugged individualism. Here is a man who has tamed a bear, who runs around the boondocks all by himself, and who doesn't need anything but a periodic delivery of six-packs. The same thing is true of the Marlboro ads on billboards. The Marlboro man is all alone on a horse out in the middle of nowhere—the picture of rugged individualism. We honor people who go across the Atlantic Ocean in a dingy, who make amazing solo flights, or who climb Mount Everest. We possess this mentality that says rugged individualism is the stuff which separates the men from the boys. We admire the scientist who walks out of his laboratory after ten years and says, "Eureka!" and receives a prize for what he has discovered. There is something that appeals to us about a person who can do something by himself and say, "I have conquered everything. I'm independent; I'm self-sufficient."

1. God's desire for dependence

Do you know why that appeals to us? We are depraved. You say, "What do you mean?" God wants us to have a tremendous sense of dependency on others. God wants us to be a family. When Cain had slain his brother Abel, God said to him, "Where is Abel, thy brother? And he said, I know not: am I my brother's keeper?" (Gen. 4:9). Ever since the Fall, man has disdained the thought of responsibility for other people. Man has definitely desired to be independent of any responsibility. That is one of the reasons that God, in the Old Testament, made any individual who sinned carry a weight of responsibility that extended to his entire family (e.g., Achan; Josh. 7). God was communicating a message: "You are your brother's keeper. You are dependent on other people. I don't want rugged individualism."

2. Satan's desire for independence

Satan, in response, has built into the heart of man this concept of independence—needing nothing and nobody—as the epitome of life. The fact is that this is the very opposite of what God wants. The philosophy of today is: "Do your own thing." The music of today is: "I did it my way." All of this echoes the same philosophy that is echoed by the man with the bear and the beer: You don't need anyone or anything—you are sufficient. It is the philosophy in the poem "Invictus," which says that I am the captain of my fate and the master of my soul.

B. The Attitude of Rugged Individualism in the Church

This attitude pervades our society to the degree that it even finds its way into the church. We tend to translate a little of this philosophy into our theology. We think that because we have Christ and the Holy Spirit, we are sufficient and we don't need anyone else. It is then that we have missed the point altogether. Since we don't live communally, as they did in the Old Testament when they lived in tribes, or as they did in the New Testament when they still lived in the father's house, Christians have fostered the same independent attitude as the world has. So in the backlash of all of this, the church struggles today to try and regain the concept that the church is one Body with many members. We have a tremendous responsibility for dependency on each other, and that has to be the general attitude for the Christian life.

1. The proponents of interdependence

a) Jesus

I suppose that there will be some people who will say, "Look at Jesus. He was a rugged individualist." Was He? Jesus spent the first thirty years of His life living with His family. I don't think He ever left and lived on His own. The next three years of His life He spent with twelve men in the midst of His ministry.

b) Paul

You say, "But Paul was a rugged individualist." No, I don't think Paul ever went anywhere without somebody going with him. I don't like to go anywhere without some company. I like to have someone to lean on, someone to minister to me, and someone to whom I can minister, pray with, share with, and labor with. I'm sure Paul felt the same. In Romans 16:1-15 Paul lists the names of the many people who helped him, who accompanied him, whom he loved, and who ministered to him, with him, and for him. In Colossians 4:7-17 there is a similar list. In 2 Timothy 4:9-21 there are more names. In the book of Acts, Paul starts out with Barnabas (Acts 13:2), then John Mark (Acts 13:13), then Silas (Acts 15:40), then Timothy (Acts 16:3), and then Luke. Someone was usually sharing in the ministry with him—someone with whom he could minister, someone to whom he could pour out his heart, and someone for whom he could be a source of strength.

There is no place in God's plan or in biblical theology for rugged individualism. There is no reason to think that you are isolated. You are your brother's keeper.

2. The problem with individualism

Sadly, many Christians today just don't get into the mainstream of this ministry. There are usually two problems:

a) The individualism of isolation

There are some Christians who feel inferior and unnecessary, so they sit on the fringe and don't ever become involved. But God loves them, and so do their brothers and sisters in Christ. They think they don't matter much, so they are just content to hang on the fringe and never get involved. But they short-circuit the ministry of the Spirit of God through their lives to somebody desperately in need of it.

b) The individualism of pride

Then there are other people who say, "Well, I am a spiritual celebrity and superstar. I don't need all these people. I can do it on my own." We all fight that kind of attitude. Sometimes, after I have preached a message, someone will come up to me and say, "You really blew it on that one." My first reaction is, "Who needs you, fella? I can handle it." Or I will come into my office on Monday and say to someone, "Great day yesterday. I really feel God blessed."

Then I open my mail and someone writes, "You so-and-so . . ." I say to myself, "Who needs it? I know what I'm doing. I don't need your criticism." But that's my first response. Then, after thinking about it, I say, "Well, Lord, they are probably right." And I begin to realize that God puts all of these people around me to minister to me and to keep things in perspective. That is the way it has to be.

You have to realize that there is no place for the individualism of isolation or the individualism of a superstar attitude. Both of those attitudes are wrong. There should be a tremendous sense of interdependence in the Body of Christ that defies the spirit of pride and the attitude of inferiority.

Review

This is Paul's major message in 1 Corinthians 12. He uses the familiar metaphor of a human body, then makes an application and a final appeal. So these are the three points we want to look at: The Analogy, The Application, and The Appeal. These three will draw a great truth out of this idea of interdependence and mutuality within the Body of Christ.

I. THE ANALOGY (vv. 12-26, 28a; see pp. 234-44)

Paul's analogy is a body. An analogy is simply another way of saying something. He wants to state a spiritual truth, but he says it in another way by using the illustration of a human body. He develops the analogy along four lines: A human body illustrates unity, diversity, sovereignty, and harmony. These four things sum up what a human body is and illustrate what the church ought to be.

A. Unity (vv. 12-13; see pp. 234-36)

"For as the body is one, and hath many members, and all the members of that one body, being many, are one body, so also is Christ. For by one Spirit were we all baptized into one body, whether we be Jews or Greeks, whether we be bond or free; and have been all made to drink . . . one Spirit."

Basically, Christians are one. There are not any upper- and lower-class Christians. There are not any highbrow and lowbrow Christians. There are no social strata involved. There is just a beautiful unity. We all have flowing through us the life of God— eternal life (Gk., *aiōnios zōē*). There is a beautiful unity in the Body of Christ, and a human body is the same. A common life principle flows through every cell in the human body.

251

B. Diversity (v. 14; see pp. 236-39)

"For the body is not one member, but many."

The body has unity and it has diversity. But it must maintain its diversity in order to experience its unity.

C. Sovereignty (vv. 18, 24b, 28a; see pp. 239-44)

"But now hath God set the members, every one of them, in the body, as it hath pleased him. . . . but God hath tempered the body together. . . . And God hath set some in the church: first apostles, second prophets, third teachers."

You can see God's sovereignty when your children are born. You wonder with your wife or your husband what your baby will look like. There are now X-rays available by means of which doctors are supposed to be able to determine many things about your child. There are many tests that can be run, but basically you don't know what your baby is going to be like until all of a sudden the life is there in front of you, and then you have to say it is by sovereign design. God put the child together. If it is a perfectly whole baby with ears that stick out a little, red hair, and a certain kind of nose, God made the baby in that way. Certainly there are genetic factors involved, but the child is still a creation of God independent of any effort on your part. A body is designed by God. If the child is born with an infirmity, or a malformation, or is malfunctioning, again that has to be assigned to the sovereign will of God—that which is beyond your ability to control.

The same thing is true of the Body of the church. The origination of the various members, their design, the way in which they are gifted, and the way they are placed into the Body are all dependent upon God.

The Dysfunction of Harmony

According to God's plan, unity, diversity, and sovereignty make the Body function. Now, where those three things function, there will be a fourth—harmony. But there will never be harmony until the other three are functioning. For example, the Corinthians:

1. Did not experience unity

Paul said to them in verses 12-13 that they ought to have unity because there was no such thing as either Jew or Greek or bond or free. They were all one. But they weren't acting that way. First Corinthians 1:10 says, "Now I beseech you, brethren, by the name of our Lord Jesus Christ, that ye all speak the same thing, and that there be no divisions among you, but that ye be perfectly joined together in the same mind and in the same judgment." In other words, get it together. According to verses 11-12 there were contentions over certain spiritual teachers. In chapter 3 he repeats the same thing, saying that they were carnal because there was envy and strife. One was saying that he was of Paul, another of Apollos—they were carnal (vv. 3-4). In chapter 4 they were glorying as if they possessed something they had earned (v. 7). They had spiritual pride. In chapter 6 they were suing each other in acts of antagonism, bitterness, resentment, and revenge. In chapter 8 they were using their liberty to defraud each other. They were stepping on the neck of the weaker brother in their pride and independence. In chapter 11 the rich came to the love feast, and instead of sharing their meal, they ate it, so that when the poor came there wasn't anything left for them to eat. So you can see that there existed anything but unity.

Implied in chapter 12 is that instead of ministering their gifts, the proud people were saying, "We are the only ones that matter." The humble people were saying, "We don't matter; we don't have the right gifts." So they were trying to seek for the ecstatic gifts and wound up with pagan counterfeits. They had destroyed the whole concept of unity.

2. Did not function in diversity

According to chapter 12, all the Corinthians were trying to obtain the same ecstatic and showy gift instead of recognizing that God had ordered them to be independent and individuals in the sense of their uniqueness. Everybody was trying to be a spiritual hotshot.

3. Denied sovereignty

Instead of accepting what God had given, they were discontent with what He had given and were seeking other gifts, manifestations, and experiences.

So they had violated all three; consequently, harmony did not exist.

Having straightened out the Corinthians about unity in verses 12-13, diversity in verse 14, and sovereignty in verses 18, 24, and 28, Paul now moves on beginning at verse 15 to talk about:

D. Harmony (vv. 15-26)

Paul dives into the concept of harmony by showing the foolishness of anything other than harmony. He covers it from two angles: first, the people who thought they were nothing and envied the ones who had the showy gifts; and second, the people with the showy gifts who thought they were something and thought the other people were nothing.

1. The disharmony of inferiority (vv. 15-20)

Here are the people who feel that they are nothing—the gripers, the envious, the ones who feel cheated.

a) The requirement in the physical body (vv. 15-17)

(1) The principle: removal is impossible (vv. 15-16)

(a) The perspective of the foot (v. 15)

"If the foot shall say, Because I am not the hand, I am not of the body; is it, therefore, not of the body?"

The foot is not particularly beautiful or lovely. If you were smart, you generally covered up your feet, especially if you happened to live in that day and age when the feet were usually exposed. The foot was considered a rather ugly thing. So the thing usually covered by dirt and not seen. When I am seen, I am not worth seeing. Since I am not a hand, I am not a part of the body."

Now, what was Paul saying—what is the principle? The principle is this: No member, by complaining and depreciating his own importance, can accomplish removal from the Body. Just because you think that you are not important, that does not eliminate your responsibility to function in the way that God called you to. You cannot sit in a corner and say, "Since I am a foot, and I don't have what some others have, I am not going to do anything or be a part of anything." That does not remove you from being a part; that only makes you disobedient. The principle is: You cannot remove yourself from a God-given responsibility simply because you are not happy with who you are. But that isn't the way it is. God made you a foot, if that is what you are, because the foot is vital—critical. To say that you don't want to be responsible for what you are doesn't relieve you of any responsibility; it only makes you disobedient.

This is exactly what was going on at Corinth. There were a lot of feet sitting in the background saying, "I wish I was an ear, or an eye—even a hand wouldn't be half bad. At least it's a little way up the ladder."

(b) The perspective of the ear (v. 16)

"And if the ear shall say, Because I am not the eye, I am not of the body; is it, therefore, not of the body?"

A little higher in the Body, and it is still relative. Some ear is saying, "I wish I could be an eye. But since I'm only an ear, I'm cutting out. They don't need me." Does that remove you from responsibility? When a foot is jealous of a hand, does that remove the responsibility of the foot from being a foot? When the ear is jealous of the eye, does that eliminate its responsibility? Not in God's eyes. Whatever your gift is, it is essential, it is needed, and God wants it. It has to be in the Body, and it has to operate. There is no sense sitting in a corner and saying, "Well, I don't have that much to offer anyway; there's no sense in me getting involved." But so many Christians do exactly that. Some of you do it. Some of you have been doing it for years. You have never known the joy of ministry because you just thought nobody wanted feet or ears. But that isn't so.

(2) The problem: reorganization is irrational (v. 17)

"If the whole body were an eye, where were the hearing? If the whole were hearing, where were the smelling?"

It would not make a lot of sense if everybody had the same gift. Yet isn't it amazing that people today keep telling us that we all need to get the same gifts? It's not true. There is no place in the Body for envying another gift. First Corinthians 13:4 says, "Charity [love] envieth not." But there is a place for contentment.

You cannot have one organ. The body cannot just be an eye, or an ear, or a nose. One organ, no matter how prominent it is, cannot survive alone. You can't cut off your ear, set it down, and say, "I have to leave. Would you hang around and listen? Maybe you can pick up some information while I'm gone." You can't pluck out your eye and have it look around for you while you are sleeping. There is no such thing as a spiritual loner.

Behind the Scenes

There is a tremendous sense of dependence in the Body of Christ. In Grace Community Church there are a number of people behind the scenes who make it possible for me to speak to you. All the people who type up things for me, all the people who give me input, and all the people who turn machines on and off make it all possible. There are many people who take upon themselves responsibilities that normally would be mine in order to free me to prepare so that I can minister to you. Without those people, I would not be able to say what I say to you, and you would not be able to receive what I say and grow. As a result, the whole purpose of ministry would be reduced.

So, Paul says that all members cannot be the same.

b) The reality in the spiritual body (vv. 18-20)

   (1) The plan of God (v. 18)

"But now hath God set the members, every one of them, in the body, as it hath pleased him."

God didn't leave the Body for us to figure out. He didn't say, "Get organized!" He said, "Be an organism, and I will run it!"

   (2) The peril of no body (v. 19)

"And if they were all one member, where were the body?"

If everyone were the same, we would not have a Body. But the Corinthians were saying, "We all have to chase after tongues. We all have to speak in prophecies. We all have to experience ecstasies." They all wanted the same gifts. So Paul says, "All that you are going to end up with is one great big eye."

256

(3) The point of Paul (v. 20)

"But now are they many members, yet but

Paul sums up his main point: Don't thi
inferior. Do not underestimate your own in

2. The disharmony of superiority (vv. 21-26)

In verses 21-26 Paul's point is: Don't think yourself superior.
Do not overestimate your importance.

a) Examining the members (vv. 21-23)

(1) The external superiority (v. 21)

"And the eye cannot say unto the hand, I have no
need of thee; nor again the head to the feet, I have no
need of you."

So far we have moved from the foot, to the hand, to
the ear, and to the eye; now we are moving from the
eye, to the ear, to the hand, to the foot. We are going
back down the Body from the viewpoint of superiority. This was what was going on in the Corinthian
assembly—many people were overestimating their
importance. The people with the fancy, showy, public
speaking gifts were assuming that they did not need
the other people—those who were nothing. They were
the superstars; they were the celebrities; they were the
superiors; they were the leaders; and they were the
hotshots. As far as they were concerned, the rest of the
people could have disintegrated into oblivion and it
would have had no effect. That isn't right. You can't
say, "I have no need of you." There is a tremendous
need for dependence in the Body.

(2) The internal support (vv. 22-23)

(a) Recognizing the necessity of the feeble members
(v. 22)

"Nay, much more those members of the body
which seem to be more feeble, are necessary."

Eyes and ears and hands and feet are nice, but you
can live without eyes, ears, hands, and feet. Even
the members that are showy, external, and strong,
you can live without. But there are weak members that you can't live without—they are more
vital.

In verse 22 Paul talks about the members of the body that are "more feeble." That means that they are weaker. Now, in this metaphor we are moving deeper into the body. Since verse 21 is dealing with hands and feet and eyes and ears (the outward), this part of the metaphor takes us deeper into the less showy, the less obvious, the less out-front, the less comely, the less prominent members. They are more feeble, but they are necessary.

What are these organs? They are the internal organs of the body—the lungs, the stomach, the liver, the kidneys, and all the other organs. These internal organs are completely hidden from view, yet they are vital and essential to sustaining life. So in this sense they are weaker. The only protection afforded them is from the other parts of the body. Paul is saying, "There are some members who are so feeble that they are totally dependent on the protection of some of the other members. They are not intended to be out front." You wouldn't live very long if you went around with your lungs hanging outside of you. They would not be able to handle the environment.

When I think about this verse, I think about the support ministries, particularly the secretaries at Grace Community Church. This church is a very intense place during the week. We have four or five crises a day. There are deadlines all the time. I believe that the secretaries, for the most part, would never be able to maintain a sense of mental balance if they didn't have some of us to protect them from the onslaught. Sometimes the frustrations mount, and since they are the gentler members of the Body, they need the protection of someone else in order to function smoothly and effectively. But if the staff walked away and left all of the onslaught to hit them, it would be difficult for them. They are the members who are necessary and vital. You don't even know who they are, but without them, I would not be able to minister.

(b) Recognizing the needs of the lesser members (v. 23)

258

"And those members of the body, which we think to be less honorable, upon these we bestow more abundant honor; and our uncomely parts have more abundant comeliness."

The Corinthians had failed to be kind, considerate, and protective of those who did not have the gift of prophecy, or the gift of languages, or the gift of healing—the out-front gifts. In addition, they had failed to protect the weaker ones, according to verse 22. So in verse 23 Paul says, "Don't you realize that even a human body compensates for its less comely members?"

Now what does Paul mean by the two terms "less honorable" and "uncomely"? About the clearest definition of "uncomely" is "ugly." Now, it doesn't mean horrible-looking, ugly things, it just means "the less beautiful parts." What do the less honorable and less beautiful parts refer to?

i) Less honorable

Most commentators assume this to be the middle part of your body—your trunk, hips, shoulders, thighs—the part you put your clothes on. Now, your face is nice to look at and enjoy, so you don't cover it up. And your hands are fine to look at, and so are your feet. But you cover up certain parts of your body because they are not as appealing. So Paul is saying that you bestow more abundant honor on your less honorable members. It is just a normal human response to fix up the part that needs it.

Some magazine articles will tell you, depending on your build, what kind of clothes to wear. If you are a little wide in a particular place, don't wear the squares, wear the stripes. That is the way people compensate for the less honorable parts—they bestow more honor on them. You might throw down your charge card and buy seventy-five dollars worth of abundant honor to drape over your less honorable parts. That is compensation. What is the principle? The less the natural grace and appeal, the greater the effort to adorn it.

So we have discussed the external, which doesn't need much adornment; then we discussed the more feeble parts—the internal organs—which are protected by the strength of the others; and then we discussed the parts of your body that you need to adorn with honor. Now Paul goes a step further.

ii) Uncomely

The Greek word for "uncomely" means "indecent." In other words, our indecent parts have more abundant comeliness. It is a normal, human reaction to cover the private or indecent parts of the human body, not just for the sake of adornment, but for the sake of modesty, with even a greater amount of effort. To show you how far away we have gone from what is normally human, just look at our society today. Those parts of the human body which mankind has long known to be private, and which ought to be covered with honor so that they can be held in modesty, are now exploited. That just shows how far our depravity has gone.

The point is this: the behind-the-scenes part of the Body should get the special attention and devotion. Paul is saying, "It is not the place for the highbrow members of the Body to say, 'I don't need you.' That member of the Body ought to say, 'I know that I am the only protection you have. I want to care for you and bestow more honor on you. And the more you need that honor, the more I want to give you that honor.' Instead of living with the attitude of spiritual, rugged individualism, we really should be busy making sure that we stop to honor the people who don't normally receive the honor." That is the kind of love that Paul talks about in 1 Corinthians 13. You should not be living with a sense of spiritual independence, but constantly acknowledging your gratitude for those parts of the church of Jesus Christ that don't receive all the glamour and appeal. They are in the church, and they are vital. They need to have the other members love them, protect them, and honor them.

So this analogy works both ways: God doesn't want the people who are sitting in the corner thinking they are nothing, and He doesn't want the other people thinking they are everything but passing around the honor where it belongs. Dr. Robert Thomas says, "It is a distorted sense of values when a Christian, well known because of his well received speaking gift, looks disparagingly at other Christians who possess no such gift. This is direct contradiction of the principle of self-concern that characterizes any body. It is far more consistent with the principle of self-preservation that members possessing greater beauty and functional ability, devote themselves tirelessly to the well-being of those not so well equipped." That is essentially what Paul is saying. Instead of thinking ourselves sufficient and independent, it is up to us to minister to others and for others to respond to that ministry by ministering to us in return. And it is also up to us to say, "We want to help you where you are weak and to strengthen you where you need to be strong." That is the kind of thing Paul wants. We ought to recognize the necessity of this, because God sees a beautiful equality in the Body.

b) Equalizing the members (v. 24)

"For our comely parts have no need; but God hath tempered the body together, having given more abundant honor to that part which lacked."

You may be a beautiful eye, ear, hand, or foot, but you could be cut off, and the rest of the body would still survive. But if you happen to be one of the vital organs, you can't be removed, because you are too important. This is how God equalizes the members. In the long run, when the judgment is in and the rewards are given, the people with the showy gifts aren't nearly as vital as the people with the support ministries.

One of the most exciting events of the ages and one of the most shocking experiences we will ever have is the *bēma* (the judgment seat of Christ), when we see who gets the rewards (1 Cor. 4:5). I think most of us will be shocked. Jesus said, "For he that is least among you all, the same shall be great" (Luke 9:48*b*), and "Whosoever of you would be the chiefest, shall be servant of all" (Mark 10:44). There are some of us who are eyes and ears and mouths and noses—we are the comely parts—but God equalizes our honor, because the less conspicuous members are the more essential to life. Nobody can see internal organs, so we usually think of people in terms of outward beauty, but that isn't what makes them what they are. The same thing is true in the church. God wants all the honor equalized.

c) Encouraging the members (vv. 25-26)

"That there should be no schism in the body, but that the members should have the same care one for another. And whether one member suffer, all the members suffer with it; or one member be honored, all the members rejoice with it."

God wants us all equalized. God wants this beautiful unity. He has designed this compensation in order that there might be a real unity. When your body suffers, you don't say, "Well, this half of me is suffering, but this half feels terrific." If any part of you suffers, your whole body suffers. And if any part of you is happy, your whole being is rejoicing. If we are truly sharing, that is the way it will be in the Body of Christ.

So Paul says, "Don't feel inferior! You are vital; you are necessary; you are important; and you are to be rewarded for faithfulness. And don't feel superior! You may be the out-front, good-looking part—that's your ministry for now, and there are certain blessings attendant with that ministry—but you cannot disdain the other parts, because they are the more necessary to life." So rivalry is impossible in the Body of Christ. The only thing that is possible is love, and that becomes Paul's theme in the next chapter.

II. THE APPLICATION (vv. 27-30)

A. Remember Your Unity (v. 27)

"Now ye are the body of Christ, and members in particular."

It is interesting that Paul calls one local congregation "the body of Christ." Is Paul saying, "You are the whole Body of Christ, and everyone else is outside of the Body?" Or is he saying, "You are one Body of Christ, and there is another Body in this town, and another Body in that town"? No, there is only one Body. Paul is saying, "You are a miniature representation of the Body of Christ. As a local assembly, you can manifest the fullness of the Body of Christ." This is so encouraging to me. In the first chapter of 1 Corinthians, Paul said, "Ye come behind in no gift" (v. 7). Isn't it thrilling to know that each local assembly of believers is given, by the Spirit of God, all that is necessary to truly represent the Body of Christ so that His image may be seen in the world? We don't need to say, "We are half of the Body over here and the other half is down there. If we could just get together, we could get the whole Body moving." God manifests the total picture in individual congregations and supplies each one with all they need. Paul says, "God has made you one, and He has poured you together in diversity. You are what you ought to be by God's sovereign will."

B. Remember Your Diversity (v. 28)

"And God hath set some in the church: first apostles, second prophets, third teachers; after that miracles, then gifts of healings, helps, governments, diversities of tongues [languages]."

C. Remember God's Sovereignty (vv. 29-30)

"Are all apostles? Are all prophets? Are all teachers? Are all workers of miracles? Have all the gifts of healing? Do all speak with tongues [languages]? Do all interpret?"

Now, what is the answer to every question? No.

So Paul says in verse 27, "Remember your unity. You are the Body I am talking about." In verse 28 he says, "Remember your diversity. You are the people with all of these different gifts." In verses 29-30 he says, "Remember God's sovereignty. He doesn't want you all to be apostles, or prophets, or teachers, or miracle workers, or healers, or all of you to speak in languages or to interpret languages." Paul confronts the Corinthians at the same three points: unity, diversity, and sovereignty. In other words, "Why are all of you trying to be noses and ears and eyes? Why do you all want to be apostles, prophets, teachers, miracle workers, tongues speakers, and healers? Don't you know that God has called some of you to be teachers and helpers and workers in the area of administration? It is all by God's sovereign design. You have nothing to seek for; you have nothing to be envious of; and you have nothing to be proud about and so disdain the others." As a result of unity, diversity, and God's sovereignty, they should experience harmony. So Paul applies the analogy.

III. THE APPEAL (v. 31)

"But covet earnestly the best gifts; and yet show I unto you a more excellent way."

When you read that verse you want to say, "You mean that Paul just spent all of his time in those verses saying to be content with the gift you have, and now he turns right around and says to covet earnestly the better gifts?" Literally, he means "the showy gifts." This verse is used by people from the Pentecostal tradition to prove that we ought to seek the gift of tongues and other gifts because this verse says to "covet earnestly the best gifts." They say that it is a command. When I look at that verse, I say, "It cannot be." Paul would not spend all this time in verses 1-30 saying, "Be content with what you have. Don't seek another gift. It has all been accomplished by God's sovereign plan. Just take the gift you have and use it. Don't feel inferior. Don't feel superior," and then say, "Go covet the showy gifts." What is Paul saying?

A. Start a New Practice (v. 31*b*)

"And yet show I unto you a more excellent way."

What was the way of the Corinthians? They had no unity, no sense of diversity (everybody was seeking the same gift), and no sense of sovereignty—they were not willing to accept God's plan. So Paul says, "I'm showing you a more excellent way— unity, diversity, sovereignty, and harmony. And then I'm going to show you that the Body functions in love" (1 Cor. 13). You say, "But what about that first statement?"

B. Stop the Old Practice (v. 31*a*)

"But covet earnestly the best gifts."

In the Greek language a statement of fact is called the indicative mood, while a command is called the imperative mood. Now, the form that each of these take in the Greek is the very same— there is no difference. So in the Greek, this verse is either a command or a statement; there is no difference in the form. It either says, "Covet earnestly the best gifts," or it says, "But you are coveting the best gifts." Now which of these do you think fits the context? There is no question: "But you are coveting the best gifts and yet I show you a more excellent way." The Greek verb *zēloō* normally has a bad connotation when it is translated *covet*.

So the indicative mood is the normal sense of the Greek in this passage and fits the context, and it should be translated this way: "But you are coveting the showy gifts, and yet I am showing you a more excellent way." Do you see the point? Paul is not saying to chase after spiritual gifts; he is saying, "You are chasing after spiritual gifts, and that is what is wrong with you. Stop doing it, and do the more excellent thing. Accept the unity, diversity, sovereignty, and harmony that God has already planned, presented, and built into the Body." And the key to all of the operation of the Body is love.

1. Why does the concept of rugged individualism appeal to people (see p. 248)?
2. What message is God trying to get across to man? What is Satan's response to that (see p. 249)?
3. Why have Christians fostered the same attitude as the world in regard to rugged individualism (see p. 249)?
4. Why would Jesus or Paul not be considered rugged individualists (see pp. 249-50)?
5. Who are the two types of Christians who do not look out for their fellow brothers and sisters in Christ? Why do they have an individualistic attitude (see p. 250)?
6. What three things must function in order for harmony to exist? Why weren't the Corinthians experiencing harmony? Explain (see pp. 252-53).
7. In what two ways does Paul cover the concept of harmony (see p. 254)?
8. What is the principle that Paul puts forward in 1 Corinthians 12:15 (see p. 254)?
9. What is the point that Paul draws out of 1 Corinthians 12:15-20 (see p. 257)?
10. What is the point that Paul wants to make in 1 Corinthians 12:21-26 (see p. 257)?
11. What exactly are the "more feeble" members of the body? What is their only protection (1 Cor. 12:22; see p. 258)?
12. What is Paul referring to by the use of terms "less honorable" and "uncomely" (1 Cor. 12:23; see pp. 259-60)?
13. What does Paul mean by the phrase "bestow more abundant honor" (1 Cor. 12:23; see p. 259)?
14. The less the _____ _____ and _____, the greater the effort to _____ it (see p. 259).
15. What kind of attitude should the members of the Body with the showy gifts have toward the weaker members (see p. 260)?
16. How does God equalize the honor for all the members of the Body (see p. 262)?
17. Why does Paul call this one local congregation in Corinth "the body of Christ" (1 Cor. 12:27; see p. 262)?
18. What three things does Paul want the Corinthians to remember in 1 Corinthians 12:27-30 (see pp. 262-63)?
19. What was the "more excellent way" that Paul was showing the Corinthians (1 Cor. 12:31; see p. 264)?
20. Is 1 Corinthians 12:31 a statement of fact or a command? How do you know? What is the best translation of this verse (see p. 264)?

Pondering the Principles

1. Do you consider yourself to be an independent or dependent person? Does the appeal of rugged individualism affect your life-style? Look up the following verses: Romans 13:1; Ephesians 5:21; 6:1; Colossians 3:22; Hebrews 13:17; 1 Peter 5:5. What do these verses tell you about the dependence Christians should have? Who should we be dependent on? Look up the following verses: Ephesians 5:25; Colossians 3:21; 4:1; 1 Peter 5:1-4. What do these verses tell you about the interdependence among Christians? Who are the subjects of these verses? Who should they be dependent on? Read Matthew 20:25-28 and Philippians 2:3-7. What should be the attitude of every Christian? Who is our example? What do you need to start doing in order to become a more dependent Christian?

2. Do you sometimes think that you have an inferiority complex? Do you feel you would like to serve the Body of Christ in some way but that in the long run you would fail? Look up the following verses: Exodus 3:2-15; Judges 6:1-16; Jeremiah 1:4-19. The great men of God mentioned in these verses each had an inferiority complex at one time. What changed their attitudes? In order to have the proper perspective on your ability to serve God, memorize 2 Corinthians 3:5: "Not that we are sufficient of ourselves to think anything as of ourselves, but our sufficiency is of God."

3. What should your perspective be on the various gifts that the various members of the Body possess? Which gifts are the most important? Which ones are necessary? Which ones can the Body survive without? In what areas do you feel God has gifted you? Are you a necessary part of the Body of Christ? What should be your attitude toward all the other members of the Body of Christ, according to 1 Corinthians 12:25? Think through some ways that you might be able to implement this perspective in your daily walk.

4. Based on this series of lessons on spiritual gifts, write down the things you have learned regarding this subject. In order to build up the fellow members of the Body, be sure to share your insights.

Scripture Index